APPLYING SOCIAL POLICY TO CRIMINAL JUSTICE PRACTICE

What Every Practitioner Should Know

Clive Sealey

P

First published in Great Britain in 2023 by

Policy Press, an imprint of
Bristol University Press
University of Bristol
1-9 Old Park Hill
Bristol
BS2 8BB
UK
t: +44 (0)117 374 6645
e: bup-info@bristol.ac.uk

Details of international sales and distribution partners are available at
policy.bristoluniversitypress.co.uk

British Library Cataloguing in Publication Data
A catalogue record for this book is available from the British Library

ISBN 978-1-4473-2405-8 paperback
ISBN 978-1-4473-2406-5 ePub
ISBN 978-1-4473-5749-0 ePdf

Cover design: Andy Ward
Front cover image: iStock/erhui1979

This book is dedicated to all those who have supported me over the last five years. Your love, support and patience has been essential to help me through this period. In particular, I would like to thank Kate Bramford, who first came up with the idea for the book and who has been there to listen to me when needed, and also Maddie Burton, for the 'inappropriate' laughs that we had that kept both of us sane during some weird times. I also give thanks to my good friends Aktar Uddin and Clement Kulang for both being there at times of need, even when going through their own difficult times. A special mention here also to Julia Smith for her kind words and support. It would be remiss of me not to mention my sister Louise Sealey and her son Braydon, who also provided me with laughter and joy whenever we met up and continue to do so. I would also like to thank my partner, Surinder Khuttan (Nikki), who has been with me through all of these times and has shown a love and understanding that has enabled us to come out on the other side happier than I would have thought possible. Thanks to Vinay and Aneesha for accepting me into their family. Finally, I dedicate the book to my two beautiful daughters, Jacintha and Annaya, for whom all of this is made worthwhile and with whom I look forward to a future that is as happy and fulfilling as possible.

Contents

Contents

List of tables, graphs and key learning boxes

Tables

Graphs

Key learning boxes

List of abbreviations

ACEs	Adverse Childhood Experiences
ADHD	Attention deficit/hyperactive disorder
ALMPs	Active Labour Market Policies
CJS	Criminal Justice System
CMI	Common mental health illness
CPS	Crown Prosecution Service
CSTRs	Community Sentence Treatment Requirements
DBS	Disclosure and Barring Service
DCLG	Department for Communities and Local Government
DLUHC	Department for Levelling Up, Housing and Communities
DWP	Department for Work and Pensions
EUCPN	European Crime Prevention Network
GDP	Gross domestic product
HB	Housing Benefit
HMICFRS	HM Inspectorate of Constabulary and Fire & Rescue Services
HMOs	Houses in multiple occupation
HMPPS	HM Prison and Probation Service
MHCLG	Ministry of Housing, Communities and Local Government
NAO	National Audit Office
NCS	National Careers Service
NFN	New Futures Network
NHS	National Health Service
NOMS	National Offender Management Service
OASys	Offender and Assessment System
OFSTED	Office for Standards in Education
OHID	Office for Health Improvement and Disparities
ONS	Office for National Statistics
SMI	Severe mental health illness
SVRU	Scottish Violence Reduction Unit
TFP	Troubled Families Programme
VAT	Value Added Tax
WHO	World Health Organization
WW2	World War Two
YTS	Youth Training Scheme

About the author

Clive Sealey is Senior Lecturer of Social Policy and Theory in the School of Allied Health and Community, University of Worcester, UK. His interests are in social policy-related issues linked to poverty, policy and theory. He teaches on a variety of courses there, from Foundation level up to PhD. He obtained his PhD in social policy from the University of Birmingham in 2009. His previous book publications are *Social Policy Simplified* (Palgrave Macmillan, 2015) and *Social Policy, Service Users and Carers* (Springer, 2022).

1

Introduction

The key objective of this book is the improvement of criminal justice practice. At this point, we can loosely define criminal justice practice as practice concerned with the prevention of crime and punishing, rehabilitating and supporting those who have contact with criminal justice individuals or organisations. The book argues that a key way in which criminal justice practice can meet these aims is by identifying and addressing key social policy issues that affect individuals and communities. Criminal justice practice can include all those individuals who work in the police, courts, Crown Prosecution Service (CPS), prison and probation. It can also include a range of non-statutory agencies such as lawyers, victims' organisations, charities such as Nacro and also research organisations such as the Centre for Crime and Justice Studies, as will be outlined in more detail later in the book.

The key objective of this book is to improve criminal justice practice by clearly outlining the significant interconnections between social policy and criminal justice practice. The book aims to show that understanding and attending to these interconnections leads to improvements in responses to crime and criminal behaviours, which has beneficial outcomes not just for criminal justice practice, but also for wider society. Understanding these interconnections is very important for anyone who has an interest in working in and improving criminal justice practice.

What is this book about?

This book aims to make clear the interconnections between social policy and criminal justice practice. Its particular focus is on highlighting how an understanding of key social policy theories, concepts and policies can better inform the work of those directly and indirectly involved in criminal justice practice. Its emphasis is on enabling those working in criminal justice practice and related sectors to recognise the importance that social policy theories, concepts and policies can have on their practice. It also provides a context to the recent changes that have occurred in the criminal justice system for students and criminal justice practitioners, thereby enabling them to make sense of these changes and reflect on their implications.

The book takes as its starting point the assertion that social policy and criminal justice practice are inextricably interconnected, meaning that the theories, policies and practices that affect social policy also affect criminal justice practice, and vice versa. However, from the author's experience of teaching both social policy and criminal justice practice to undergraduate students, it is evident that students do not initially understand this interconnection, thus highlighting a need to make this interconnection more readily apparent. However, as students progress through their course and gain more extensive practice and sector experience, these interconnections become more evident to them. In particular, students begin to see that some of the important concepts that are relevant to social policy such as equality, prevention, well-being, needs, redistribution, universalism, poverty, power and stigma have very important implications when working with individuals and groups within criminal justice practice. This leads directly to the belief that it is important for all those working directly and indirectly within criminal justice practice to understand and apply social policy concepts to their work.

These interconnections become particularly evident when studying the seven pathways to reducing reoffending that were set out by the then National Offender Management Service (NOMS) in 2004 (Home Office, 2004) and reinforced by NOMS in 2009 (NOMS, 2009). These focus on accommodation, education, training and employment, health, drugs and alcohol, finance benefit and debt, children and families, and attitudes, thinking and behaviour. While some organisations have argued that these pathways are no longer officially used (Barnardo's/ HM Prisons and Probation Service, 2018), the Home Office/Ministry of Justice (2015) reinforced them in the outline for the Integrated Offender Management model and described them as established pathways. Additionally, the criminal justice system and other agencies still use them. As an example, some prisons have a 'champion' for each of the pathways, and these pathways are also frequently referred to in terms of resettlement and rehabilitation of offenders (Barnardo's/ HM Prisons and Probation Service, 2018). More significantly, the main probation assessment tool currently in use in England and Wales is the Offender Assessment System (OASys), which is concerned with documenting an offender's criminal history. This involves economic and social characteristics such as accommodation, education, training and employment, lifestyles and associates, relationships, and drug and alcohol misuse, which broadly reflect the seven pathways.

The key point that should be noted here, as set out in more detail in Chapter 2, is that the seven pathways relate to issues that are core aspects of social policy. Accommodation, education, training and employment, health, drugs and alcohol, finance benefit and debt, children and families, and attitudes, thinking and behaviour are all key social policy areas, thus emphasising the interconnection between social policy and criminal justice practice.

Additionally, since 2010 there have been some significant changes in government policy, largely driven by the emphasis on **austerity** (Key Learning Box 1.1) in all sectors of government expenditure, including the criminal justice system, and particularly in social policies. This has meant that there has been a transformative shift in the focus, delivery and funding of social policies, which has affected not just the economic circumstances of individuals, but also their social and personal circumstances. What is often not acknowledged is the impact that these changed social policies have had in terms of increasing the potential for involvement with the criminal justice system, either directly or indirectly, particularly in relation to efforts to reduce reoffending.

> **KEY LEARNING BOX 1.1** AUSTERITY
>
> Austerity in this context refers to where, since 2010, successive UK governments have decreased, and still continue to decrease, both the funding and scope of government spending, especially in areas relevant to social policy and criminal justice practice. As an example, since 2010, the government has cut funding to the police, the courts, the prison system and the probation services. As a specific consequence, the backlog of cases in the courts has grown, meaning that it is taking longer to progress them through the CJS. This has had a negative effect not only on those accused of crimes, but also on those who are victim of crimes, as it takes longer for them to access justice.

As a specific example of this, there is the fact that changes that have been occurring specifically in social policy since the 1980s have now started to trickle down into criminal justice practice, with important practice implications. This includes the more recent Transforming Rehabilitation Agenda, which, in emphasising a focus on a greater diversity of providers in delivering the seven pathways, presents opportunities for a more 'mixed economy of criminal justice' (Buck and Corcoran, 2011). For example, since 2010, the prison service has increased its use of private prisons, and the government has effected a series of transformational changes in the probation service, from public control to private control and back to public control. This echoes the emphasis on the mixed economy of welfare in social policies since the 1980s, which has had important outcomes and problems for services (Sealey, 2015). It is likely that this changing context for criminal justice practice will result in significant transformation in the structure, function and nature of criminal justice practice.

Who is this book for?

This book is primarily about how social policy and criminal justice practice are fundamentally linked. I hope that it will be relevant to those not only studying in an academic context, but, just as importantly, to those working in criminal justice practice in policy and practice contexts. This can include students, those working or planning to work directly in the criminal justice system such as in the police, probation, Youth Offending Teams, prisons, HM Courts and Tribunals Service and the CPS. It can also include those working in criminal justice allied sectors such as local authorities, drug and alcohol rehabilitation services and voluntary sector organisations involved in housing and homelessness, substance misuse, welfare and advocacy. The book may also be of interest to students and practitioners who are concerned with related subjects, such as social work, youth justice, policing and law.

There are several features of this book that distinguish it from others about either social policy or the criminal justice system. First, its main aim is to articulate the principle that social policy and criminal justice practice share a common concern with improving outcomes for individuals, groups and communities, and this cannot be seen as separate. Secondly, it specifically relates that attention to social policy issues is a prerequisite for improvements to criminal justice practice. This highlights that improvements within criminal justice practice require a move away from a narrow focus on crime and criminality to a wider focus that attends to the social policy needs that individuals, groups and communities have. This makes the book of particular relevance to both criminal justice practitioners and policy makers.

The structure of the book

The book is divided into two parts, with a focus on identifying the interconnections between social policy and criminal justice practice in the Part I, and outlining what these interconnections are in Part II.

Part I – Understanding the interconnection between social policy and criminal justice practice

The focus in this part is on defining what social policy and criminal justice practice refer to in this book, and detailing how they are interconnected. The part also explores the relevance of this link between social policy and criminal justice practice.

Chapter 2: What is social policy, and why is it relevant to you?

This chapter provides a brief overview of social policy and its practical relevance to everyday life. Social policy is a term that you may not have come across, but which is nonetheless likely to have had a significant impact on your everyday life, as it can impact on your welfare and well-being in numerous ways. This is because at the heart of social policy is a range of measures that can affect the levels and quality of healthcare you receive, the type of education you have access to, the quality of housing that you live in, the amount of income you have and the type of social care that is available to you. These are all issues that matter to you, your family and the community in which you live. The chapter outlines key features and concepts within social policy, and also details why understanding and studying social policy is relevant to you.

Chapter 3: What is criminal justice practice, and what is the rationale for working to improve it?

This chapter provides the rationale for the book's key aim, that of working to improve criminal justice practice. It provides a brief and concise outline of what criminal justice practice does. It then details key observations about criminal justice practice, in terms of the importance of the law, the importance of social norms and the current punitive context in which criminal justice practice operates. The chapter then outlines the current crisis within criminal justice practice and the direct and indirect costs of crime, which provide a clear rationale for improving criminal justice practice. This is to make it clear that this book is about more than providing an understanding of what criminal justice practice is. Its key focus is on improving criminal justice practice by showing how social policy and criminal justice practice are theoretically and functionally interconnected, and how understanding this interconnection is important for improving criminal justice practice.

Chapter 4: What is the interconnection between social policy and criminal justice practice?

This chapter presents evidence for the book's key rationale: that identifying and working with the interconnections between social policy and criminal justice practice has beneficial outcomes for both criminal justice practitioners and service users. While the interconnections between social policy and criminal justice practice may not be obvious, this chapter argues that they are linked by five important concepts. These are justice, security, equality, making a meaningful contribution and rights. These provide the key rationale for the book, as they indicate there are solid links between the two fields. This suggests that aiming to improve criminal justice practice by reference to social policy is achievable.

Part II – The importance of social policies to criminal justice practice

This part details the importance of specific social policy issues to criminal justice practice, and outlines the ways in which understanding this can improve criminal justice practice outcomes in these areas.

Chapter 5: Housing, criminal justice practice and social policy

This chapter's focus is on the changes since the 1980s in housing and housing policy that have had significant actual or potential implications for criminal justice practice and practitioners. The chapter details how the significant changes in housing tenure over this period are impacting on criminal justice practice in significant ways, either directly or indirectly, through, for example, issues such as homelessness and residualisation. The chapter concludes with the argument that there are a number of ways in which social policy could improve criminal justice practice, such as a particular focus on the individual and structural causes of homelessness and housing need, and policies that emphasise the prevention of homelessness.

Chapter 6: Employment, criminal justice practice and social policy

The importance of employment to criminal justice practice is perhaps most evident in that it is often the case that a standard requirement for probation or parole is involvement in employment as a route towards rehabilitation. It is also relevant to note that rehabilitation through employment is one of the very few types of rehabilitation programmes for which there is definitive evidence that it works – for most types of rehabilitation programmes there is mixed or no evidence (Ministry of Justice, 2013). The chapter begins with an outline of the evidence of a link between employment and positive criminal justice outcomes, wherein employment has been shown to both increase desistance and reduce recidivism. The chapter then considers specific factors that limit the effectiveness of employment for criminal justice practice, before detailing the importance of employment to social policy outcomes, together with the changes in policy since the 1980s which are impacting on the nature of employment policies. Finally, the chapter analyses what criminal justice practice can learn from this changed context, in order to identify ways in which social policy can improve criminal justice practice.

Chapter 7: Physical /mental health, criminal justice practice and social policy

This chapter begins by discussing the evidence for a criminogenic link between physical and mental health and criminal justice outcomes, and also the factors that increase the likelihood of CJS involvement, such as comorbidity, dual diagnosis and Adverse Childhood Experiences (ACEs). There is then an analysis of how the CJS manages those with physical and mental health conditions, with a particular focus on the cost of prison, but also noting the wider costs to the CJS. The chapter then presents an outline of measures that have been identified as ways to improve CJS outcomes for those with physical and mental health conditions. Finally, the chapter outlines how a social policy approach to dealing with physical and mental health, focused on universalism, citizenship, equivalence and integration, could improve the outcomes for criminal justice practice.

Chapter 8: Substance abuse, criminal justice practice and social policy

This chapter opens by highlighting the high prevalence of substance abuse in the CJS, despite the general decreasing trend in society as a whole since the 1990s. This, together with the criminogenic nature of substance abuse, means this is a particular concern for criminal justice practice. The chapter analyses the punitive approach of the CJS when dealing with substance abuse alongside other alternative approaches, such as harm reduction, decriminalisation and regulation of the drug market. This leads to an analysis of how a social policy focus could improve current criminal justice practice. The focus is on detailing the need for a move away from an individualised and narrow approach to risk management towards an approach that focuses on social harm and the comprehensive causes of substance abuse, including personal, social, financial and emotional factors. This emphasises a criminal justice practice that seeks to provide a broad range of measures and services to prevent and break the cycle of substance abuse.

Chapter 9: Low income and poverty, criminal justice practice and social policy

There are a number of criminological and non-criminological theories that make an explicit link between crime and poverty. The chapter analyses evidence for and against such a link between poverty and crime, which shows that crime and its effects hurt those living in poverty the most, a fact should lead to a primary focus on what can be done to stop those living in poverty from being victims of crime. However, criminal justice practice strongly emphasises crime prevention through what is typically referred to as crime reduction strategies, particularly situational crime prevention. The chapter analyses the limitations of this approach, leading to an outline of how a social policy focus on the social problems that lead to poverty, particularly a lack of power, can improve criminal justice practice outcomes.

Chapter 10: Children and families, criminal justice practice and social policy

To analyse the CJS approach to children and families, this chapter begins by outlining how children and families are defined both legally and socially, and makes key observations about the criminal age of responsibility in England and Wales, and the historic importance to policy of the nuclear family. When considering how the CJS engages with children and families, it becomes evident that the emphasis is primarily negative, with the focus being on their 'delinquent' and 'troublesome' nature, as expressed through the notion of intergenerational transmission, which has led the CJS to a more punitive approach to children and families. The chapter analyses evidence for and against this approach, together with its wider implications. The chapter concludes by detailing what criminal justice practice can learn from the lessons of the punitive approach in social policy, as expressed through the Troubled Families Programme (TFP).

Chapter 11: Ten ways in which a social policy focus can improve criminal justice practice

The concluding chapter draws together the key issues from the previous chapters to provide ten key ways in which understanding and applying key social policy concepts can improve criminal justice practice. The key objective of this book is the improvement of criminal justice practice by clearly outlining that there are significant interconnections between social policy and criminal justice practice. Understanding and working with these connections leads to improved responses to crime and criminal behaviours, which has beneficial outcomes not just for criminal justice practice, but also for wider society. Understanding these interconnections is very important for anyone who has an interest in working in and improving criminal justice practice.

The use of key learning boxes

The book uses key learning boxes to make key issues and concepts clearer. Where an issue or concept has a key learning box, it is highlighted with bold text. In many instances, key learning boxes appear in another chapter. Please refer to the list of key learning boxes.

References

Barnado's/HM Prisons and Probation Service (2018) 'Reducing reoffending children and families pathway'. Available from: https://www.nicco.org.uk/directory-of-resources/reducing-reoffending-children-and-families-pathway [Accessed 17 April 2023].

Buck, G. and Corcoran, M. (2011) 'The mixed economy of criminal justice: The challenges of contestability, privatisation and partnership working'. *The Third Sector in Criminal Justice Seminar Four – 24 November 2011*. University of Leeds: ESRC Seminar Series.

Home Office (2004) *Reducing Re-Offending: National Action Plan*, London: Home Office.

Home Office/Ministry of Justice (2015) *Integrated Offender Management Key Principles – Supplementary Information*. London: Home Office/Ministry of Justice.

Ministry of Justice (2013) *Transforming Rehabilitation: A Summary of Evidence on Reducing Reoffending*. London: Ministry of Justice.

NOMS (National Offender Management Service) (2009) *The National Reducing Re-Offending Delivery Plan*. London: Home Office.

Sealey, C. (2015) *Social Policy Simplified*. Basingstoke: Palgrave Macmillan.

PART I

Understanding the interconnection between social policy and criminal justice practice

2

What is social policy, and why is it relevant to you?

This chapter aims to:

- provide a brief overview of what social policy is;
- outline key social policy features and concepts;
- detail why understanding and studying social policy is relevant.

Introduction

This chapter aims to provide a brief overview of what social policy is and its practical relevance to your everyday life. Social policy is a term that you may not have come across, but which is likely nonetheless to have a significant influence on your everyday life, impacting on your welfare and well-being in numerous ways. This is because at the heart of social policy is a range of measures that can affect levels and quality of healthcare, type of education that is available, quality of housing, income and social care. These are all issues that matter to individuals, families and communities. The chapter aims to outline key features and concepts in social policy, and also why understanding and studying social policy is relevant to you.

What is social policy?

The origins of today's social policies can be traced back to the publication of a report in 1942, during **World War Two** (WW2) (Key Learning Box 2.1) by William Beveridge (Beveridge, 1942), which is commonly referred to as the *Beveridge Report*. This was ordered by the government to provide a vision for the type of society that they wanted to reconstruct after WW2 had ended, a society that they hoped would be considerably better than what had existed before.

KEY LEARNING BOX 2.1 WORLD WAR TWO

WW2 occurred between 1939 and 1945. As the deadliest military conflict in history so far, it had a huge impact on society: it is estimated that 3 per cent of the world's population died as a consequence. To put this in context, at the time of writing this book, the population of the world is estimated at 7.7 billion. If the same percentage of this population were to die as during WW2, this would mean the deaths of 231 million people, or almost four times the population of the UK. This meant that WW2 touched the lives of almost all individuals in British society, most obviously through death, but also through conscription (men), employment in war industries (women), evacuation (children and older people) and rationing (everyone). Richard Titmuss (1960) refers to the effects of WW2 as 'total war', because of the major impact it had on the whole population.

The horrors of WW2 shone a light on the social and economic circumstances in which the majority of the population were living at that time, and these circumstances were not very pleasant. For many, hunger, ill health, unemployment, illiteracy and living in slums were normal. There were very limited systems of social and economic assistance for the population at large, as people were to a great extent expected to look after and look out for themselves. As an example, there was no national state healthcare, most doctors were private and people were expected to pay for both consultations and treatment. However, this was unaffordable for many, and as a consequence treatment was not sought for curable diseases such as diphtheria and tuberculosis (Rivett, 1998).

It was in this context that the government asked Beveridge to consider ways in which the social and economic circumstances of the population could be improved in the period of reconstruction after the war. He carried out a comprehensive investigation and analysis of living conditions, and from his findings argued that the goals of post-war reconstruction should be the elimination of what he termed 'five giant evils'. These were Want, Disease, Ignorance, Idleness and Squalor. Beveridge argued that this was an important aim because these factors had held back the social and economic development of the country before WW2, and would do so again if not dealt with.

When WW2 ended, the new post-war government specifically used the *Beveridge Report* as their model for post-war reconstruction. They did this by putting in place a range of social and economic policies that they specifically designed to improve society's welfare in relation to the five giant evils, hence the term social policy. Crucially, it was Beveridge's emphasis on the elimination of these evils that was at the heart of the government's aim to improve the economic and social conditions of the population. In practical terms, this meant that the government put in place a wide range of specific social policies and measures to enable individuals to overcome the negative effects of Beveridge's five giant evils. In relation to health, for example, the government created the National Health Service (NHS) to provide free, comprehensive and universal healthcare for all; in relation to housing, the government built approximately a million council houses; in relation to social security, the government introduced a universal child allowance; in relation to employment, the government created jobs to reconstruct the country after the war; and in relation to education, the government made secondary schooling free for all. Together, these changes constructed what we now know as the post-war welfare state. They are summarised briefly in Table 2.1.

Table 2.1 Links between Beveridge's five giant evils and post-war social policies

Beveridge's giant evils	Social policy area	Post-war social policies
Want	Social security	• universal child allowance • sickness benefit • unemployment benefit • pension • maternity and widows' allowance • guardians' allowance (for orphans) • death grant (for funerals) • means-tested national assistance for those not entitled to social insurance
Idleness	Employment	• increased government spending overall • nationalisation of coal, electricity, rail, steel, iron and gas industries, canals, airlines and Bank of England
Disease	Health	• introduction of the NHS in 1948, making healthcare free, comprehensive and universal
Ignorance	Education	• secondary education provided as a right, free and universally • raising of school leaving age to 15 • tripartite school system (grammar, secondary technical and secondary modern) introduced
Squalor	Housing	• over a million permanent new homes built between 1945 and 1951

Source: Created using data from Sealey (2015)

As we can see in Table 2.1, most of these social policies are still relevant today. The most obvious example is the creation of the NHS, which remains a source of free, comprehensive and universal healthcare. Additionally, a range of social security policies can trace their origins to this period, such as Child Benefit. This shows that while the five giant evils are no longer explicitly spoken about, they remain the foundational basis of our current welfare state.

We can therefore define social policy according to its historical origins as a set of policies that aim to improve the social and economic well-being of individuals and society. Defining social policy in this way enables us to answer a number of key questions about it.

Who receives social policy?

As stated earlier, the main aim of post-war welfare policies was to improve the social and economic well-being of society through the elimination of a wide range of harmful social and economic circumstances, such as ill health, unemployment, poverty, homelessness and lack of education. These are social and economic needs that most individuals have or are likely to experience at some point in their life. For example, it is very likely that all individuals will have a need for healthcare, housing, and education, and may have a need for financial assistance because of unemployment or a low income at some point during their life.

Social policy enables individuals to access services that meet needs as required throughout their lifetime, from when they are born to when they die. As an example, when you are born, you become entitled to health care services such as post-natal maternity care, and may also be entitled to specific benefits such as Child Benefit. Throughout your childhood, you are entitled to access primary and secondary education as well as continuous health care services. When you become an adult, and throughout your working life, you are entitled to benefits to maintain your income such as Jobseeker's Allowance/Universal Credit and also access to higher education, as well as continued access to healthcare services. Once you retire, you are entitled to the basic State Pension, and also access to social care and continued access to healthcare services, which continues until you die. We can term this **cradle to grave entitlement** (Key Learning Box 2.2). Social policy therefore provides entitlement to a wide range of services and benefits throughout a citizen's life.

KEY LEARNING BOX 2.2 CRADLE TO GRAVE ENTITLEMENT

The term cradle to grave refers to the fact that there is an entitlement to social policy benefits and services from birth to death. This can be through access to healthcare, education, income maintenance benefits such as tax credits, and social care such as nursing home care. The extent of social policy benefits and services is extensive over a lifetime.

Entitlement refers to the right to access and receive social policy services and benefits, either in the form of services or as specific cash and non-cash benefits. Sometimes entitlement can be very broad and simple to understand. For example, for most people, entitlement to receive NHS services occurs simply from being ill. However, not all social policy entitlement is so simple. Entitlement can be based on age such as Child Benefit; level of income such as Universal Credit; occupation such as student maintenance loans; or whether contributions have been paid such as the full basic State Pension.

A key point to note is that a wide variety of social policies have the potential to impact on welfare and well-being. Given all the entitlements to services and benefits that social policy provides, it is very likely that most, if not all, people have received or are receiving some type of social policy. This can either directly through services such as access to schools or healthcare, or indirectly through legislation that ensures a basic standard of living, such as the National Minimum Wage, or regulation that ensures minimum standards, such as access to schools that are inspected by the Office for Standards in Education (OFSTED).

Therefore, the answer to the question of who receives social policy is that we all do.

How does social policy provide social policies?

As has been stated, social policy meets the wide range of individual welfare needs that you have in a variety of ways. This is not just through providing money, but also through access to services. For instance, social policy provides specific **cash benefits** (Key Learning Box 2.3) to give individuals a basic level of income, an example being Universal Credit; and social policy provides **non-cash benefits** (Key Learning Box 2.3) in the form of services such as free childcare or education. Social policy therefore provides access to a wider range of benefits than you might have previously thought. The key point to take from this is that when we consider both the cash and non-cash benefits of social policy, the extent of social policy on our lives increases significantly. This highlights that social policy benefits are received by all sections of society, not just lower income groups.

> **KEY LEARNING BOX 2.3** CASH BENEFITS VERSUS NON-CASH BENEFITS
>
> Social policy provides services and benefits in two main ways. Social policy provides benefits such as Child Benefit, Universal Credit, State Pension and Student Maintenance Loans in the form of cash. Social policy also provides non-cash benefits in the form of services such as the NHS, and primary, secondary and further education. Non-cash benefits can also include regulations to ensure that people's living standards are met, an example being the National Living Wage/ National Minimum Wage. Non-cash benefits also include regulations to limit what people can or cannot do in order to protect their welfare, an example being the smoking ban. They also include ensuring that services provide minimum standards for specific services, through organisations such as OFSTED. Social policy therefore provides benefits in a variety of cash and non-cash ways, with non-cash benefits such as services, regulations and minimum standards perhaps not always being thought of as social policies.

For example, the NHS is used not just by lower income groups, but also by middle and higher income groups. Similarly, education is used not just by lower income groups. Indeed, higher education is most likely to be used by higher rather than lower income groups (Goldstone, 2021). The way in which higher income groups make extensive use of social policy is specifically highlighted when we consider the **inverse care law** (Key Learning Box 2.4). It is true to say that some groups of people, such as pensioners and children, are more likely to be in receipt of social policy services and benefits than others, but everyone at some point experiences the circumstances in which people need social policy services and benefits, such as ill health, and so everyone is likely to need social policy services and benefits at some point.

> **KEY LEARNING BOX 2.4** THE INVERSE CARE LAW
> The inverse care law refers to Tudor Hart's (1971) observation that because income and resources are important factors in health use, there is a contradictory relationship between the need for healthcare and its actual use. This means that those who least need healthcare are most likely to use it, and those who most need healthcare are least likely to use it. In other words, welfare services such as health are more likely to be used more often and/or more effectively by those with higher income and resources, and less likely to be used more often and/or more effectively by those with lower income and resources. When someone is poor, they are less likely to adequately identify and access the healthcare they need, whereas a richer person is more likely to adequately identify and access the healthcare they need. The inverse care law has also been observed in other social policy areas. For example, it is better-off people who use and benefit the most from education services, as richer families are more likely to move to areas with better schools, and children from these families are three times more likely to go to university (and the more elite universities) than poorer families (Independent Commission on Fees, 2014).

Who pays for social policy?

As noted earlier, social policy provides entitlement to a wide range of services and benefits that meet an individual's welfare needs. These services and benefits have to be paid for, and this is done mainly through **taxation** (Key Learning Box 2.5).

> **KEY LEARNING BOX 2.5** TAXATION
> A simple definition of taxation is a compulsory charge that a government imposes on individuals in order to pay for government services. Usually, this means that an individual is legally required to pay money to the government, and in return the government provides services. As taxation is compulsory not optional, non-payment involves the possibility of prosecution.

The most well-known tax is probably Income Tax, but depending on circumstances, individuals can be responsible for paying a range of other taxes, as shown in Table 2.2. Taxes enable the government to pay for and provide the range of social policy services and benefits previously discussed. A key point to note from Table 2.2 is that everyone pays tax, regardless of their income. This includes the young, the unemployed, the sick and the old, the rich and

Table 2.2 Main types of taxes

Tax type	Explanation	Who pays
Income Tax	Paid from your earnings from employment	These who earn above £12,570 a year
National Insurance	Paid from your earnings from employment	These who earn above £12,570 a year
Value Added Tax (VAT)	Paid when you buy most things, for example, goods such as some food, clothes and TVs; and services such as cleaning, repairs and maintenance	Anyone who buys relevant goods and services
Council Tax	Paid depending on where you live	Those who live in a household (although some groups are exempted, such as students)
Excise Taxes	Paid when you buy and use certain goods and services	Those who buy cigarettes, alcohol, fuel, most motor vehicle users, BBC TV users

the poor. This is because taxes are paid not just through work, but also when goods are bought. For example, a tax such as VAT means that even those who you would not normally think of paying tax, such as the unemployed or even ten-year-old children, do so, for example when buying a soft drink. This means that everyone to a greater or lesser extent pays for social policy services and benefits such as the NHS. This is important to note given that some groups of people, such as the unemployed, are often portrayed as less deserving of social policy services and benefits than others because they are wrongly perceived to not pay tax.

It is also important to remember that most people pay considerably less tax than they receive in social policy services and benefits. In most circumstances, paying directly for the welfare services and benefits that social policy provides is prohibitively expensive. An example of this is private education. The average cost of a year's education at a private day school is £15,192 per person, and the fees for private boarding schools are considerably higher, at £36,000 (Independent Schools Council, 2021). Most people with one child would not be able to afford this, even less so if they had more than one child. As a consequence, most people send their children to state schools, which are funded by the taxes they pay. The average tax paid per person in a year is £16,821 (ONS, 2020), which is below the amount that they would need to pay for a child at a private boarding school, not including other social policy benefits and services that would be accessed over a year.

Although taxation is usually an individual affair, with everyone responsible for paying their own taxes, it can be regarded as something that not only directly benefits the individual, but also the wider community and society. As an example of this, consider that being educated in schooling that is paid for by taxation not only benefits the individual, but also the community in which they live, in terms of leading to greater prosperity and the creation of goods, ideas and services that further benefit society. In this context, paying tax represents a **public good**, as paying it funds social policies to provide goods and services that benefit the community and the society in which the individual lives (Key Learning Box 2.6). To exemplify this point, we only need a simple consideration of the state of countries where education is not provided through taxation but where individuals are wholly responsible for paying for education to see the important part that paying taxation plays in terms of the public good.

KEY LEARNING BOX 2.6 PUBLIC GOOD

A public good broadly refers to a good or service that has the potential to benefit the whole of society, not just those who directly use or fund them. A good example of this is in relation to education, which provides a direct benefit not just to those who are educated, but also to those who do not use education, through enabling the wider social and economic development of society. This is why things that are deemed a public good, such as education, are often provided by the government, to ensure that are accessible to as many people as possible, so that their wider benefits occur as widely as possible.

So we all pay for social policy, and for most people it functions as a form of social insurance, as you pay tax in order to have access to services and benefits that meet welfare needs now and in the future. This is especially relevant when the cost of these needs, such as education, are unaffordable for most people.

How does social policy benefit me?

We have seen that social policy comprehensively covers everyone's life, defined here as from cradle to grave, through a wide variety of services and benefits. This is because the welfare needs that people have tend to be greatest when they are least able to pay for them, for example when they are very young or very old. It is very unlikely that a new-born would be able to afford the cost of post-natal health care if it was not provided, and being unable to do so would significantly reduce the chance of survival through the early years, as can be seen in many countries where child mortality is very high. Social policy therefore benefits everybody, because in the absence of the services and benefits it provides, your welfare needs would not be met, or at least not as extensively as they are currently.

Social policy is also important in terms of improving health and well-being throughout the life course. For example, the healthcare provided by the NHS means that citizens are less likely to die young and more likely to live to the age of 100 than before the NHS was created. Similarly, the expansion of secondary further and higher education means that levels of illiteracy and innumeracy are lower than they very likely would be in the absence of education. This point is reinforced if the relatively positive welfare and social circumstances in the UK are compared with those of developing countries with less comprehensive social policy services and benefits. This highlights that social policy is important to you as it enables you to improve your health and well-being in important ways.

Why is understanding social policy relevant to me?

The brief history of social policy provided here indicates that the post-war welfare state emerged from real social and economic problems, in particular high levels of poverty and disease. History also shows that social policy measures put in place to deal with these problems had beneficial outcomes for the individual, communities and society (Greve, 2022). This reinforces the fact that social policy made and continues to make a real difference to the lives of many people, and contributes significantly to the social and economic development of society.

However, at the time of writing this book, we are living at a time of major social and economic problems, similar to the end of WW2. We have just come through the COVID-19 pandemic, and have gone straight into a cost of living crisis. This means that currently, rising poverty and inequality are arguably the most serious societal problems.

Unlike at the end of WW2, however, the UK is experiencing a period of **austerity** in government spending, meaning there has been a decade of continual reductions and cuts to the amount that the government spends on providing services and benefits, as shown in Graph 2.1. The decade between 2010 and 2020 has seen public expenditure fall significantly, by as much as 15 per cent. This means that the government is spending less money on public services in general, and specifically on many social policy services and benefits.

Graph 2.1 UK public expenditure as a percentage of GDP, 2010–2020

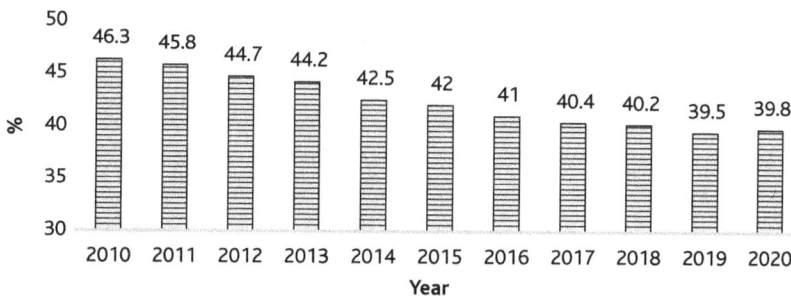

Source: HM Treasury (2021)

The lessons from history as detailed above tells us that the absence of social policy can lead to significant social problems such as poverty, ill health and homelessness, which have the potential to affect a wide range of people, including those who may not consider themselves to be so affected. For example, rising poverty indirectly has the potential to affect the quality of a neighbourhood, social relationships and whether individuals feel safe and secure. This is especially relevant in the current context of austerity.

However, the past also shows us that while these problems are significant, they are not unsolvable if the will and determination exist to address them. It is possible to construct policies that benefit social and economic needs. This is where studying social policy becomes relevant. Creating policies that may solve such problems is the essence of social policy. Studying the subject allows deep and meaningful engagement with these issues, and can make a real difference to many people in many ways.

In essence, the study of social policy is a study of ways to improve your life. This goes a long way to answering the question of what social policy is, and makes it clear why understanding social policy is so relevant.

Summary

The main aim of this chapter has been to briefly outline what social policy is. It has done this by detailing some key elements and also key ways in which social policy is relevant to individuals, families and the communities in which we live.

We can simply define social policy as policies that aim to improve the social and economic well-being of individuals and society. Defining social policy in this way enables us to analyse how social policy works and functions, and also to consider its relevance. It also shows us that the key aim of social policy is to find answers and solutions to social problems that affect us all in order to improve our social and economic well-being.

To do this, social policy provides cradle to grave entitlement. This means it can meet the wide range of welfare needs that individuals have. The significant consequence of this is that most, if not all, individuals are receiving and/or will receive social policy benefits.

We can also see that social policy provides for aspects of welfare that we could not otherwise afford, education being a good example of this. In the absence of social policies, it is very likely that your welfare needs would not be met, or not met as extensively as they are now. This highlights that social policy is important to everyone.

The period of austerity that the UK is experiencing is likely to lead to rising social problems such as poverty and inequality. These problems have the potential to negatively impact on individuals and communities directly and/or indirectly. However, the study of social policy is a study of ways to improve your life, and this is what makes studying social policy relevant to you.

References

Beveridge, W. (1942) *Beveridge Report.* CMD 6404. London: HMSO. Available from: https://www.parliament.uk/about/living-heritage/transformingsociety/livinglearning/coll-9-health1/coll-9-health/ [Accessed 19 July 2022].

Goldstone, R. (2021) 'Is social class relevant in higher education today?', LSE Higher Education, 11 February. Available from: https://blogs.lse.ac.uk/highereducation/2021/02/11/is-class-still-relevant-today/ [Accessed 19 July 2022].

Greve, B. (2022) *Rethinking Welfare and the Welfare State.* Cheltenham: Edward Elgar Publishing Limited. Available from: https://public.ebookcentral.proquest.com/choice/PublicFullRecord.aspx?p=7009119 [Accessed 19 July 2022].

HM Treasury (2021) *Public Expenditure Statistical Analyses 2021.* London: HM Treasury.

Independent Commission on Fees (2014) *Analysis of Trends in Higher Education Applications, Admissions, and Enrolments.* London: The Sutton Trust. Available from: https://www.suttontrust.com/wp-content/uploads/2019/12/ICoF-Report-Aug-2014-1.pdf [Accessed 23 January 2023].

Independent Schools Council (2021) *ISC Census and Annual Report 2018.* London: Independent Schools Council. Available from: https://www.isc.co.uk/research/annual-census/isc-annual-census-2018/ [Accessed 19 July 2022].

ONS (Office for National Statistics) (2020) 'Effects of taxes and benefits on UK household income – Office for National Statistics'. Available from: https://www.ons.gov.uk/peoplepopulationandcommunity/personalandhouseholdfinances/incomeandwealth/bulletins/theeffectsoftaxesandbenefitsonhouseholdincome/financialyearending2019 [Accessed 19 July 2022].

Rivett, G. (1998) *From Cradle to Grave: Fifty Years of the NHS.* repr. London: King's Fund.

Sealey, C. (2015) *Social Policy Simplified: Connecting Theory with People's Lives.* London; New York: Palgrave Macmillan.

Titmuss, R.M. (1960) *Essays on 'The Welfare State'.* London: George Allen & Unwin.

Tudor Hart, J. (1971) 'The inverse care law', *The Lancet*, 297(7696): 405–412. https://doi.org/10.1016/S0140-6736(71)92410-X.

3

What is criminal justice practice, and what is the rationale for working to improve it?

> **This chapter aims to:**
>
> - provide a brief overview of what criminal justice practice is;
> - detail key features of criminal justice practice;
> - outline the key focus of the rest of the book on improving criminal justice practice.

Introduction

The likelihood is that you picked up this book because you have at least a passing interest in criminal justice practice. Perhaps you are considering working in criminal justice practice or already work in that field. At this point, it is important to highlight that there is not one system of criminal justice across the UK but three, which are separate but linked. These are for:

- England and Wales
- Scotland
- Northern Ireland

There are important differences in the way these three systems operate, and therefore differences in criminal justice practice. For example, the age of criminal responsibility, which means the age at which a person can be held responsibility for committing a criminal act, is 12 in Scotland, but 10 in England and Wales and in Northern Ireland. These differences are important because they lead to different outcomes in the criminal justice system (Garside and Ford, 2015). Because of these differences, only the English and Welsh system of criminal justice is covered in this chapter and elsewhere in this book, unless otherwise specifically stated.

This chapter provides the rationale for the key aim of the book, that of working to improve criminal justice practice. First, the chapter provides a brief and concise outline of what criminal justice practice does, to detail its key aims and objectives. The chapter then outlines key and interrelated observations about criminal justice practice, showing the importance of the law and social norms to criminal justice practice and the current punitive context in which criminal justice practice operates.

The chapter then outlines the current crisis within criminal justice practice and the direct and indirect costs of crime, which provides a clear rationale for improving criminal justice practice. This clarifies that the book is about more than providing an understanding of what criminal justice practice is. Rather, its key focus is on improving criminal justice practice by showing how social policy and criminal justice practice are theoretically and functionally interconnected, and that is important to understand this interconnection in order to improve criminal justice practice.

What is criminal justice practice?

In trying to determine what criminal justice practice is, we can start by making a distinction between criminal justice and civil justice, as the focus of this book is solely on criminal justice practice, and sometimes the distinction between the two is not as clear cut as it should be. There are three key differences between criminal justice and civil justice:

1. Criminal justice is concerned with when someone does something or is suspected of having done something that the government has deemed is against the interests of society and therefore some form of punishment is necessary, as set out in the laws made by government. Criminal justice cases are brought by the government against the parties concerned, primarily by the Crown Prosecution Service (CPS). If it is determined that a crime has been committed, then there is a penalty associated with the crime that is administered by the government. This penalty is set in law and can have serious implications for the individual concerned.
2. Civil justice refers to when a disagreement or a dispute that is not a crime in law occurs between individuals or groups. Although no crime has been committed, there is a disagreement about what to do or someone feels they have been wronged. Issues concerning divorce, debt and contracts are all examples. In most civil justice cases, courts deal with cases brought by private individuals or organisations, as the dispute primarily affects only the parties concerned and no one else. This means that the penalty is usually less serious than for crimes, and this is usually a financial penalty or an order to change behaviour.
3. A key difference between criminal justice and civil justice is the burden of proof required. Criminal justice requires that the facts of a case are proved to have happened beyond a reasonable doubt, meaning that the facts suggest there is only one logical explanation. This means that a crime is only deemed to have happened if this can be proved beyond reasonable doubt. Civil justice requires that the facts of a case are proved to have happened on the balance of probabilities, meaning that what one party says happened is more likely than what the other party says happened.

These key differences enable us to identify some key legally required organisations in criminal justice practice. The legally required organisations include, of course, the police, the courts and prisons. Their legal functions respectively are to investigate, prosecute and punish crime, and these are probably what most people would consider as criminal justice practice, as it is principally through these organisations that law enforcement occurs. These bodies, together with others such as the probation service, youth justice service and the CPS, and the Home Office and Ministry of Justice government departments, are what are commonly referred to as the Criminal Justice System (CJS) (Clinks, 2022). This is because they officially function together as a 'single system', meaning that their actions are closely linked and these bodies work in an almost sequential manner (Pope et al, 2020). For example, when a suspected crime occurs, first, the police carry out the investigation; secondly, the CPS decide whether to charge; thirdly, the courts oversee the prosecution of the alleged crime in court and if the CPS prove the crime, whether the perpetrators should be sentenced; and fourthly, if the court sends the perpetrators to prison, the prison service oversees this, and finally, the probation service may be involved in their release. By simply looking at these legally required organisations and what they do, we can narrowly define criminal justice practice as the work of these and other legally required organisations such as government departments, the police, judges/magistrates, CPS lawyers, prison officers and probation officers in response to crime.

However, such a narrow focus omits some important individuals and groups. The most obvious omission is lawyers who do not work for the CPS, such as defence lawyers. Also missing are charities and campaigning organisations such as Nacro, the Howard League for Penal Reform and Victim Support, and also research organisations such as the Centre for Crime and Justice and criminologists, which have all made important contributions to the development of criminal justice practice. An example of this is the successful campaign in 2014 by the Howard League for Penal Reform to overturn the ban on prisoners having access to books – a specific example of a campaigning organisation from outside the legally required CJS changing practice within the CJS. This highlights that individuals and organisations who work outside the legally required CJS also affect criminal justice practice, so it is important to include them as part of criminal justice practice. This means that while statutory organisations are the largest part of criminal justice practice, they are not the only element – there are many other organisations, each with a specific purpose, all of which inform and influence criminal justice in significant ways. The key point is that criminal justice practice is wider than just the legally required CJS. This distinction is shown in Table 3.1.

From Table 3.1, we can make a distinction between the statutory organisations of the CJS, which refers to the legally required bodies, and non-statutory organisations, which are not legally required but which nonetheless often have a significant impact on the workings of the CJS. For the purposes of this book from this point onwards, the term CJS refers specifically to the statutory organisations as detailed in Table 3.1, while the term criminal justice practice refers to both the statutory and non-statutory organisations listed in Table 3.1.

Table 3.1 Criminal justice practice

Statutory organisations (CJS)	Non-statutory organisations
• Government departments, eg Home Office, Ministry of Justice, Attorney General's Office • Police • CPS • HM Court and Tribunal Service • Probation Service • Magistrate and Crown Courts • Prison Service • Youth Justice Board • Youth Offending Services • Police and Crime Commissioners	• Criminal defence lawyers • Victims' organisations, eg Victim Support • Campaigning organisations, eg Nacro • Research organisations, eg Centre for Crime and Justice • Criminologists, eg university lecturers • Voluntary sector organisations, eg Clinks • Rehab services, eg Turning Point Please note that this list is not exhaustive

Having clarified these distinctions between criminal justice and civil justice, and statutory and non-statutory organisations, we can begin to see, in the simplest terms, that criminal justice practice is concerned with dealing with crime. While there is no universal definition of crime, we can provide a working definition of crime as *an action that is deemed to be against the laws of a country and therefore requires some form of sanction or punishment*. This is very simplistic, but we can use it to outline some key features of criminal justice practice, to understand more clearly what it is. Three key features that are relevant to this follow.

Criminal justice practice is largely determined by what the law says is a crime

The working definition of crime noted above states that crime is an action. However, for something to be deemed a crime, it has to be defined in law that this is the case (Marsh, 2011). There are some actions that are evident as crime to most people, such as murder and theft, but there are lots of other things that, if we did them, would mean that we are committing a crime. Examples are driving without a valid licence, smoking indoors and drinking under the age of 18. Conversely, ensuring that our children are protected from harm, paying Council Tax and having a TV licence to watch live TV are all things which, if we did not do them, would also be crimes.

It is also important to note that as Lamond (2007) highlights, almost anything can be a crime, as we can see by looking at what has been historically deemed as such in England and Wales. For example, heresy (having a religious belief other than that defined by the state) was illegal in the 16th century, the Vagrancy Act 1824 effectively made it a criminal offence to be poor during the 19th century and both abortion and homosexuality were crimes until the 1960s. Additionally, things that have not been criminal historically can also become a crime, such as domestic abuse and driving offences related to mobile phone use. The important point here is that changes in the law lead to changes in criminal justice practice.

As an example, the gradual change in the law concerning domestic abuse as a crime has led to the growth of criminal justice practices such as victim support, lawyers and training. Criminal justice practice is therefore something that changes over time as the law changes. This point also reinforces the significance of the CJS as stated earlier, wherein criminal justice law usually only changes owing to CJS organisations, primarily the Home Office and the Ministry of Justice.

Criminal justice practice differs from country to country

As noted in the previous section, there are lots of actions in our daily lives that can be deemed crimes and so are relevant to criminal justice. Additionally, some acts become crimes or cease to be so. This leads to the question of why some things are deemed to be crimes and others not (Craven, 2015)? The answer is easy when we look at something like murder, as this is something that, as Ashworth and Horder (2013:2) observe, 'most people would agree represents a serious wrong against an individual or against some fundamental social value or institution'. This notion of a 'serious wrong' can therefore be regarded as important when determining why some things are deemed crimes.

However, this notion cannot explain all crimes. The example of requiring a licence to watch live TV is an example of something that it would be hard to argue is a serious wrong, but which is nonetheless a crime. This leads to the question of why this is deemed a crime and other actions that are equally less serious are not. To answer this question, we need to ask another: who decides what a serious wrong is? If we can answer this question, it may help us to understand why some actions become crimes and others do not.

Ashworth and Horder (2013:2) argue that 'The boundaries of the criminal law are explicable largely as the result of exercise of political power at particular points in history.' By this they mean that there is no definitive answer to our question of why some things become crimes and others do not. Determining what is a crime is a human process that is determined not so much by logic but by who has the appropriate power, meaning that what a society determines as a crime is reflective of the power relations within that society. An example of this is the previously mentioned crime of heresy in 16th-century England and Wales. This was deemed a crime because of the power of the Church at the time, but as this power decreased, so the view that heresy was a crime also decreased, until the law was finally **repealed** (Key Learning Box 3.1), meaning that heresy was no longer a crime.

> **KEY LEARNING BOX 3.1** REPEAL OF A LAW
>
> Sometimes a law is no longer relevant and so is no longer used. This means it is removed from the list of laws that apply, meaning that the law is dead and can no longer be used. This is known as repeal. Examples of laws that have been repealed are the Slave Trade Act 1807, the Treason Act 1817 and the Vagrancy Act 1838. More recently, the European Union (Withdrawal) Act 2018 repealed many laws related to

the EU after Brexit. Often, a repealed law is replaced by an updated version. For a law to be repealed, it has to go through a specific process. Unless this takes place, a law is still live and can still be used, however obscure the law.

Additionally, if we consider the crime of watching TV without a licence, we can observe that the requirement to have a licence exists despite the fact that other options that do not criminalise watching TV exist, such as having a tax on every broadband connection (Weeds, 2016). In other words, it is only a crime because a decision was made by those in power to make it a crime. It is possible to imagine that in an alternate universe watching TV without a licence is not a crime, and indeed this is the case in some other countries. This supports the point that determining what is a crime is not determined by logic.

This view is also supported by the fact that a crime in one country is not necessarily a crime somewhere else. An example of this is rape, as in some countries this is not deemed a crime when it occurs between a married couple. Another example is the crime of heresy, which still exists in some countries. Even the act of killing someone is not always deemed illegal, as, in the US, some states allow a homeowner to kill an intruder on their private property without it being a crime, and in some countries the killing of a female relative is not pursued as a crime if it is deemed to have taken place to maintain family honour. What this shows is that there is clearly no worldwide consensus about what acts are crimes, but, rather, definitions are dependent on a country's social norms, and are designed to uphold those social norms. We can define social norms as 'the informal rules that govern behaviour in groups and societies' (Bicchieri et al, 2018). They can be determined at family level (for example, the importance of family relationships), community level (for example, the importance of raising children in a certain way) and society level (for example, the importance of religion). The key point about social norms is that they function to restrict behaviour, so that the social norm is reinforced.

The obvious question to ask is who determines social norms at the societal level. An obvious answer to this would be the family, communities or society, depending on the type of norm. However, it is important to note that social norms are not universally acceptable to all, as for example in relation to the importance of religion. There may be some who do not wish to be religious. However, when the social norm is reinforced through the law, making it a crime to behave in a less religious way, then it is very hard not to follow the social norm. Breaking the social norm is not only seen as deviance from that norm, but also becomes a crime. We can therefore see that what is deemed a crime is often the breaking of a social norm.

The other key point about social norms is that they often represent the norms of the most powerful within society. It is rare that the opposite is true. Therefore, when something becomes a crime, it is typically a crime against the norms of the most powerful. An example of this is discrimination. In the UK, this mainly affects those with limited power, and so is more likely to be committed against those with little or no power by those with power. However, discrimination is a civil offence, not a criminal offence, as evident in the Equality Act 2010. This brings us back to the quote from Lamond that anything can be a crime, to which we can now add that what becomes a crime is reflective of the dominant power held in a society.

The relevance here is that, as previously discussed, criminal justice practice is largely determined by what the law says, and the law itself is determined by the norms of the society. This means that if we want to truly understand criminal justice practice within a society, we need to understand how society itself functions and particularly what its norms are.

Criminal justice practice operates in a more punitive CJS context now than in the recent past

As we have noted, punishment or sanctions are integral to dealing with crime. Punishing someone who commits a crime means that they are being punished for violating a particular social norm. Punishment as an important, if not the most important, aspect of criminal justice is evident when we consider that many parts of the CJS, such as the police, the CPS, the courts service, the prison service and the probation service, have punishment as their key focus.

The act of punishing can be justified in two ways. First, it is necessary to deal with violations in a proportionate manner, and secondly, punishment acts as a deterrent, and so limits the occurrence of crime (Carvalho et al, 2020). In other words, in the absence of punishment by society, disproportionate punishment could be carried out by others in the form of revenge, or the crime rate could be higher because crimes would go unpunished. Furthermore, the deterrent effect of punishment ensures that the social norm is maintained and societal stability is maintained. This is a point made by Robinson and Cussen (2017:153), who argue that 'A civilised society requires a government to develop laws for its citizens to be able to live in collective harmony and a government requires various systems (or departments) that can enact and administer these laws.' This view is supported by the observance of the chaos that occurs in societies in which law and order has broken down and crime is left to go unpunished, as occurred in Iraq in the 2000s and Afghanistan in 2021.

However, there are a number of problems with this argument. The first is that it is very hard to quantify that a punishment is proportionate to a crime. Sometimes it can be seen that punishment is disproportionate, for example where physical punishments such as manual labour are used for crimes such as theft. Secondly, it cannot be said that punishment actually works as a deterrent if a clear punishment exists in relation to a crime and yet that crime still occurs, for example murder. Thirdly, if we accept the point that crimes are defined in order to reinforce social norms, then we can argue that punishment is simply

Graph 3.1 England and Wales prison population per 100,000 of the population, 1901–2020

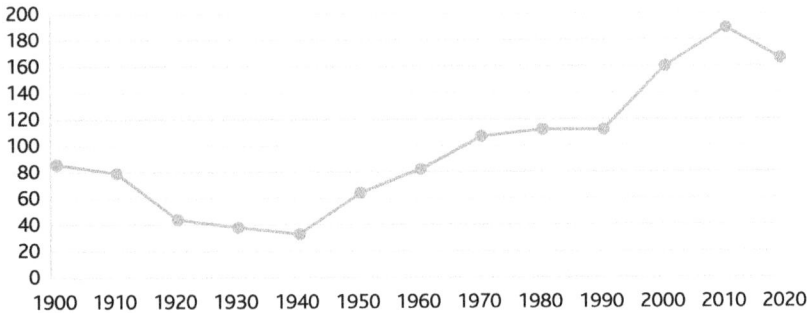

Source: MoJ (2021)

the reinforcement of a social norm by powerful groups over less powerful groups (Ashworth and Horder, 2013).

Despite these problems, the notion that it is necessary to punish crimes, and specifically that punishment is a deterrent, dominates CJSs in almost all parts of the world, including in England and Wales. More specifically, the emphasis in the CJS is primarily on punitive forms of punishment. In the past, this was in the form of public beatings, prison and capital punishment, but today the emphasis is largely on prison, and specifically long prison sentences. This is shown in Graph 3.1, which shows the prison population of England and Wales as a proportion of the population between 1901 and 2020. Graph 3.1 shows that even when taking the increased population into account, the prison population has seen consistent increases from the 1940s onwards, and it is only recently that this increase has ceased.

One possible explanation for this increase is that there is more crime now than there was in the past, resulting in the need to imprison more people. However, this is not supported by the evidence, which shows that, since the mid-1990s at least, recorded crime has been falling (ONS, 2022). This should have meant a fall in the rate of imprisonment, but instead it has risen dramatically in this period. An alternative explanation is that the nature of crimes has changed, meaning that the types of crimes that occur now are those that require imprisonment, such as violent crimes. Again, though, this explanation does not stand up to scrutiny. The data show that while the rate of murder increased until the mid-1990s, it fell after that (Allen and Zayed, 2021), at just the same time that the prison population increased. Similarly, data also show an overall fall in violent crime since the mid-1990s (ONS 2021), suggesting that this explanation is not valid.

This leads to an alternative explanation – that the CJS has become harsher, or more punitive, in nature. This can be viewed in two ways. First, the punishment for crimes has been increased, resulting in longer prison sentences. An example is the recent increase in sentencing for carrying knives and other offensive weapons.

Secondly, more crimes are punished severely, meaning that crimes that might not have resulted in a prison sentence now do so. An example of this is the introduction of Civil Injunctions and Criminal Behaviour Orders (previously known as Anti-Social Behaviour Orders (ASBOs)), a breach of which can lead to a prison sentence.

This evidence indicates that the CJS has indeed become more punitive since the mid-1990s, and this is the context within which criminal justice practice now operates.

Having defined the three key features of criminal justice practice, we can return to our basic definition of crime and redefine it as *an action which at the time is deemed by those in power to be against the social norms of a society and therefore requires some form of sanction or punishment by society, usually punitive in nature.*

Why is improving criminal justice practice relevant?

The previous sections have provided an outline of what criminal justice practice is. However, this book is about more than what criminal justice practice is. It is about improving criminal justice practice. It starts from two assumptions. The first is that criminal justice practice requires improvement, and the second is that improvement is a desirable outcome. Either way, this book aims to get you thinking about the kind of criminal justice practice you want to be involved in.

In relation to the first of these assumptions, even if you only have a passing interest in criminal justice issues, it would have been hard not to have noticed since 2010 that there have been problems within all areas of the CJS and criminal justice practice that are impacting on criminal justice. There is evidence of a 'justice gap' wherein 'the criminal justice system has become slower and less effective' (Redgrave, 2021:3). This has affected all aspects of the CJS. For instance, there has been a problem with confidence in police practice, as a consequence of their handling of the murder of Sarah Everard in 2021 by an off-duty police constable and the identification of cultures of misogyny (HMICFRS, 2022) and racism (Casey, 2022). In relation to the CPS, there has been an issue of confidence in the way decisions are made about whether to prosecute particular crimes such as rape, and specifically the low conviction rates for this offence. In relation to the courts, there have been problems with how they have dealt with the case backlog that has accrued over the years. In the prison service, there has been a problem with overcrowding and the resulting treatment of prisoners and prison safety. In the probation service, there has been a problem with the assessment and release of high-risk prisoners. These and other problems highlight the general public's overall lack of confidence in the CJS, especially among those who have been victims of crime (Marsh et al, 2019). These concerns have led Pope at al (2020) to observe that there are concerns about the overall effectiveness of the CJS as a whole, while the Law Society goes further by arguing that there is a need to 'fix the broken system' that is the CJS (Law Society, 2022). It is clear that most of these are systematic problems that can be seen as interrelated. As an example, the lack of confidence from those who have been victims of crime occurs from the way in which crime is investigated by the police, the length of time taken in deciding whether to bring charges by the CPS, the experience of delays in the court process, the early release of prisoners and the lack of supervision after release (Marsh et al, 2019). Often, these issues occur because of the lack of joined-up working within the CJS, meaning

> the different agencies that make up the justice system – the police, the courts, the probation service, prison. At the moment they are a loosely collected affiliation of agencies that work in silos and that don't really talk to each other. That cannot continue in a world where demand is going up and resources are going down. (Redgrave, 2017)

For those in criminal justice practice who work outside the CJS, this lack of working together must be an even more pressing issue. The key point here is that there are currently major problems with the CJS that affect criminal justice practice as a whole, and in order to improve criminal justice practice, it is necessary to understand what these problems are.

The second assumption of this book, that improving criminal justice practice is desirable, starts from the premise that even if we do not actually experience crime ourselves, improving criminal justice outcomes benefits not just those who are the victims of crimes but all of us. Criminal justice is something that affects us not only directly, but also indirectly. As an example of this, consider the rise in cybercrimes, particularly those related to sexual images such as revenge porn. Someone who is a victim of revenge porn is a direct victim of the crime, but there are also indirect victims, most obviously friends and family. If the crime affects the victim's health and well-being, limiting their participation in their community, then the crime has a wider indirect effect on society. As Maximo (2014) states:

> All criminal behaviour imposes direct costs to the victim and indirect costs to society at large. Some secondary impacts are harder than others to verify, however, in particular the wider economic effects that can ripple outward after a crime. Residents can avoid dangerous neighbourhoods, go outside less or move elsewhere, but research has shown that criminal activity can shift between neighbourhoods in ways that resemble infectious diseases. Surveillance systems have been shown to reduce crime, but only in certain contexts, and questions of whether they merely displace crime require more study.

The key point here is that the focus of effective criminal justice practice should be on both the direct and indirect costs of crime, as they can both have significant impacts on the individual and the community. We can also rationalise the improvement of criminal justice outcomes from a purely financial

Graph 3.2 Public sector spending, 2021–2022

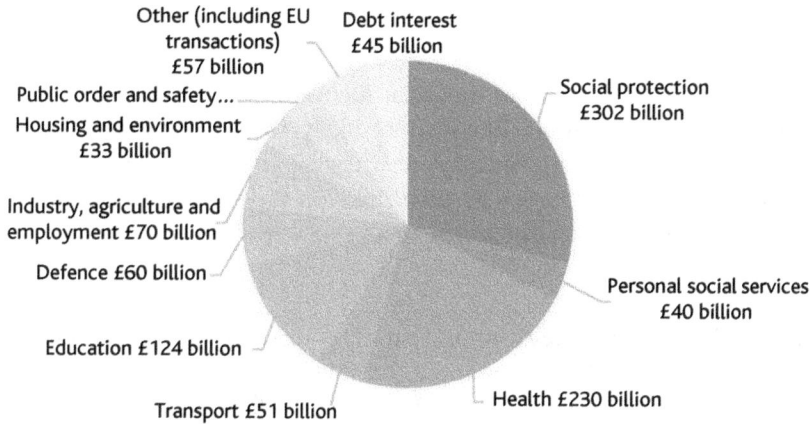

Other (including EU transactions) £57 billion

Debt interest £45 billion

Public order and safety...

Housing and environment £33 billion

Social protection £302 billion

Industry, agriculture and employment £70 billion

Defence £60 billion

Personal social services £40 billion

Education £124 billion

Transport £51 billion

Health £230 billion

Source: HM Treasury (2021)

perspective. Graph 3.2 shows how much the government spent on public services in 2020–2021, including the category of Public Order and Safety, which relates to spending on criminal justice practice.

As Graph 3.2 shows, £41 billion was spent on Public Order and Safety, which by any account is a huge amount of money – it represents spending £112 million every day for a year! Remember, this is just spending by the government on the CJS, it does not include spending by other criminal justice practice organisations, such as charities and private sector organisations. The general point is that criminal justice costs a lot of money. The other point is that this expenditure by government is borne by us, as almost all government expenditure is paid for by taxation, which, as detailed in Chapter 2, involves the general population (Sealey, 2015). We can conclude that improving criminal justice practice in terms of making it more cost-effective is beneficial to all of us, from a financial perspective.

At this point it is important to note that the punitive approach detailed earlier is not the only way in which criminal justice practice can deal with crime. The key point about the punitive approach is that it is not concerned with trying to deal with the underlying causes of crime, it is focused on either deterring crime from occurring or punishing crime after it has happened, neither of which deal with crime's underlying causes. An alternative approach to dealing with crime would consider these underlying causes and deal with them so crime does not occur in the first place. This is known as a preventive approach, as it is concerned with preventing either the opportunity or the circumstances for crime (United Nations Office on Drugs and Crime, 2002). It sees crime as a societal rather than an individual problem, so problems need to be solved at a societal level. The objective is to alter the conditions that allow crime to occur. This includes policies that focus on improving the social aspects of society, such as equality, inclusion and opportunity. This is acknowledged even by the police themselves, as evident in the quote from Neil Basu, who as Britain's most senior counter-terrorism officer stated that:

> Policies that go towards more social inclusion, more social mobility and more education are much more likely to drive down violence … than all the policing and state security apparatus put together. It is much more likely to have a positive effect on society. The prescription for me is around social inclusion – it's social mobility, it's education, it's opportunity. (Dodd, 2019)

This quote captures the key theme that runs through this book, that of the importance of dealing with issues at the social level before they become criminal justice issues. As detailed in Chapter 2, dealing with social issues is at the core of social policy, and this book's core argument is that the key way in which criminal justice practice can be improved is through a clear understanding of the interconnection between social policy issues and criminal justice practice.

Summary

This chapter has provided a brief overview of criminal justice practice, as relevant to this book. The focus has been on criminal justice in England and Wales, as opposed to civil justice. A key point is that while the CJS's legal bodies are very important to criminal justice, there are other relevant organisations. For the purposes of this book, the term criminal justice practice refers to all individuals and groups, including the CJS, that work within the field of criminal justice.

The chapter has highlighted some key and interrelated observations about criminal justice practice. First, criminal justice practice is defined by the law, meaning that what is a crime and is therefore the focus of criminal justice practice is determined by the law. Secondly, the law itself is largely determined by the norms of society, and so will differ within each society. This is evident if we consider that some laws do not exist in all countries. Thirdly, the CJS, and by extension criminal justice practice, currently operates in a largely punitive context, with the emphasis on punishment and sanctions. All these points contribute to an understanding of what criminal justice practice is.

However, this book is about more than understanding what criminal justice practice is. Its key focus is on improving criminal justice practice. The current context provides two key rationales for this. The first is that criminal justice practice is in a state of crisis, as numerous issues are impacting its effectiveness. The second is that improving criminal justice practice is desirable, because as crime has both direct and indirect effects, an improvement to criminal justice will benefit everyone. A purely financial consideration of the cost of criminal justice makes this evident. In the rest of this book, we focus on showing how social policy and criminal justice practice are theoretically and functionally linked, and how understanding this link can benefit criminal justice practice. In particular, we will highlight how developing a more comprehensive understanding of this link can lead to better outcomes for criminal justice practitioners, and therefore for society as a whole.

References

Allen, G. and Zayed, Y. (2022) *Homicide Statistics. Number 8224, 25 May 2021*. London: House of Commons Library. Available from: https://commonslibrary. parliament.uk/research-briefings/cbp-8224/ [Accessed 21 July 2022].

Ashworth, A. and Horder, J. (2013) *Principles of Criminal Law*. Seventh edition. Oxford: Oxford University Press.

Bicchieri, C., Muldoon, R. and Sontuoso, A. (2018) 'Social norms', *Stanford Encyclopaedia of Philosophy* [Preprint] (Winter). Available from: https://plato. stanford.edu/archives/win2018/entries/social-norms/ [Accessed 21 July 2022].

Carvalho, H., Chamberlen, A. and Lewis, R. (2019) 'Punitiveness beyond criminal justice: Punishable and punitive subjects in an era of prevention, anti-migration and austerity', *The British Journal of Criminology*, 60(2): 265–280. https://doi. org/10.1093/bjc/azz061.

Casey, L. (2022) *Baroness Casey Review – Interim Report on Misconduct*. Available from: https://www.met.police.uk/police-forces/metropolitan-police/areas/ about-us/about-the-met/bcr/baroness-caseys-report-misconduct/ [Accessed 3 November 2022].

Clinks (2022) *Navigating the Criminal Justice System*. Available from: https:// www.clinks.org/publication/navigating-criminal-justice-system [Accessed 21 July 2022].

Craven, S. (2015) *What is Crime?* University of Glasgow: Scottish Centre for Crime and Justice Research.

Davies, N., Pope, T. and Guerin, B. (2020) *The Criminal Justice System*. Available from: https://www.instituteforgovernment.org.uk/publications/criminal-just ice-system [Accessed 21 July 2022].

Dodd, V. (2019) 'Counter-terror chief says policing alone cannot beat extremism', *The Guardian*, 6 August. Available from: https://www.theguardian.com/uk- news/2019/aug/06/counter-terrorism-chief-calls-for-greater-social-inclusion [Accessed 21 July 2022].

Garside, R. and Ford, M. (2015) *The Coalition Years: Criminal Justice in the United Kingdom 2010 to 2015*. London: Centre for Crime and Justice Studies.

HM Treasury (2021) *Budget 2021: Protecting the Jobs and Livelihoods of the British People*. London: HM Treasury.

HMICFRS (HM Inspectorate of Constabulary and Fire & Rescue Services) (2022) 'An inspection of vetting, misconduct, and misogyny in the police service'. Available from: https://www.justiceinspectorates.gov.uk/hmicfrs/publ ication-html/an-inspection-of-vetting-misconduct-and-misogyny-in-the-pol ice-service/ [Accessed 3 November 2022].

Lamond, G. (2007) 'What is a crime?', *Oxford Journal of Legal Studies*, 27(4): 609–632. https://doi.org/10.1093/ojls/gqm018.

Law Society (2022) 'Fix the broken system – back our criminal justice campaign'. Available from: https://www.lawsociety.org.uk/campaigns/criminal-justice [Accessed 6 April 2023].

Marsh, I. (ed.) (2011) *Crime and Criminal Justice*. Abingdon; New York: Routledge.

Marsh, N., McKay, E., Pelly, C. and Cereda, S. (2019) *Public Knowledge and Confidence in the Criminal Justice System and Sentencing. A Report for the Sentencing Council*. London: Sentencing Council.

Maximo, M. (2014) *The Impact of Crime on Property Values: Research Roundup – the Journalist's Resource*. Available from: https://journalistsresource.org/economics/the-impact-of-crime-on-property-values-research-roundup/ [Accessed 21 July 2022].

Ministry of Justice (2021) 'Annual Prison Statistics'. Available from: https://assets.publishing.service.gov.uk/government/uploads/system/uploads/attachment_data/file/1006269/Population_30June2021_quarterly.ods [Accessed 21 July 2022].

ONS (Office for National Statistics) (2021) *Crime in England and Wales: Year Ending March 2021*. London: Office for National Statistics. Available from: https://www.ons.gov.uk/peoplepopulationandcommunity/crimeandjustice/bulletins/crimeinenglandandwales/yearendingmarch2021. [Accessed 6 April 2023].

ONS (Office for National Statistics) (2022) 'Crime in England and Wales – Office for National Statistics'. Available from: https://www.ons.gov.uk/peoplepopulationandcommunity/crimeandjustice/bulletins/crimeinenglandandwales/yearendingseptember2021 [Accessed 21 July 2022].

Redgrave, H. (2017) *Why the CJS Is in Trouble*. Crest. Available from: https://www.crestadvisory.com/post/why-the-criminal-justice-system-is-in-trouble-harvey-redgrave-on-the-factors-challenging-the-cjs [Accessed 21 July 2022].

Redgrave, H. (2021) *The Justice Gap*. Institute for Global Change. Available from: https://institute.global/policy/justice-gap [Accessed 21 July 2022].

Robinson, S. and Cussen, T. (2017) *The Criminology and Criminal Justice Companion*. London: Macmillan Education.

Sealey, C. (2015) *Social Policy Simplified: Connecting Theory with People's Lives*. London; New York: Palgrave Macmillan.

United Nations Office on Drugs and Crime (2002) 'Crime Prevention, Crime Prevention'. Available from: https//www.unodc.org/unodc/en/justice-and-prison-reform/CrimePrevention.html [Accessed 21 July 2022].

Weeds, H. (2016) 'Is the television licence fee fit for purpose in the digital era?', *Economic Affairs*, 36(1): 2–20. https://doi.org/10.1111/ecaf.12166.

4

What is the interconnection between social policy and criminal justice practice?

This chapter aims to:

- outline the significant interconnections between social policy and criminal justice practice;

- detail the relevance of these interconnections to improving criminal justice practice.

Introduction

The focus of this book is on improving criminal justice practice. The book's core argument is that the key way in which criminal justice practice can be improved is through a clear understanding of its interconnection with social policy. Chapters 2 and 3 outlined key features of social policy and criminal justice practice. In this chapter and throughout the rest of this book, we focus on showing how social policy and criminal justice practice are theoretically and functionally interconnected, and how understanding this interconnection can improve criminal justice practice. In particular, the chapter highlights five key conceptual interconnections between social policy and criminal justice practice, and shows how developing a more comprehensive understanding of interconnections can lead to better outcomes for individuals, communities and society. The chapter also outlines key issues that are addressed later in the book.

How are social policy and criminal justice practice interconnected, and why is this important to understand?

In Chapter 2, we define social policy as a set of policies that aim to improve the social and economic well-being of individuals and society. Social policies refer to services (such as the National Health Service, NHS), financial benefits (such as Child Benefit) or legislation (such as the National Living Wage legislation). Defining social policy in this way enables us to analyse how it works and functions, and also enables us to consider the wider relevance of social policies to individuals, families and communities. It also shows that the key aim of social policy is to find answers and solutions to social problems and thereby to improve social and economic well-being.

In Chapter 3, criminal justice practice is defined broadly as any practice that works within criminal justice, including not only statutory bodies such as the police, the Crown Prosecution Service (CPS), the courts and the prison service, but also non-statutory groups such as campaigning groups, third sector and research organisations. There are also some key and interrelated observations about criminal justice practice, such as that it is defined by the law, which is largely determined by social norms, and it operates in a largely punitive context.

On the face of it, there do not appear to be many links between these two fields, as they appear to be concerned with different issues, concepts and outcomes. For example, social policy is primarily concerned with welfare issues such as poverty, equality and meeting needs, while criminal justice practice is concerned with crime, the law and dealing with offenders. Additionally, while it is true that most people receive some form of social policy services or benefits in their lifetime, it is less likely that someone will have contact with the Criminal Justice System (CJS). And, linked to this, is that while it is possible to go through life with no contact with a criminal justice practitioner, it is impossible to go through life with no contact with a social policy practitioner, as these include teachers, doctors and social care workers. This suggests that there are clear differences between social policy and criminal justice practice that deny their interconnection.

However, I argue that there are five key concepts that indicate social policy and criminal justice practice are interconnected, and these are analysed here.

The concept of justice

The notion of justice is at the heart of criminal justice practice. It is concerned with the effective detection, prosecution and conviction of crime, and ensures that 'due process' is followed in the criminal justice process (Ellis and Savage, 2013). Due process means that a fair and just process applies to all, and that everyone is treated in the same way throughout the criminal justice process. In this way, criminal justice contributes to the creation of a fair and just society, which benefits all. In the absence of due process, criminal justice outcomes would be determined according to the resources that individuals have and who they know, which would run counter to the notion of justice.

Justice is also an important concept in social policy, through the notion of social justice, which commonly refers to the way in which resources in society are distributed (Lister, 2010). For social policy, a focus on social justice is about improving outcomes for the least able in society, and the rationale for this emphasis is that this leads to an improvement in society that benefits all of society. As set out in Chapter 2, the current structure of social policy in the UK has its origins in the 'cradle to grave' welfare state that the Clement Atlee government created in 1945 in the aftermath of World War Two (WW2) following the *Beveridge Report*. A key point about this welfare state was its comprehensive nature, in terms of its attempt to deal with the five so-called 'giant evils' in a wide ranging and detailed way, as opposed to being limited and selective in its scope and provision. This is exemplified by the emphasis that Beveridge and the Attlee government gave to the social policy areas of health, education, housing, employment and social care, regarding them as 'pillars of the welfare state', and therefore essential to its effective functioning.

This presents the first key link between social policy and criminal justice practice, whereby it can be argued that ensuring social justice is essential to ensuring due process, and vice versa (Behan et al, 2016). In the absence of a social policy focus on social justice, due process is hard to achieve, and in the absence of a criminal justice focus on due process for all, social justice is hard to achieve. So we can say that although social policy and criminal justice practice have different conceptions of what justice means, they are interdependent on each other and the ultimate outcomes for both are the same, in terms of working towards the creation of a fair and just society. This is because social policy and criminal justice both require adequate access to services and benefits for justice if they are to be achieved. For instance, without adequate access to social policy services such as healthcare, then the health and well-being of individuals are severely limited. Similarly, without adequate access to criminal justice practices such as legal aid, the possibility of getting fair treatment is also severely limited.

The concept of security

The notion of security is a key aspect of the CJS and therefore criminal justice practice. Security here usually refers to 'the safety of individuals in their everyday life' (Zedner, 2003:153), and the CJS includes a range of measures that ensure this security, which include laws that restrict gun ownership, risk assessment for probation, stop and search for knife crime and measures against the threat of terrorism. The key point about the emphasis on security that runs through the CJS is that criminal justice practice is concerned with protection from threats to physical existence, however defined. Conversely, insecurity in CJS terms is something that is harmful to individuals, communities and society.

Security is also an important aspect of social policy, but in a different sense. The focus is on social security, meaning protection from harms such as poverty, unemployment and ill health through a range of measures, as set out in Chapter 2. These threats are seen as harmful to the individual, communities and society. The key interconnection here is in relation to the notion of protection from harm, as both criminal justice practice and social policy are concerned with this.

The concept of equality

The Equality and Human Rights Commission (2018) defines equality as 'ensuring that every individual has an equal opportunity to make the most of their lives and talents. It is also the belief that no one should have poorer life chances because of the way they were born, where they come from, what they believe, or whether they have a disability.' This acknowledges that society is not equal and that there are inequalities between groups. These can relate to income, gender, race, geography, education and health, for example. Social policy aims to ensure a level of equality within society so that that the gaps between individuals and groups do not become too wide. This acknowledges the fact that a lack of equality has the potential to cause divisions in society, which can potentially lead to tension and strife.

What is often not well known is that at the same time as the Attlee government put in place social policy measures for the post-war welfare state as detailed in Chapter 2, it also made significant changes to the civil justice system and CJS, through the Legal Aid and Advice Act 1949:

> An often-overlooked additional pillar of the Clement Attlee government's post-war welfare state is the provision for free access to justice, through what we now know as legal aid. Up to and during WW2, there was very limited legal assistance for impoverished defendants in criminal case, while legal advice for poorer individuals in civil cases (that is where there is a non-criminal dispute between two parties, for example in divorces or housing) relied heavily on the good will of lawyers prepared to work for free. Changes made in 1949 gave 80% of the population free access to legal aid not just in criminal cases, but also in civil cases, which was a very significant shift. (Sealey, 2015:52)

The aim of these changes was to make access to both the civil justice system and CJS an additional pillar of the welfare state, and the effect was to provide free access to civil and criminal justice for the majority of the population. This was done by enabling the state to pay private lawyers to provide legal advice and represent civil and criminal justice applicants. This was in contrast to the previous system that was in place where the vast majority of people had to pay privately for legal advice. The changes meant that access to civil and criminal justice became an almost universal component of the post-war welfare state for the majority of the population, just like the social policy service and benefits such as the NHS. The Attlee government rationalised this change to the provision of legal aid as: 'to provide legal advice for those of slender means and resources, so that no one would be financially unable to prosecute a just and reasonable claim or defend a legal right; and to allow counsel and solicitors to be remunerated for their services' (Brooke, 2017:5).

The key point that the Attlee government wanted to make was that equal access to civil and criminal justice was just as important as equal access to social policy for the simple reason that the two cannot be separated. By this is meant that equal access to civil and criminal justice makes equal social policy outcomes more probable and, vice versa, equal access to social policy service and benefits makes equal access to civil and criminal justice more probable. For example, consider how much harder it would be to get justice without the benefit of education to know your rights to criminal justice services. Borrowing from Cohen (2010), consider the circumstances of two individuals together in the CJS for the same offence, the difference between them being that one is poor and the other is rich. While they will face the same judge and/or jury, they will very likely have different levels of representation based on their income, and this could very well impact on the outcomes. As Cohen (2010) observes, however, the provision of equal access to justice is designed to negate the impact that social advantage or disadvantage has on the life chances of individuals. More specifically, it relates to the fact that having equality before the law is ineffective without the resources to ensure that those rights are enforced. Resources could be in the form of education, so that the legal process can be understood, as provided by social policy, or they could be in the form of income, so that an individual can afford a better lawyer, also provided by social policy.

Thus, the key rationale of the Attlee government for the need to provide equal access to justice at the same time as equal access to social rights was to ensure that those who would be unable to afford legal assistance owing to inadequate resources would be given an equal footing in the justice system. This acknowledges that criminal justice practice operates in a world that is laden with inequalities, and that measures are needed to overcome such inequalities. There is a wealth of data showing that inequalities are still highly prevalent in criminal justice practice, including inequalities of race (Lammy, 2017), religion (Livingstone and Mullen, 2015), health (Anders et al, 2019) and income (Duque and McKnight, 2019). Moreover, research from Wilkinson and Pickett (2010) outlines several clear links between equality and positive social policy outcomes. This includes the observation that more equal countries tend to have an increased life expectancy, lower infant mortality, higher educational outcomes, higher social mobility, less poverty and lower rates of mental illness. The research also outlines a clear link between equality and positive criminal justice practice outcomes, as more equal countries tend to have a lower prison population, a lower murder rate and lower drug use. For example, if we consider two countries where one is highly equal and the other is highly unequal, Wilkinson and Pickett (2010) outline that trust between individuals in the former is higher than in the latter. It is feasible to imagine that in the latter there is a social divide between individuals, less optimism among those who are experiencing a lack of equality and also the feeling they have no power. As an example of this, the experience of the **2011 English riots** (Key Learning Box 4.1) has shown that where such a lack of trust exists within communities and society, it can be the catalyst for violent action and strife (Sutterluty, 2014). The negative impact of this lack of trust does not need to be so spectacular as rioting, but can result in smaller scale acts of crime such as theft, violence and civil disobedience (Wieshmann et al, 2020).

KEY LEARNING BOX 4.1 THE 2011 ENGLISH RIOTS

In August 2011, there were riots in a number of English cities, most notably London and Birmingham, which cased approximately £200 million worth of damage. The riots followed the death by shooting of Mark Duggan by police while they were carrying out an operation to arrest him. A number of explanations have been given for the cause of the riots, but among the rioters themselves, poverty was noted as the prime cause, with other socio-economic issues such as unemployment and inequality also featuring prominently (Lewis et al, 2011).

Furthermore, in Chapter 3, we note that crime has both direct and indirect consequences. If we consider the consequences of the absence of equality, we can see that criminal justice practice does not just affect those who experience inequality. For example, consider a situation where due process is not followed and individuals are prosecuted and convicted for a crime they did not commit, such as in relation to the **Birmingham Six miscarriage of justice** (Key Learning Box 4.2) following the pub bombings of 1974. The implication of that case was not only significant to the individuals concerned, but also in a wider context because it led to a section of society, namely the Irish community, mistrusting not just the criminal justice process but also the wider political process, which had significant implications for many years.

KEY LEARNING BOX 4.2 THE BIRMINGHAM SIX MISCARRIAGE OF JUSTICE

This refers to six Irishmen who were accused of bombing two pubs in Birmingham in 1974 and killing 21 people. The six men were subsequently convicted of terrorism offences and sent to prison for life. At the time, all the men protested their innocence and continued to protest their innocence after their conviction. Then, 17 years after their imprisonment, the convictions were quashed because the police had fabricated and suppressed evidence, and the confessions had been obtained in an unacceptable manner. All six men were freed. The Guildford Four and Maguire Seven are similar cases where there were miscarriages of justice in the prosecution of Irish individuals for terrorist offences that were subsequently quashed.

On the other hand, consider the situation where due process is not followed and individuals are not prosecuted for a crime they did commit because of a lack of racial equality, such as in relation to the murder of **Stephen Lawrence** (Key Learning Box 4.3). Again, the implications of this miscarriage of justice were not just felt by the family, but also by the wider Black community in the form of mistrust of the CJS and the wider political system. It is likely that such incidents will also reduce the actual or perceived safety and security of all individuals in society (Boutellier, 2001).

KEY LEARNING BOX 4.3 STEPHEN LAWRENCE

The Black teenager Stephen Lawrence was murdered in London in 1993 while waiting for a bus. It emerged that the murder was wholly racially motivated, as he was killed simply because he was Black. Following the murder, the police arrested but did not charge six suspects, and the murder remained unsolved. Following public pressure, a public inquiry was held to explore why this was the case. The inquiry's Macpherson Report stated that the murder remained unsolved because the police investigation had been incompetent, and that this was because of the police's institutionally racist attitudes. Put simply, it was the fact that Stephen Lawrence was Black that affected the incompetent way in which the police carried out the investigation. Following this report, the investigation was reopened and two men were eventually convicted of the murder.

The link between social policy and tension and strife may not be as evident, but its impact is very similar. Social policy provision exists to facilitate equality, and where an individual does not feel that they are being treated equally, the consequences can be wide ranging. For example, imagine someone who is in a job where their pay is much less than their peers despite doing the same work. It is quite possible that this lack of equality could lead to anger and resentment, and also stress and anxiety. This could also lead to tension and strife in the workplace, and then wider resentment and anger within the community, owing to feeling powerless. To return to the 2011 English riots, the key reason given by participants was high levels of poverty, highlighting how a lack of social equality can become a criminal justice problem.

To summarise, both social policy and criminal justice practice work towards equality, and the absence of equality leads to anger, mistrust and feelings of powerlessness, which can have a significant negative effect on outcomes for both social policy and criminal justice practice.

The concept of making a meaningful contribution to society

In relation to this concept, from a social policy perspective, we can take the example of someone who is physically disabled and unable to access either cash benefits in the form of Personal Independence Payment or non-cash benefits because of the absence of regulations that prohibit discriminations based on their disability. This would mean that this person would not be able to participate as fully as possible in society. Now it might be the case that this person, given the chances and resources that social policy services and benefits provide, would be able to contribute significantly to the development of society: the most outstanding example being **Professor Stephen Hawking** (Key Learning Box 4.4). Another good example is J.K. Rowling, the author of the Harry Potter books. She has spoken about the importance of the social policy services and benefits she received while writing her first book during a sustained period that involved divorce, single parenthood and poverty.

KEY LEARNING BOX 4.4 PROFESSOR STEPHEN HAWKING

Stephen Hawking, who died in 2018 aged 76, is still one of the world's most famous scientists. His work contributed significantly to our understanding of the universe. He was diagnosed with a form of motor neurone disease at the age of 21, and was given a life expectancy of two years. The disease affected his physical abilities but not his mental capacity. As a consequence, he was able to use various adaptations in order to continue his work and make the contributions for which he became famous. Hawking was clear about the impact that social policy provision in the form of healthcare had on enabling him to achieve his potential. When it was claimed by an American publication that his physical condition made his life essentially worthless in the UK, he responded by saying that 'I have had a lot of experience of the NHS and the care I received has enabled me to live my life as I want and to contribute to major advances in our understanding of the universe' (Triggle, 2017).

Similarly, if we consider this notion of making a meaningful contribution to society in relation to criminal justice practice, we could take the case of someone who has committed a crime and served their sentence. In the absence of criminal justice practice focused on rehabilitation, it would be harder for this person to integrate back into society, meaning that the potential that they have to make good for the crime that they committed would be limited, and so their ability to contribute to society would also be limited. However, with an emphasis on rehabilitation, there is the potential for individuals to contribute meaningfully to society. An example of this is **The Clink restaurants** (Key Learning Box 4.5).

What this shows is that a key interconnection between social policy and criminal justice practice is an emphasis on enabling individuals to make a meaningful contribution to society, with the core belief that this is beneficial not just for individuals but also for the communities in which they live and wider society.

KEY LEARNING BOX 4.5 THE CLINK RESTAURANTS

The Clink restaurants is a group of restaurants run in prisons by The Clink charity. The aim of the restaurants is to reduce the rate of reoffending by helping prisoners to secure employment after release by providing vocational training in catering, front of house and cleaning for accredited City and Guilds and NVQ qualifications. The results of an evaluation of the scheme showed that 'those who took part in the programme were less likely to reoffend than those who did not' (Ministry of Justice, 2018), which suggests a specific beneficial outcome in relation to its stated aims.

The concept of rights

Rights are at the core of both social policy and the criminal justice practice, including the right to social policy services such as healthcare and the right to criminal justice practice that is fair, such as a fair trial. The key point is that without such rights, the possibility of achieving the outcomes already outlined such as equality would be seriously limited. It is interesting to consider what would happen in the absence of either social policy or criminal justice rights. For example, it might be the case that you are entitled to a certain service, but are denied it for an administrative reason. Without access to legal assistance, it becomes very hard to ensure that your rights are respected and your needs are met. This links in to T.H. Marshall's ([1950] 1973) conceptualisation of citizenship, which argued that to be a complete citizen, not only are civil and political rights necessary, but also social rights to ensure that these other rights are attainable. Marshall relates access to justice as a crucial element of civil rights, and defines social rights as rights to provision such as health, housing, social security and education. In his words, 'the right to freedom of speech has little real substance if, from a lack of education, you have nothing to say that is worth saying, and no means of making yourself heard if you have to say it' (Marshall, [1950] 1973:151). This means that without having access to and the benefits of important social policy rights such as education, access to justice becomes less possible if not impossible. The point can also be made in relation to the importance of other social policy services, such as good health, a decent income, decent housing and good social relationships, which are all conducive to being able to access justice. When your rights to these services are not being met, it is the right to justice that enables you to enforce these rights. This makes the link between rights, social policy and accessing criminal justice practice highly evident and relevant.

Summary

While the interconnections between social policy and criminal justice practice may not be obvious, this chapter has argued that the they are actually linked by five important concepts. The first is justice, which is significant to both social policy and criminal justice. In particular, although social policy and criminal justice practice conceive of justice differently, they are interdependent on each other and the ultimate outcomes for both are the same in terms of working towards a fair and just society.

Secondly, social policy and criminal justice practice are linked by security, as they are both concerned with protecting the individual, communities and society from harm. Thirdly, both social policy and criminal justice practice aim to ensure there is equality in the provision of services, acknowledging that equality has beneficial outcomes for society while inequality has the potential to cause divisions, which can potentially lead to negative criminal justice practice outcomes. Linked to this is, fourthly, enabling individuals to make a meaningful contribution to society so they can reach their full potential, which means that society benefits from the skills they possess. Finally, there is a concern with rights that ensure the principle of equality before the law occurs within criminal justice practice, as the absence of social rights severely impacts this.

These interconnections provide the key rationale for the book, as they present concrete links between the two fields, suggesting that aiming to improve criminal justice practice by reference to social policy is feasible. The lack of acknowledgement of these interconnections makes it harder for criminal justice practice to achieve its aims and objectives.

The rest of the book outlines key topics of concern for criminal justice practice, as summarised in Chapter 1. These topics are analysed in terms of the key issues in relation to criminal justice practice, and show how a social policy focus could improve outcomes for individuals, communities and society.

References

Anders, P., Jolley, R. and Leaman, J. (2019) *A Resource for Directors of Public Health, Police and Crime Commissioners and Other Health and Justice Commissioners, Service Providers and Users*. London: Revolving Doors.

Behan, C., Sloan, J., Bennett, C., Shapland, J. and Farrall, S. (2016) *Justice Is More than Just Criminal Justice: Perspectives on Criminal Justice Institutions and Citizen Participation*. London: Howard League for Penal Reform.

Boutellier, H. (2001) 'The convergence of social policy and criminal justice', *European Journal on Criminal Policy and Research*, 9(4): 361–380. https://doi.org/10.1023/A:1013118803610.

Brooke, H. (2017) *The History of Legal Aid 1945–2010*. London: Fabian Society. Available from: https://www.fabians.org.uk/wp-content/uploads/2017/09/Bach-Commission-Appendix-6-F-1.pdf [Accessed 22 July 2022].

Cohen, M. (2010) 'T.H. Marshall's "Citizenship and social class"', *Dissent Magazine*, Fall 2010. Available from: https://www.dissentmagazine.org/article/t-h-marshalls-citizenship-and-social-class [Accessed 22 July 2022].

Duque, M. and McKnight, A. (2019) *Understanding the Relationship between Inequalities and Poverty: Mechanisms Associated with Crime, the Legal System and Punitive Sanctions*. CASEpaper 215/LIPpaper 6. London: London School of Economics.

Ellis, T. and Savage, S.P. (eds) (2011) *Debates in Criminal Justice*. London; New York: Routledge.

Equality and Human Rights Commission (2018) 'Understanding equality'. Available from: https://www.equalityhumanrights.com/en/secondary-education-resources/useful-information/understanding-equality [Accessed 22 July 2022].

Hobbs, S. and Hamerton, C. (2014) *The Making of Criminal Justice Policy*. Abingdon: Routledge, Taylor & Francis Group.

Lammy, D. (2017) *Lammy Review: Final Report.* Available from: https://www.gov.uk/government/publications/lammy-review-final-report [Accessed 22 July 2022].

Lewis, P., Newburn, T., Taylor, M., Greenhill, A., Frayman, H. and Proctor, R. (2011) *Reading the Riots: Investigating England's Summer of Disorder.* London: The London School of Economics and Political Science and *The Guardian.* Available from: http://www.guardian.co.uk/uk/series/reading-the-riots [Accessed 22 July 2022].

Lister, R. (2010) *Understanding Theories and Concepts in Social Policy.* Bristol: Policy Press.

Livingstone, I. and Mullen, J. (2015) *Tackling Inequality in the Criminal Justice System.* London: Clinks. Available from: https://www.clinks.org/publication/tackling-inequality-criminal-justice-system [Accessed 22 July 2022].

Marshall, T.H. (1973) *Class, Citizenship, and Social Development: Essays.* Westport, CT: Greenwood Press.

Ministry of Justice (2018) *Justice Data Lab Analysis: Reoffending Behaviour after Participation in The Clink Restaurant Training Programme (2nd Analysis).* London: Ministry of Justice. Available from: https://assets.publishing.service.gov.uk/government/uploads/system/uploads/attachment_data/file/699335/clink-report.pdf [Accessed 18 June 2022].

Sealey, C. (2015) *Social Policy Simplified: Connecting Theory with People's Lives.* London; New York: Palgrave Macmillan.

Sutterlüty, F. (2014) 'The hidden morale of the 2005 French and 2011 English riots', *Thesis Eleven*, 121(1): 38–56. https://doi.org/10.1177/0725513614528784.

Triggle, N. (2017) 'Stephen Hawking: I'm worried about the future of the NHS', *BBC News.* Available from: https://www.bbc.com/news/health-40967309 [Accessed 22 July 2022].

Wieshmann, H., Davies, M., Sugg, O., Davis, S. and Ruda, S. (2020) *Violence in London: What We Know and How to Respond.* London: Behavioural Insights Team. Available from: https://www.bi.team/publications/violence-in-london-what-we-know-and-how-to-respond/ [Accessed 25 January 2023].

Wilkinson, R.G. and Pickett, K. (2010) *The Spirit Level: Why Equality is Better for Everyone; [With a New Chapter Responding to their Critics].* Published with a new postscript. London: Penguin Books.

Zedner, L. (2003) 'The concept of security: An agenda for comparative analysis', *Legal Studies (Society of Legal Scholars)*, 23(1): 153–175. https://doi.org/10.1111/j.1748-121X.2003.tb00209.x.

PART II

The importance of social policies to criminal justice practice

5

Housing, criminal justice practice and social policy

This chapter aims to:

- provide an understanding of key contemporary issues related to housing;

- detail the interconnection between housing and criminal justice practice;

- outline how a social policy focus can improve criminal justice practice.

Introduction

This chapter outlines key issues related to housing, and how these impact on criminal justice practice. In particular, the focus is on changes since the 1980s in housing and housing policy that have had significant actual or potential implications for criminal justice practice and practitioners. While there have been some positive developments in housing during this time, the notion that there is a 'housing crisis' is something that has made itself apparent both politically and among the wider public. The chapter details that the crisis specifically linked to social policy issues of costs, quality and quantity, and argues that these issues are having important implications for the Criminal Justice System (CJS) and therefore for criminal justice practice. Finally, the chapter outlines a number of ways in which a social policy focus on housing could improve criminal justice practice.

What is housing and why is it important?

For most people, housing is the most expensive thing they will ever buy. This is because the lifetime cost of a house will in most circumstances outstrip everything else, meaning that housing is the single biggest outgoing expenditure, and is prioritised over and above all other expenses (Poll and Rodgers, 2019). Furthermore, as Lowe (2011:1–2) argues, 'the significance of housing to people's welfare and well-being – having a roof over our heads – is hard to beat in terms of its significance ... [home is] the central focus of most people's lives ... and in many ways define who we are as individuals'.

At a basic level, housing provides physical shelter against the elements, so its absence poses a real risk of serious harm, especially in the winter, when it can lead to death. For this reason, housing can be categorised as a 'subsistence need', meaning that it is something required to avoid serious harm or death to the individual (Sealey, 2015).

Housing is important to a person's general well-being. It provides basic needs such as shelter, warmth and sanitation, as well as less obvious requirements such as privacy and security. It is both a physical asset and enhances non-physical conditions that affect an individual's welfare. By this is meant that if we think about health, this is something that we experience as an emotional state of being healthy. In contrast, not only do we experience housing in terms of its emotional quality physically, but we also live in houses from day to day, meaning that both the quantity and quality of housing can have a huge impact on our emotional well-being.

At a less basic level, housing also provides personal space, privacy and security. This relates to housing beyond that of shelter, as a home (Commission on Housing and Wellbeing, 2015). As King (2009:50) states, 'It provides the existential and emotional space in which we can share our lives with those most significant to us.' So not only do we need houses to live in, we also need housing to be of sufficient quality, as both of these can impact on the quality of our lives. A house provides a range of other important emotional and welfare outcomes that are associated with well-being. Emotionally, privacy and security involve the freedom we have to live in a property alongside how much control we have about when to move on (Corlett and Judge, 2017:3). They also refer to the creation of our own self-identity, as home is the place where most of our social life is played out, and therefore it is where we tend to be most comfortable being 'ourselves' (Lowe, 2011).

However, a home also provides less obvious welfare outcomes. For example, good-quality housing that is not cramped or damp, is free from pests such as rats and is warm is not only important to good health, but is also important to facilitating positive educational outcomes (Commission on Housing and Wellbeing, 2015). These impacts are felt at the personal level but also at the societal level. Additionally, the financial cost to society of poor housing in terms of the increased costs of healthcare and the reducing educational outcomes and therefore reduced earnings over a lifetime has been calculated at £14.8 billion a year (Lund, 2011), which is a significant figure. Inadequate housing can also have a wider impact on health, for example, a lack of either cooking or dining facilities can lead to unhealthy eating and/or ill health, especially in relation to children (Clair, 2019). As well as being important to physical health, housing is also important to mental health, as research shows that people with housing problems are at a greater risk of mental health problems (Savage, 2016). Concerns about housing are a significant cause of stress and anxiety, making people feel either physically ill or impacting on their mental health (Shelter, 2020).

The notion of home can also be translated to communities. A positive notion of home can enable people to develop positive relationships with their neighbours and others within the community, which benefits well-being. This can lead to positive criminal justice outcomes, such as the formation of Neighbourhood Watch schemes. Therefore, the emotional and welfare consequences that housing can have on well-being are just as important as the physical outcomes (Somerville, 2013).

What are the recent trends in housing?

A key difference between housing and other social policy areas such as health and education is that while these are mainly provided by the state, housing is largely provided by the private sector. By this is meant that you are more likely to be living in a private property than a state-provided property. The state contributes to housing needs, mainly through Housing Benefit (HB)/Universal Credit, but these are largely paid to private landlords. This means that individual income plays a more important part in ensuring individuals' and families' housing needs are met than in some other social policy areas.

The last 40 years has seen the nature of housing change significantly in terms of its type, referred to as **housing tenure** (Key Learning Box 5.1), costs and quantity.

KEY LEARNING BOX 5.1 HOUSING TENURE

There are three main ways in which people live in housing, known as housing tenure. These are owner occupier, social renting and private renting.

Owner occupier is where the person lives in the housing they own. They can own it having paid for it in full or they can own it with a mortgage. The main advantage of this form of tenure is the ability to choose your housing based on income.

Social renting is where housing is rented from either a local authority (typically referred to as council housing) or a housing association. The main advantage of this tenure is that it is cheaper than the others.

Private renting is where housing is rented from an individual or a private company. The main advantage of this is ease of access in comparison to the other types of tenure, in terms of income and eligibility criteria.

Changes in housing tenure

An important point to note is that housing tenure has changed significantly over the last century and even over the last 40 years, as shown in Graph 5.1.

As seen in Graph 5.1, private renting was the most common type of housing tenure just before World War Two (WW2). However, this declined significantly over the next 40 years to become the least common. It has increased significantly in recent years to become the second most common housing tenure. In the UK as a whole, the private rented sector increased from 2.8 million households in 2007 to 4.5 million in 2017, an increase of 1.7 million (63 per cent) (ONS, 2019). Young people aged 16–24 are more likely to be in private rentals than other age groups, and this trend has been increasing since 2010 (DWP, 2019).

Graph 5.1 Housing tenure by percentage, 1939–2021 (England and Wales)

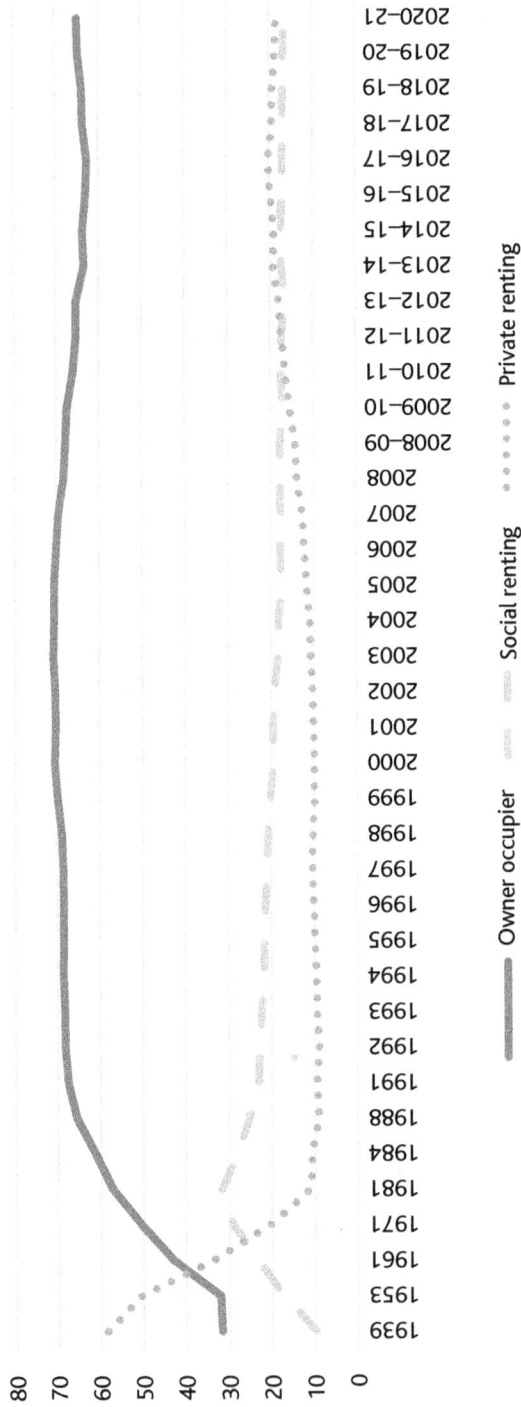

Owner occupier ——— Social renting - - - Private renting • • •

Source: DLUHC (2022)

More specifically, the number of 35–44 year olds in the private rented sector has increased from 13 per cent to 28 per cent since 2010. This means that it is no longer a temporary stopgap between leaving university and buying a home (Poll and Rodgers, 2019). It should also be noted that social renting is the tenure that is concentrated in the lowest income groups, while owner occupiers are concentrated in the highest income quintile groups (MHCLG, 2020). Moreover, since 2000, social renters have seen the proportion of income that they pay in housing costs increase from 15 per cent to 19 per cent. This is in contrast to private renters who, during the same period, have seen the proportion of income they pay in rent effectively remain stable, while for owner occupiers the proportion of income they pay as a mortgage has fallen (Judge et al, 2021).

Conversely, owner occupier became the most common form of housing tenure in the 1960s, where it has remained since, although it has declined since then as private renting has increased. This could also explain that the reason why house prices remain so high is because demand is high. It should be noted that the initial cost of buying a house outweighs the initial cost of renting, and so requires a higher level of savings. The significance of this is that as owner occupier has become the most common type of housing tenure, in the context of a rising population, more homes have to be built to buy, as opposed to rent.

Graph 5.1 also shows that social renting saw a significant rise in the 1940s in the aftermath of WW2, but has declined since the 1980s and is at the time of writing the least common type of housing tenure. Exemplifying this is the fact that between June 2018 and June 2019, only about 19 per cent of homes were built by social renting landlords such as housing associations and local authorities (MHCLG, 2019).

A key feature of the rise of private renting over the last 15 years has been the boom of **houses in multiple occupation** (HMOs) (Key Learning Box 5.2) (Morley, 2016). HMOs are a type of shared accommodation, and their boom has been driven by financial pressures in the housing market that have led to both high property prices for those wishing to buy and high rental prices. HMOs offer a cheaper housing alternative to buying a property or renting a whole property.

KEY LEARNING BOX 5.2 HOUSES IN MULTIPLE OCCUPATION

A House in Multiple in Occupation, or HMO, is a type of shared accommodation where at least three people live in the same house but not as a household, and, despite living separately, share toilet, bathroom and kitchen facilities. This usually means that they pay rent separately. Students have historically been the most common group living in HMOs. However, couples and families can also live in HMOs, and this is an increasing feature of HMOs, meaning that that they are housing groups that in the past would not have been housed in them.

However, a key point about HMOs is that they can be occupied by some of the most vulnerable people in society, in properties that were not built for multiple occupation, and the risk of overcrowding and fire can be greater than with other types of accommodation (MHCLG, 2018:4). Additionally, the living space that HMOs provide is typically less than for other types of accommodation, and this can lead to stresses and strains associated with living in cramped accommodation.

Changes in housing costs

Perhaps the most noteworthy trend in housing since the 1980s has been the large increase in its cost. As has been detailed, owner occupation is now the most common form of tenure. This is despite the cost of buying property increasing significantly. For example, in 1990 the average house price in the UK was equivalent to £118,485 in today's money. However, in 2018, the average price of a house was £214,578, which is an increase of approximately 80 per cent, greater than for any other Western democratic country (Rees-Mogg and Tylecote, 2019). To put this into context, in the 2000s the average working family needed to save for 3 years to afford a deposit to buy a home, while today, they must save for 19 years (Corlett and Judge, 2017). Put another way, while in 2002 the average cost of a house in England and Wales represented just over five times an average person's annual income, in 2018 the cost of a house in England and Wales represented nearly eight times a person's annual income (ONS, 2019a). This exemplifies both the huge increase in house prices and also the increasingly significant cost of housing over this period. The effect is that home ownership and housing more generally is becoming unaffordable for large swathes of citizens (Ryan-Collins, 2019).

This increased cost of housing relates to both owner occupied and rental housing. Since 2000–2001, housing costs for households on low incomes who rent in the private and social rented sectors have risen higher than housing costs for people paying a mortgage and outright owners (Barry et al, 2020). In particular, since 2011, private sector rents have increased more than wages (ONS, 2019), meaning that people are paying 34 per cent of their annual income in rent as opposed to the average mortgaged household spending 12 per cent of their income on housing (Monbiot, 2019). It should be noted that renting council housing is cheaper than renting from private landlords (Pickvance, 2012), and that private renters consistently spend a higher proportion of their incomes on housing than any other tenure group. This has negative implications for both their immediate and longer-term living standards.

The increased cost of renting is reflected in the increased cost of HB. HB is an income-related benefit that helps households pay their rent in both the private and social-rented sectors. However, HB can vary from individual to individual, depending on a number of factors such as household income and where they live, and it usually does not pay all rent, just a portion of it. The key point is

Table 5.1 Housing Benefit expenditure, 1988–2018

	1988	2018
Amount	£3.7 billion	£21 billion
% Increase	——	560%

Source: DWP (2019), table 1a

that since the late 1980s, expenditure on HB has increased both as a proportion of gross domestic product (GDP), and in terms of the actual amount, as shown in Table 5.1.

As Table 5.1 shows, HB expenditure has increased by nearly 600 per cent since 1988. This has occurred at a time when the social rented sector has declined, as shown in Graph 5.1. However, Graph 5.1 also shows the growth of the private rented sector at the expense of the social rented sector, and as rents in the former are more expensive than in the latter, this is a significant reason for the increase. As housing costs have increased since the 1980s, there has been a significant impact on the income that individuals are able to spend on other aspects of their life after paying for housing. For instance, while the average family spent just 6 per cent of their income on housing costs in the early 1960s, this has now trebled to 18 per cent, meaning that housing costs are taking up a growing proportion of disposable income from one generation to the next (Corlett and Judge, 2017). This means that increases in income are being swallowed up by increases in housing cost.

Changes in housing quantity

Another significant change is in the number of houses being built, which has caused a significant mismatch between housing demand and supply. A key outcome of the development of the welfare state after WW2 was the building of over 1 million new council houses between 1945 and 1951, and this was important in meeting the considerable need for housing. However, since the 1970s, the number of houses built by both council and private builders combined has been nowhere near the number after WW2, despite the increased population, and this accounts for the ever-present housing shortage (Commission on Housing and Wellbeing, 2015). For example, during 2017/18, there were 6,434 homes built for social rent in England, despite the fact that there was a need for 90,000 homes in this category (Greaves, 2019). According to the National Housing Federation (2019), 3.6 million people in England would have their housing needs best met by social rented housing.

The clear and obvious indication of a lack of housing is increased **homelessness** (Key Learning Box 5.3), as since 2010, the number of people declaring themselves to be homeless has increased. In 2010, 97,210 households declared themselves to be homeless in England (MHCLG, 2019a), but by 2020, this had increased to 290,820 households (DLUHC, 2022a), an almost 300 per cent increase in a decade. This means that more people than ever are experiencing homelessness. Perhaps not surprisingly, there has also been an increase in the number of rough sleepers during the same time, as shown in Graph 5.2.

KEY LEARNING BOX 5.3 WHAT IS HOMELESSNESS?

Homelessness can be defined in absolute, narrow or broad terms.

An absolute definition of homelessness determines that only those who are without any type of accommodation are homeless. This means that only those who are roofless and/or rough sleeping are homeless. This definition has the advantage of being easy to understand, as it is easy to see who does not have a roof over their head.

A narrow definition of homelessness determines that those without the right to occupy any type of accommodation are homeless. This includes people who live in temporary accommodation such as shelters, as their right to occupy this type of property is very limited and they can be asked to leave at any time. More people would be classified as homeless than in the absolute definition. This is the definition of homelessness that is most similar to current homeless legislation (Lund, 2011).

A broad definition of homelessness determines homelessness through reference to the suitability of accommodation for the needs of an individual. If, for example, a house is overcrowded, lacks basic amenities such as heating or is unsuitable for the occupant (perhaps because of age), the occupant may be classified as homeless. This can include 'hidden homelessness', where people are living with friends as they cannot find or afford suitable accommodation. An example of this is 'sofa surfing' (Sanders et al, 2020). This definition of homelessness classifies many more people as homeless.

As Graph 5.2 shows, although there was a fall in rough sleepers in 2018, the trend between 2010 to 2021 has been upwards, with the number increasing by over two and a half times. The figures have fallen from 2017 onwards, but are still significantly higher than in 2010. It should be noted that these figures are likely to grossly underestimate the true number of rough sleepers (Syal, 2021). The key point about these figures is that they have both been on an upward trend since 2010, which suggests a general shortage of housing. It should also be noted that the numbers are regarded as an under-representation of the true number of both homeless and rough sleepers (Booth, 2020).

Beside homelessness, another clear but perhaps less visible outcome from the lack of house building is overcrowding. According to the National Housing Federation (2019a), overcrowding affects nearly 3 million people in England, of

Graph 5.2 Rough sleeping in England, 2010–2018

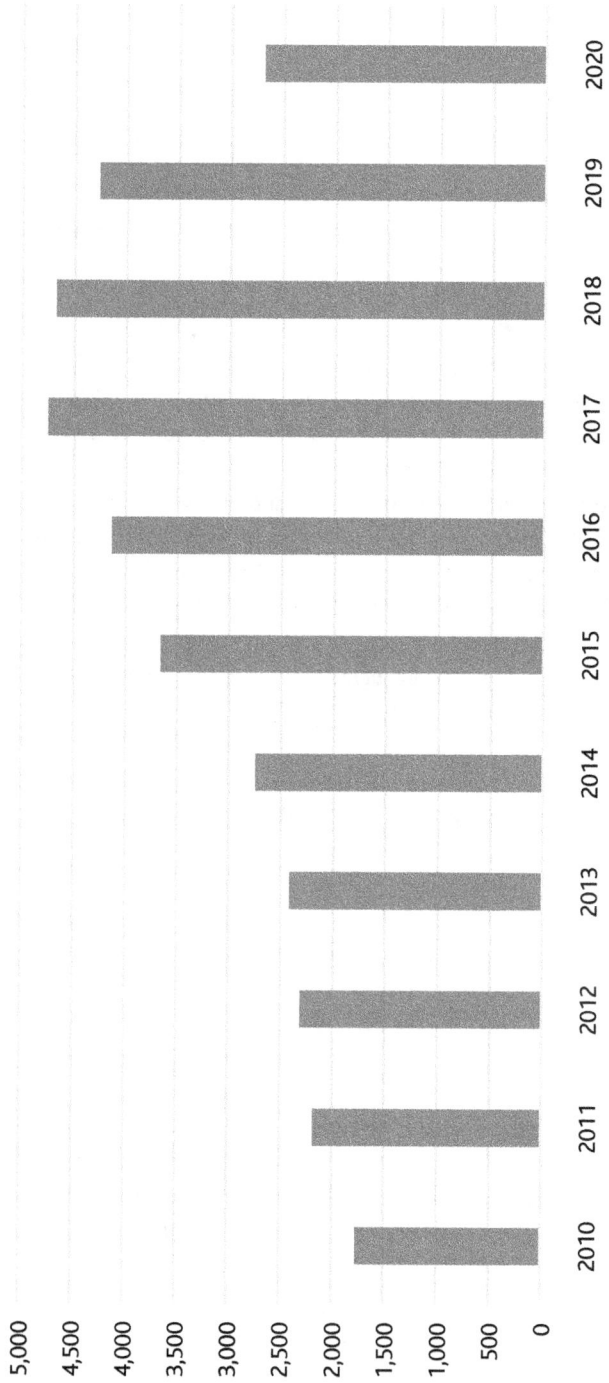

Source: MHCLG (2021)

which approximately 1.3 million are children. For nearly half of these children, this entails sharing a room with an adult, while for a quarter of children, this means sharing a bed with another person. The negative impact of this includes struggling to do homework, arguments, ill health, mental health issues and lack of friendships. For adults, the impact can also include deteriorating partner relationships and separation (Sanders et al, 2019). Additionally, according to the Centre for Ageing Better (2020:8), 'poor housing can create or worsen health conditions, reduce a person's quality of life, cause poverty and even premature death'. This is evident from the death of **Awaab Ishaak** (Key Learning Box 5.4) in 2020.

KEY LEARNING BOX 5.4 AWAAB ISHAAK

Awaab Ishhak was a two year old who died in Manchester in 2020. At the inquest, the coroner determined that his death was caused by extended exposure to harmful toxic black mould in the one-bedroom flat that he lived in with his mother and father. The family had raised the issue of mould in the flat on numerous occasions, but were continually told to take remedial action themselves, such as painting over it. The inquest identified that the property had inadequate ventilation, which contributed to the build-up of mould, and that this had led directly to the development of a severe respiratory condition that was the cause of Awaab's death. This case highlights how living conditions can significantly affect health and well-being.

Additionally, the lack of good-quality, affordable housing can result in negative gendered outcomes, such as 'women not declaring themselves homeless and instead staying in abusive relationships ... [they] believe that their situation and responsibilities mean that they cannot walk away and subject their children to hostel life and temporary accommodation' (Smith 2017:159). A more direct consequence of either homelessness, rough sleeping and living in temporary accommodation is an increased risk of death compared with the general population (ONS, 2021).

One obvious consequence of the lack of social housing has been the increased use of temporary housing such as bed and breakfast accommodation by local authorities to house families in need. This has increased significantly over the past decade (Wilson and Barton, 2019). Along with significant financial implications, this also has important negative social implications for those affected, such as lack of space and lack of amenities such as cooking facilities.

What is the relevance of housing to criminal justice practice?

We have identified a number of issues related to housing, including quantity, quality and cost. Housing can have a direct impact on the physical and mental health, education, employment and caring needs of individuals. To understand the relevance of housing to criminal justice practice, it is important to outline the specific links between housing and crime. In particular, the changes in housing over the last 30 years or so detailed above can be shown to have the potential to impact on criminal justice practice in significant ways, either directly or indirectly.

Direct relevance of housing to criminal justice practice

Recent years have seen significant increases in homelessness and rough sleeping. In relation to criminal justice practice, Bramley and Fitzpatrick (2017) identify that having a criminal record is the strongest predictor to being homeless when compared with other factors such as unemployment, age and income. This suggests that the CJS has an important impact on homelessness. One reason for this is that entitlement to HB stops for all sentenced prisoners who are expected to be in prison for more than 13 weeks. Many of them therefore have very little chance of keeping a tenancy open until the end of their sentence and risk losing their housing. This could explain why so many prisoners leave prison as homeless.

Research shows that homeless people are more vulnerable and at risk of crime than other groups in society, with more than three-quarters of people who sleep rough having been a victim of crime or antisocial behaviour over the period of a year (McCulloch, 2019). These crimes include theft, property damage, burglary, violence and sexual assault. For all of these, with the exception of theft, the perpetrator is usually a member of the public and not another homeless person. Perhaps even more significant is the fact that the estimated number of deaths among homeless people has generally been on an upward trend, peaking in 2019 at 788 deaths, equivalent to 2 per day (ONS, 2021). This suggests that there is an increased risk of death from being homeless.

Despite these factors, homeless people are typically labelled and stereotyped as dangerous and therefore to be avoided, meaning that rather than preventative measures being taken, the emphasis in the CJS is on surveillance and security against them (Muncie and McLaughlin, 2001). An example is the 'zero tolerance' approach towards street homelessness, with the aim of forcing homelessness 'out of sight' (Dean, 2012:101). Because of the stereotyping that takes place, the vulnerability of homeless people is not clearly evident. Instead, they are treated as offenders and their victimisation and their constant feelings of vulnerability are overlooked (McCulloch, 2019). This is compounded because homeless people tend not to report crime or to access services that could help them, probably for the reasons outlined here (Newburn, 2017).

It is also important to note that homelessness can affect access to other services. For example, having a fixed address is important when gaining employment and certain services and benefits, and to ensure correspondence relating to these is maintained. Additionally, homeless people are often illegally turned away from registering with a GP (Healthwatch, 2018), which compounds their poor health status. This is exemplified by the fact that the average age of death of a homeless person is 47 years and even lower for homeless women at just 43 years, compared with 77 years for the general population (Thomas, 2011).

Prison statistics show that housing has a direct effect on the CJS in terms of the link with reoffending. For example, prisoners are more likely to have been homeless than the general population, and people who are homeless are much more likely to be reconvicted than people who are not homeless (Ministry of Justice, 2010). One possible reason for this is the lack of suitable housing for prisoners when they are released. Approximately 13 per cent of people leaving prison do so as homeless or as rough sleepers, while a further 10 per cent leave prison to live in 'unsettled accommodation', defined as transient/short-term accommodation that does not provide a long-term solution to housing need (Ministry of Justice, 2018). This means that nearly a quarter of people leave prison without permanent and independent housing.

Indirect relevance of housing to criminal justice practice

It is obviously the case that individuals in all types of housing commit crime. In addition, burglary is one of the most frequently occurring crimes, making housing a key concern of the CJS. However, there are certain aspects of housing that link specifically to criminal justice practice.

Most people in the UK are housed as owner occupiers. Initial access to this form of tenure is highly income contingent, as noted earlier, because of the need for a deposit. This is less relevant for renting, meaning it is lower income groups that tend to take this route. This is especially the case for social housing, which tends to have lower deposits and rents than private housing. Social housing therefore tends to be concentrated in lower income groups than other housing tenure types. This is known as **residualisation** (Key Learning Box 5.5), which refers to social housing tenants in general and council housing tenants in particular being less affluent, from lower income groups, older people, outside the labour market and the non-working poor (Murie, 1997). This process has been compounded by **Right to Buy** (Key Learning Box 5.6) policies, which has seen better-off tenants able to purchase better social housing at a discount rate, leaving the worse-off tenants and worst housing in the social housing sector. Sometimes, residualisation directly leads to **gentrification** (Key Learning Box 5.5), which is essentially its reverse, and this also has implications for poorer individuals.

> **KEY LEARNING BOX 5.5** RESIDUALISATION AND GENTRIFICATION
>
> Residualisation is the process by which social policies becomes eligible to only a narrow group of people rather than a broad mix of groups. This usually takes place when the rules about who can access social policies are changed, to make it harder for some groups to access services and for other groups to be targeted. The UK provides an example of this, with council and housing association provision having

moved away from being available to all the population to only the most vulnerable and lowest income groups (Angel, 2021). The key point about residualisation is that it is a deliberate process, actively undertaken.

Gentrification is where an area that was previously poor and neglected undergoes development so it becomes less deprived and more desirable for outsiders. It may take place as better houses are built, existing houses are refurbished, a retail complex is developed or a public amenity such as a school or hospital is built. As a consequence, there is an influx of usually better-off outsiders, resulting in an increase in the cost of living and working in the area, and this means it becomes too expensive for existing residents, who then have to move out – being forced to move to poorer areas. This directly leads to residualisation, so there is a larger concentration of poorer people living in poor areas and a higher concentration of richer people living in rich areas. The key point about gentrification is that it potentially reinforces segregation between the rich and the poor.

Additionally, residualisation is also evident in the fact that both unemployment and economic inactivity are far higher among social renting tenants living in housing association and council properties in comparison with the rest of the population (Dromey et al, 2018). Moreover, where social renting tenants do work, their income tends to be significantly less than that of owner occupiers (Dromey et al, 2018). This suggests that they are more disadvantaged than the population in general and owner occupiers in particular.

KEY LEARNING BOX 5.6 RIGHT TO BUY

Right to Buy is a policy that was introduced in 1980, giving those who lived in council housing the right to buy their home. Its key feature was that it gave a significant discount on the purchase price, meaning those living in a council house were given the right to buy at up to 50 per cent less than the market price of the house, while those living in council flats were given a right to buy discount of up to 70 per cent of the market price. The policy was hugely significant in that it led to a change in tenure for nearly 2 million homes (Murie, 2015). Right to Buy is still a live policy in England, but not in Wales and Scotland.

The key point about housing residualisation is not that it is something that individuals have chosen to do to themselves, but that it has been a deliberate policy to segregate and divide communities into rich and poor, and it is this deliberate policy that has led to the problems we have identified. The implication of this is that the living environments of people who are left behind in these areas is less than optimal. In effect they become socially excluded from many facets of society that others take for granted, such as access to well-paid jobs, services such as shops, transport links, leisure and other facilities. Consequently, as Murie (1997:30) observes:

> These problems create huge pressures on family and community life, can lead to tensions between neighbours and together with high population turnover, mean that residents are vulnerable to crime and the fear of crime. ... They contribute in turn to a lack of political clout, no market to attract quality goods and services, overstretched public services, the stereotypes which reinforce isolation and lack of access to jobs and capital, poor health, low self-esteem and crime.

Murie's observation is supported by social disorganisation theory. This argues that economically disadvantaged communities foster crimes, as a consequence of the lack of informal controls that normally exist to control the behaviour of individuals. In particular, it is the concentration of disadvantaged individuals within a community that specifically inhibits social controls. Research has supported this theory in a British context (Akers et al, 2017). The implication is simply that the composition of housing in a neighbourhood can significantly contribute to crime, and therefore that concentrating the poorest into poor neighbourhoods can lead to crime. The key point is that it is not individuals' characteristics that contribute to crime, but the characteristics of the neighbourhood in which they live, as a consequence of their social exclusion (Wieshmann et al, 2020). Crime is unevenly distributed among income groups, with lower earners being more likely to be victims of crime than higher income groups (Sprigings, 2005). This is important in the context of housing tenure, as low-income groups tend to be concentrated in social housing. Additionally, renting tends to be more transient and short term than owner occupier tenure, meaning that the social bonds that bind communities together and act to prevent crime, through the formation of neighbourhood community groups, for example, are less likely to emerge. This is highly significant in the context of the growth of private renting. As Barry et al (2020:72) observe:

> Private renters, who move more often than social renters, also incur the costs of frequently moving house and risk losing rental deposits. This legal insecurity can feed into a wider insecurity, which may undermine their ability to 'feel at home' and their willingness to invest in their home and local community. For renters with children, this can cause particularly acute problems, such as having to move children out of school and other supportive social networks.

How could a social policy focus on housing improve criminal justice practice?

Criminal justice practitioners should recognise the significance that housing issues and circumstances can have on criminal justice practice. In particular, the changes in housing detailed here potentially impact on criminal justice practice in significant ways, either directly or indirectly. This has important implications.

The first is that paying attention to housing needs can be an important way to limit criminal activity, in terms of both perpetrators and victims. An example of this is the importance of housing in rehabilitation. Research has shown that providing appropriate and accessible accommodation is crucial to successful criminal justice outcomes such as rehabilitation (Home Office, 2004). For example, providing relevant accommodation can reduce reoffending by up to 20 per cent. This is because of its importance to sustaining employment, treatment, family support and finances. However, only a third of prisoners return to some form of settled accommodation on release.

Additionally, criminal justice practitioners such as social workers and police officers may come across individuals for whom attention to housing problems at an early stage may limit the need for criminal justice action later on. As a simple example of this, Sanders et al (2020) outline how sofa surfing negatively impacts on both the mental and physical well-being of individuals, as a result of living conditions that are often poor and dangerous and lack access to basic amenities. Sofa surfing can also result in exposure to others' antisocial behaviour, which can lead to other forms of antisocial behaviour, and potentially to troublesome and/or illegal activity.

Housing insecurity can make itself apparent in many other ways, such as those relating to tenure and finances. This can impact on an individual in ways that negatively impact on their well-being and potentially lead to exposure to illegal behaviour. Criminal justice practitioners therefore need to be aware of and act to mitigate this insecurity.

Additionally, there needs to be acknowledgement that being homeless is a key feature of people who have contact with the CJS, and is therefore an important consideration for criminal justice practice. The most simplistic explanation for homelessness and rough sleeping is a lack of housing. However, the process by which this comes about can range from debt, unemployment, divorce and family conflict to substance misuse, low income and being in prison. A report by Alma Economics (2019) identifies a number of both **structural and individual causes of homelessness** (Key Learning Box 5.7). It makes the key point that while the cause varies by individual, it is structural factors such as lack of affordable housing and poverty, and individual factors such as relationship breakdown that predominate as the causes of homelessness.

KEY LEARNING BOX 5.7 STRUCTURAL AND INDIVIDUAL CAUSES OF HOMELESSNESS

There are two main ways in which explanations of homelessness can be categorised.

Structural explanations of homelessness locate the cause to factors outside the control of individuals, such as lack of housing, low wages and unemployment.

Homelessness is the consequence of wider issues over which the individual has no power.

Individual explanations locate the cause to factors within the control of individuals, such as their personal characteristics, behaviours and vulnerabilities. Homelessness is the consequence of an individual's actions.

However, it is often very hard to directly attribute homelessness to one specific cause, as causes are often interrelated (Lund, 2011). What might present as an individual cause of homelessness, such as substance misuse, may have been triggered by a non-individual cause such as unemployment following from redundancy, and so a focus on individual causes of homelessness without considering non-individual causes can mean that the real focus of the issue is missed. The key point for practice is that these causes are very likely to be compounded among those in contact with the CJS, so criminal justice practice needs to reflect them.

Over the last 30 years or so, the primary focus of the CJS and other related criminal justice practice when dealing with homelessness has been a concentration on issues that affect the individual rather than the structural cause of homelessness itself. This means that priority has been given to addressing issues that may lead to an individual's homelessness, such as substance misuse or mental health issues, and to make a staged transition from homelessness to permanent housing. The rationale for this is that not dealing with these issues simply leads to the recurrence of homelessness. However, more recently, the Housing First approach has provided housing for the homeless on the basis that after stable housing has been delivered, other issues can then be dealt with. The key difference between these two approaches is that permanent housing is provided as the first priority in the latter. As Loubière et al (2020:2) state, 'Housing First operates on the assumption that access to independent and permanent housing (as a basic human right) offers a secure foundation from which to address other social and health related problems, along with concurrent support from a dedicated medical and social team.' There is evidence suggesting the Housing First approach provides a number of benefits, including those that specifically relate to criminal justice outcomes such as reductions in offending behaviours and decreased workloads for criminal justice practitioners (Homeless Link, 2019). Recent legislation has supported this preventative approach, with the Homelessness Reduction Act 2017 giving prisons and probation providers a new duty to refer people who might be at risk of becoming homeless to the local housing authority. This provides all criminal justice practitioners with the opportunity to foreground the prevention of housing problems as a practice objective.

Summary

This chapter has outlined key issues related to housing, and how these impact on criminal justice practice. Changes since the 1980s in housing and housing policy that have had significant impact on criminal justice practice and practitioners have been detailed. In particular, it is apparent that there has been and continues to be a housing crisis that has had significant implications for the CJS, and therefore for criminal justice practitioners. Increased housing costs, lower housing quality and reduced housing quantity have all contributed in significant ways to the prevailing crisis.

What should have become apparent is the linkage of these issues to criminal justice practice. In particular, changes in housing provision have the potential to impact criminal justice practice in significant ways, either directly or indirectly. Directly, there is a strong link between homelessness and having a criminal record, as well as the homeless being more likely to be victims of crime. Indirectly, this relates to the residualisation of housing, which has socially excluded individuals and communities from many facets of society that are often taken for granted, such as access to well-paid jobs, services such as shops, transport links, leisure and other facilities, and this in turn leads to a greater risk of crime, as supported by social disorganisation theory.

There are a number of ways in which a social policy focus could improve criminal justice practice. The most obvious is that criminal justice practitioners should recognise that dealing with housing issues can improve their practice. This means a focus on how housing insecurity can impact the individual in ways that negatively affect their well-being and potentially lead to exposure to illegal behaviour, and on the structural causes of homelessness and housing needs. The Homelessness Reduction Act 2017 provides a focus on prevention, as does the Housing First approach, and both of these make evident how meeting housing needs through social policy can improve criminal justice practice.

References

Akers, R.L., Sellers, C.S. and Jennings, W.G. (2017) *Criminological Theories: Introduction, Evaluation, and Application*. Seventh edition. New York: Oxford University Press.

Alma Economics (2019) *Homelessness. Causes of Homelessness and Rough Sleeping. Rapid Evidence Assessment*. London: Alma Economics. Available from: https://assets.publishing.service.gov.uk/government/uploads/system/uploads/attachment_data/file/793471/Homelessness_-_REA.pdf [Accessed 20 March 2020].

Angel, S. (2021) 'Housing regimes and residualization of the subsidized rental sector in Europe 2005–2016', *Housing Studies*, 0(0): 1–21. https://doi.org/10.1080/02673037.2021.1921122.

Barry, A., Bennett, S., Collingwood, A., Drake, B., Easton, S., Goulden C., Innes, D., Leese, D., Matejic, P., Schwendel, G. and Wenham, A. (2020) *UK Poverty 2019/20*. York: Joseph Rowntree Foundation. Available from: https://www.jrf.org.uk/report/uk-poverty-2019-20 [Accessed 25 July 2022].

Booth, R. (2020) 'UK's official rough sleeping numbers "far lower than reality"', *The Guardian*, 26 February. Available from: https://www.theguardian.com/uk-news/2020/feb/26/uks-official-rough-sleeping-numbers-far-lower-than-reality [Accessed 25 July 2022].

Bramley, G. and Fitzpatrick, S. (2018) 'Homelessness in the UK: Who is most at risk?', *Housing Studies*, 33(1): 96–116. https://doi.org/10.1080/02673 037.2017.1344957.

Centre for Ageing Better (2020) 'Home and dry: The need for decent homes in later life'. Available from: https://ageing-better.org.uk/resources/home-and-dry-need-decent-homes-later-life [Accessed 25 July 2022].

Clair, A. (2019) 'Housing: An under-explored influence on children's well-being and becoming', *Child Indicators Research*, 12(2): 609–626. https://doi.org/ 10.1007/s12187-018-9550-7.

Commission on Housing and Wellbeing (2015) 'A blueprint for Scotland's future: The importance of housing for general wellbeing in Scotland'. Available from: https://www.housinglin.org.uk/Topics/type/A-blueprint-for-Scotla nds-future-The-importance-of-housing-for-general-wellbeing-in-Scotland/ [Accessed 25 July 2022].

Corlett, A. and Judge, L. (2017) *Home Affront: Housing across the Generations • Resolution Foundation*. London: The Resolution Foundation/Intergenerational Commission. Available from: https://www.resolutionfoundation.org/publicati ons/home-affront-housing-across-the-generations/ [Accessed 25 July 2022].

Dean, H. (2012) *Social Policy*. Second edition. Cambridge: Polity.

DLUHC (Department for Levelling Up, Housing and Communities) (2022) *Table FT1101 (S101): Trends in Tenure*. London: DLUHC. Available from: https:// assets.publishing.service.gov.uk/government/uploads/system/uploads/atta chment_data/file/1088765/FT1101_Trends_in_tenure.ods [Accessed 4 November 2022].

DLUHC (Department for Levelling Up, Housing and Communities) (2022a) 'Statutory homelessness live tables July to September 2021 England'. Available from: https://www.gov.uk/government/statistical-data-sets/live-tables-on-homelessness [Accessed 25 July 2022].

Dromey, J., Snelling, C. and Baxter, D. (2018) *Building Communities that Work: The Role of Housing Associations in Supporting Employment*. London: IPPR. Available from: https://www.ippr.org/research/publications/building-communities-that-work [Accessed 25 July 2022].

DWP (Department for Work and Pensions) (2019) 'Benefit expenditure and caseload tables 2019'. Available from: https://www.gov.uk/government/publi cations/benefit-expenditure-and-caseload-tables-2019 [Accessed 25 July 2022].

Graves, F. (2019) 'Rethinking allocations'. Chartered Institute of Housing. Available from: https://thinkhouse.org.uk/site/assets/files/1378/cih0919.pdf [Accessed 27 July 2022].

Healthwatch (2018) 'Three common issues homeless people face when trying to access care'. Available from: https://www.healthwatch.co.uk/news/2018-12-21/three-common-issues-homeless-people-face-when-trying-access-care [Accessed 25 July 2022].

Home Office (2004) *Reducing Re-Offending National Action Plan*. London: Home Office.

Homeless Link (2019) *Housing First and Its Impact in the Community*. London: Homeless Link. Available from: https://homelesslink-1b54.kxcdn.com/media/documents/Housing_First_and_its_impact_in_the_community_2019.pdf [Accessed 25 July 2022].

Judge, L., Odamtten, F. and Shah, K. (2021) 'Housing outlook Q4 2021 – resolution foundation', *The RF Housing Outlook*, Quarterly Briefing: Q4 2021. Available from: https://www.resolutionfoundation.org/publications/housing-outlook-q4-2021/ [Accessed 25 July 2022].

King, P. (2009) 'Using theory or making theory: Can there be theories of housing?', *Housing, Theory and Society*, 26(1): 41–52. https://doi.org/10.1080/14036090802704296.

Loubière, S., Taylor, O., Tinland, A., Vargas-Moniz, M., O'Shaughnessy, B., Bokszzanin, H., Bernad, R., Wolf, J., Santinello, M., Loundou, A., Ornelas, J. and Auquier, P. (2020) 'Europeans' willingness to pay for ending homelessness: A contingent valuation study', *Social Science & Medicine*, 247: 112802. https://doi.org/10.1016/j.socscimed.2020.112802.

Lowe, S. (2011) *The Housing Debate*. London: Policy Press.

Lund, B. (2011) *Understanding Housing Policy*. Second edition. Bristol; Portland, OR: Policy Press.

McCulloch, D. (2019) 'More than three quarters of people sleeping rough have been victims of crime or anti-social behaviour in the past year', in J. Treadwell and A. Lynes (eds) *50 Facts Everyone should Know about Crime and Punishment in Britain*. Bristol; Chicago, IL: Policy Press, pp. 232–236.

MHCLG (Ministry of Housing, Communities and Local Government) (2018) *Houses in multiple occupation and residential property licensing reform: guidance for local housing authorities*. London: Ministry of Housing, Communities & Local Government. Available at: https://assets.publishing.service.gov.uk/government/uploads/system/uploads/attachment_data/file/925269/HMOs_and_residential_property_licensing_reforms_guidance.pdf [Accessed 5 January 2022].

MHCLG (Ministry of Housing, Communities and Local Government) (2019) *Rough Sleeping in England – Street Counts, Evidence-Based Estimates, and Estimates Informed by a Spotlight Street Count, Autumn 2010–2018*. London: Ministry of Housing, Communities and Local Government. Available from: https://assets.publishing.service.gov.uk/government/uploads/system/uploads/attachment_data/file/781567/Rough_Sleeping_Statistics_2018_release.pdf [Accessed 25 July 2022].

MHCLG (Ministry of Housing, Communities and Local Government) (2019a) *Statutory Homelessness Main Duty Decision and Outcomes April to December 2018*. London: Ministry of Housing, Communities and Local Government.

MHCLG (Ministry of Housing, Communities and Local Government) (2020) *English Housing Survey 2018 to 2019: Headline Report*. London: Ministry of Housing, Communities and Local Government. Available from: https://www.gov.uk/government/statistics/english-housing-survey-2018-to-2019-headline-report [Accessed 25 July 2022].

MHCLG (Ministry of Housing, Communities and Local Government) (2021) *Rough Sleeping Snapshot in England: Autumn 2020*. London: Ministry of Housing, Communities and Local Government. Available from: https://assets.publishing. service.gov.uk/government/uploads/system/uploads/attachment_data/file/963 703/infographic_2020.pdf [Accessed 25 July 2022].

Ministry of Justice (2010) *Compendium of Reoffending Statistics and Analysis 2010*. London: Ministry of Justice. Available from: https://www.gov.uk/government/ statistics/compendium-of-reoffending-statistics-and-analysis-2010 [Accessed 25 July 2022].

Ministry of Justice (2018) *Homelessness on Release from Prison by Quarter – a Freedom of Information Request to Ministry of Justice*, WhatDoTheyKnow. Available from: https://www.whatdotheyknow.com/request/homelessness_on_release_f rom_pri [Accessed 25 July 2022].

Monbiot, G. (ed.) (2019) *Land for the Many: Changing the Way Our Fundamental Asset Is Used, Owned and Governed*. London: Labour Party.

Morley, E. (2016) 'HMO market set to boom, but how are they valued?', *Landlord News*, 26 April. Available from: https://www.landlordnews.co.uk/hmo-mar ket-set-boom-valued/ [Accessed 25 July 2022].

Muncie, J. and McLaughlin, E. (eds) (2001) *The Problem of Crime*. Second edition. London; Thousand Oaks, CA: SAGE Publications in association with the Open University.

Murie, A. (1997) 'Linking housing changes to crime', *Social Policy & Administration*, 31(5): 22–36. https://doi.org/10.1111/1467-9515.00073.

Murie, A. (2015) 'The right to buy: History and prospect', History & Policy. Available from: https://www.historyandpolicy.org/index.php/policy-papers/ papers/the-right-to-buy-history-and-prospect [Accessed 4 November 2022].

National Housing Federation (2019) *Briefing: How Many People Need a Social Rented Home?* Understanding Society. London: National Housing Federation. Available from: https://www.understandingsociety.ac.uk/research/publications/ 525872 [Accessed 25 July 2022].

National Housing Federation (2019a) 'Briefing: Overcrowding in England'. Available from: http://s3-eu-west-1.amazonaws.com/doc.housing.org.uk/Ove rcrowding_briefing_2019.pdf [Accessed 25 July 2022].

Newburn, T. (2017) *Criminology*. Third edition. London; New York: Routledge.

ONS (Office for National Statistics) (2019) *UK Private Rented Sector – Office for National Statistics*. London: Office for National Statistics. Available from: https:// www.ons.gov.uk/economy/inflationandpriceindices/articles/ukprivaterentedsec tor/2018 [Accessed 25 July 2022].

ONS (Office for National Statistics) (2019a) *House Price to Residence-Based Earnings Ratio – Office for National Statistics*. London: ONS. Available from: https://www.ons.gov.uk/peoplepopulationandcommunity/housing/datas ets/ratioofhousepricetoresidencebasedearningslowerquartileandmedian/current [Accessed 25 July 2022].

ONS (Office for National Statistics) (2021) *Deaths of Homeless People in England and Wales – Office for National Statistics*. London: ONS. Available from: https://www.ons.gov.uk/peoplepopulationandcommunity/birthsdeathsandmarriages/deaths/bulletins/deathsofhomelesspeopleinenglandandwales/2020registrations [Accessed 25 July 2022].

Pickvance, C. (2012) 'Housing and housing policy', in J. Baldock (ed.) *Social Policy*. Fourth edition. Oxford; New York: Oxford University Press, pp. 314–368.

Poll, H. and Rogers, C. (2019) *Getting the House in Order: How to Improve Standards in the Private Rented Sector*. Citizens Advice. Available from: http://www.citizensadvice.org.uk/about-us/our-work/policy/policy-research-topics/housing-policy-research/getting-the-house-in-order-how-to-improve-standards-in-the-private-rented-sector1/ [Accessed 25 July 2022].

Rees-Mogg, J., Radomir, T. and Ashmead, S. (eds) (2019) *Raising the Roof: How to Solve the United Kingdom's Housing Crisis: A Collection of the 2018 Richard Koch Breakthrough Prize Essays*. London: The Institute of Economic Affairs.

Ryan-Collins, J. (2019) *Why Can't you Afford a Home?* Cambridge; Medford, MA: Polity Press.

Sanders, B., Boobis, S. and Albanese, F. (2019) *It was Like a Nightmare – the Reality of Sofa Surfing in Britain Today*. London: Shelter. Available from: https://www.crisis.org.uk/media/241555/it_was_like_a_nightmare_the_reality_of_sofa_surfing_in_britain_today_2019.pdf [Accessed 25 July 2020].

Savage, J. (2016) *Mental Health and Housing*. London: Mental Health Foundation.

Sealey, C. (2015) *Social Policy Simplified: Connecting Theory with People's Lives*. London; New York: Palgrave Macmillan.

Shelter (2020) 'Two million renters in England made ill by housing worries', Shelter England. Available from: https://england.shelter.org.uk/media/press_release/2_million_renters_in_england_made_ill_by_housing_worries [Accessed 25 July 2022].

Smith, J. (2017) 'Housing, gender and social policy', in P. Somerville and N. Sprigings (eds) *Housing and Social Policy: Contemporary Themes and Critical Perspectives*. London; New York: Routledge, pp. 150–165.

Somerville, P. (2013) 'Understanding homelessness', *Housing, Theory and Society*, 30(4): 384–415. https://doi.org/10.1080/14036096.2012.756096.

Sprigings, N. (2017) 'Housing policy and social justice', in P. Somerville and N. Sprigings (eds) *Housing and Social Policy: Contemporary Themes and Critical Perspectives*. London; New York: Routledge, pp. 43–68.

Syal, R. (2021) 'Covid: Officials underestimated number of rough sleepers in England needing help', *The Guardian*, 14 January. Available from: https://www.theguardian.com/society/2021/jan/14/covid-officials-underestimated-number-of-rough-sleepers-in-england-needing-help [Accessed 25 July 2022].

Thomas, B. (2011) *Homelessness: A Silent Killer (2011) | Crisis | Together We Will End Homelessness*. London: Crisis. Available from: https://www.crisis.org.uk/ending-homelessness/homelessness-knowledge-hub/health-and-wellbeing/homelessness-a-silent-killer-2011/ [Accessed 25 July 2022]

Wieshmann, H., Davies, M., Sugg, O., Davis, S., and Ruda, S. (2020) *Violence in London: What We Know and How to Respond*. London: Behavioural Insights Team. Available from: https://www.bi.team/publications/violence-in-london-what-we-know-and-how-to-respond/ [Accessed 25 January 2023].

Wilson, W. and Barton, C. (2019) *Households in Temporary Accommodation (England)*. Briefing Paper Number 02110. London: House of Commons Library.

6

Employment, criminal justice practice and social policy

This chapter aims to:

- outline the evidence of a link between employment and positive criminal justice outcomes;

- detail factors that constrain these positive criminal justice outcomes;

- analyse ways in which a social policy focus on employment can improve criminal justice practice.

Introduction

A standard requirement of probation or parole is involvement in employment, making evident employment's importance to criminal justice practice as a route towards rehabilitation. It is also relevant to note that while there is mixed or no evidence that most rehabilitation programmes work, rehabilitation through employment is one of the few types of rehabilitation activities that does actually work (Ministry of Justice, 2013). The chapter begins with an outline of the evidence of a link between employment and positive criminal justice outcomes, with employment having been shown to increase desistance and reduce recidivism. The specific factors that limit the effectiveness of employment for criminal justice practice are then considered. The importance of employment to social policy outcomes is detailed, together with the changed context over the last 40 years that is impacting the nature of employment policies. Finally, the chapter considers what criminal justice practice can learn from this changed context, in order to identify ways in which social policy can improve criminal justice practice.

What is employment?

The definition of employment that is used in this chapter is employment as work carried out formally in exchange for pay or profit, which can include part-time or full-time employment (ILO, 1988). Voluntary work and work carried out informally, such as working without contract, are excluded from this definition – meaning, for example, that someone working for cash in hand is not included.

Why is employment important?

Chapter 2 sets out the significance of the *Beveridge Report* to the development of post-war social policy in the UK, a significance that remains to this day. Idleness was one of Beveridge's five giant evils, and a key aspect of post-war social policy was employment, regarded as important both in financial and social terms. From a social perspective, employment is important as it improves well-being, health and psychosocial needs (Sage, 2015). Conversely, a lack of employment leads to 'social exclusion, poor physical health, low subjective well-being, and life satisfaction, lack of personal autonomy and suspended human capital development' (Sage, 2015:322). As a consequence, employment remains central to contemporary social policy. There is also a specific economic reason why this is the case, namely that those in employment are more able to provide for themselves financially, and pay taxes that fund social policies, meaning that without a certain level of employment, social policy benefits and services are constrained. This is evidenced by times of high unemployment, such as during the economic crisis after 2008 that saw government expenditure in most areas reduced but particularly in social policy areas (Poinasamy, 2013).

To show how central employment is to social policy, we can examine policies around those who become unemployed. The main unemployment benefit paid since the *Beveridge Report* has changed from unemployment benefit to Jobseeker's Allowance to Universal Credit. Regardless of name changes and structural alterations, the key point about unemployment benefits is that they have never been paid at a rate that matches employment wages. This is a deliberate policy, stemming from the belief that employment should be incentivised and unemployment disincentivised, thus reinforcing the fact that work remains central to social policy.

However, it is important to observe that the labour market was considerably different 70 years ago. At the end of World War Two (WW2), employment policy was geared towards (male) **full employment** (Key Learning Box 6.1), meaning that it included almost the whole male population. Consequently, the government took an active role in ensuring that employment was available through the nationalisation of important sectors such as energy, the railways, telecommunications and the iron and steel industries (Kelf-Cohen, 1973). This not only improved the quantity of jobs, but also their quality (Millward, 1997). These conditions were encapsulated in the notion of a 'job for life' that existed in the 20–30 years after WW2 (Gilbert, 1998), meaning not just continuous employment throughout the life course if so desired, but also the ability to walk straight into a new job if unemployment was unavoidable (McDowell, 2002). The period was also characterised by improvements in work conditions, and has been defined as a 'golden age' for the labour market in particular (Hatton and Boyer, 2005).

KEY LEARNING BOX 6.1 FULL EMPLOYMENT

There are many definitions of full employment, but the one that was used at the end of WW2 was an unemployment rate no higher or lower than 3 per cent of the

---

population. This was regarded as the point when everyone who was willing to have a job would have one. It took into consideration the fact that some groups, such as stay-at-home parents and students, might not be looking for a job, which together was thought to represent 3 per cent of the population. An unemployment rate higher than 3 per cent was seen as having a negative impact on the country and the economy. On the other hand, an unemployment rate lower than 3 per cent also had negative implications such as increasing the power of workers over their employers, thus leading to high wage increases and voluntary unemployment.

It is also relevant to note that also important to the emphasis on full employment in social policy after WW2 was the specific belief that education improves the employment outcomes for individuals and society (Marginson, 2019). This was built on a belief that education could improve labour quality, and therefore enhance economic growth (Wang and Lui, 2016). In particular, policy was specifically focused on equality of opportunity and social mobility, the aim being to 'create a fairer and more efficient society, in which educated merit and hard work would determine success, rather than prior family position' (Marginson, 2019:288). For this reason, policies focused on providing choice in education that nodded towards social mobility, such as comprehensive schooling, and further and higher education to build employment skills.

What is the evidence of a link between employment and positive criminal justice outcomes?

The positive outcomes of employment as relevant to criminal justice practice can be seen in increasing **desistance** (Key Learning Box 6.2) and reducing **recidivism** (Key Learning Box 6.3).

KEY LEARNING BOX 6.2 DESISTANCE

Desistance refers to an individual with a record of offending who stops participating in crime. This usually refers to the long term, rather than a short period. It would therefore not apply to someone who has not committed a crime for a week, but would to someone who has not committed a crime for a year. The notion of desistance is important as it reflects one of the key aims of criminal justice practice, that of stopping crime.

A key focus of criminal justice practice when working with those who have committed criminal acts is to facilitate desistance from crime. There is good evidence that employment in particular is important in this respect. For example, it has been observed in particular that adults who are involved in the Criminal Justice System (CJS) 'are more likely to desist when they achieve employment, particularly when that employment pays relatively well and provides favourable working conditions' (Duwe and Clark, 2017:657). This effect has been established 'fairly consistently' in international contexts, and suggests that employment has a long-term positive benefit on desistance (Apel and Horney, 2017). It is important to note, though, that this effect is regularly noted as being age-specific, meaning that it only relates to those who are over a certain age, from mid to late 20s, suggesting that stable work histories, career growth and higher earnings levels, which all relate to age, are the reasons why employment is important to desistance (Adeling-Judge, 2021).

Where employers take on ex-offenders, the evidence for beneficial outcomes is strong. Atherton and Buck (2021) note that employers use terms such as trustworthy, loyal and hardworking to describe ex-offenders they employ. Evidence to support this is provided by Timpson, an employer that has publicly taken a stance of employing ex-offenders. The company claims that it has employed 1,500 ex-prisoners in its shops, and only four of them have gone back to prison (Allison, 2019), which if true is an astonishingly low rate. This supports the claim that employment is strongly linked to desistance.

KEY LEARNING BOX 6.3 RECIDIVISM

Recidivism is the opposite of desistance, as it refers to where an individual returns to crime either after having stopped or after having been punished for it. Sometimes, individuals do not commit crimes for a long time after they have been punished or for a long time after they have committed a previous crime, and then they commit a crime or crimes again. This is recidivism. Understanding what causes recidivism is important because when it occurs, it can result in an expensive cost to the CJS, and therefore criminal justice practice.

The opposite of desistance is recidivism, where a person relapses into crime. Employment has been strongly negatively linked to recidivism for a number of reasons, including a reduction in economic need, an engendering of informal social control and positive peer associations (McNeeley, 2021). It has been observed that reoffending rates are higher among those who do not work compared to those to those who do work (Adeling-Judge, 2021). Van der Geest et al (2011) observe that full-time employment in particular has a sizeable independent effect on the reduction in reoffending, when compared with being unemployed. The evidence also shows that of those who are reconvicted within a year of release from prison, the majority had failed to find work (Allison, 2019). Being denied employment opportunities can result in re-engagement in crime, owing to the depression and self-defeating behaviours this can lead to (Obastusin and Ritter-Williams, 2019).

Being in prison has been shown to not only reduce the probability of employment, but also to increase the length of unemployment and reduce the wages earned from employment (Apel and Sweeten, 2010). This is because 'time out' from the labour market results in the erosion of skills and gaps in employment history, which both negatively affect labour market participation, as an individual's reputation is negatively affected, and reduce the possibility of successful reintegration into the community (Apel and Sweeten, 2010). However, employment has been shown to help with adjustment to civilian life, thereby reducing recidivism, in a number of ways, such as providing structured activities, building social contacts, status and the opportunity for an individual to prove that they have changed (Obastusin and Ritter-Williams, 2019). Employment can also alter the types of crimes that are committed, as someone who is employed is less likely to commit 'predatory' crimes such as burglary (Berg and Huebner, 2011).

It is also important to highlight the importance of education to employment. Lochner (2008) argues that education has a negative effect on crime: it 'socialises' individuals so they become better citizens and so move away from crime, it increases returns available from non-criminal activity, it teaches individuals to consider the consequences of crime and it also encourages them to become more risk averse and so less likely to commit crimes. Evidence supports a link between education and crime, in that a disproportionate number of prisoners 'have low levels of literacy (62 per cent) which is four times higher than in the general population and there are even lower levels of numeracy. Around 47 per cent of people entering prison have no prior qualifications' (Prisoner Learning Alliance, 2020). As a consequence of these educational deficiencies, many prisoners lack stable employment histories, or indeed any employment history (Berg and Huebner, 2011), meaning that they lack job training and vocational skills (McNeeley, 2021). The low education attainment level of those who commit crimes limits their ability to gain employment.

There are a number of criminological theories that seek to explain the reasons why employment has such an important impact on desistance and recidivism. These are summarised in Table 6.1. There are two key points to make from this simplified summary. The first is that most of the theories outline the beneficial impact of employment, in terms of their focus on desistance rather than recidivism. This suggests that employment works in a positive rather than a negative way in terms of beneficial criminal justice outcomes. The second is the importance of an economic and social perspective when explaining the relationship between employment and crime, showing how it is this perspective rather than others, such as for example the psychological perspective, that explains the link (Mesters et al, 2014). By this is meant that social and economic factors such as money and social ties seem to be more important to desistance and recidivism than psychological factors such as positive reinforcement.

What are the factors that limit the positive criminal justice outcomes of employment?

Research shows that the **stigma** (Key Learning Box 6.4) of being an offender or ex-offender has a significant impact on employment. Being an offender or

Table 6.1 Simplified summary of theories that focus on the importance of employment to desistance and recidivism

Theory	Explanation for desistance	Explanation for recidivism
Rational choice theory	Employment provides (financial) gains to the individual that outweigh those from crime	
Social control theory	Employment ties individuals to social networks, controlling the temptations to commit crime	
Strain theory		Exclusion from work motivates individuals towards criminal behaviour
Interactionist theory	Employment transforms the social outlook of individuals away from crime	
Learning theory	The workplace provides exposure to positive reinforcement of law-abiding behaviours	
Routine activities theory	Employment provides a routine activity that limits the opportunity for crime	

Source: Created using data from Apel and Horney (2017)

ex-offender is highly stigmatised, not just by the general public but also by employers, and this has a debilitating effect in terms of finding work (Berg and Huebner, 2011). Stigma therefore creates an informal barrier to employment, one that is very hard to overcome (Adeling-Judge, 2021). Employers even refuse to employ offenders or ex-offenders, in the knowledge that such overt discrimination is not illegal (Atherton and Buck, 2021). For example, an experiment by Savolainen et al (2018) observed that if an applicant had a criminal record, the probability that an employer would respond to their job application was reduced by 50 per cent. Berg and Huebner (2011:388) report that 'employers were unwilling to hire those with a reported criminal record even when they exceeded the qualifications for a post'.

KEY LEARNING BOX 6.4 STIGMA

Stigma refers to negative attitudes towards and/or beliefs about a person, group or place. The key point is that this negativity can often lead to discrimination and other negative behaviours, meaning that the stigmatised person's position is made worse. Stigma can lead to rumours and myths, which can also lead to discrimination. In relation to criminal justice practice, there is a stigma associated with having being in prison, meaning that prisoners and ex-prisoners are often viewed and treated worse than the general population, thus limiting the possibility of positive outcomes.

It is important to note that having been in prison acts to reinforce the employment disadvantage of individuals, so it is harder to get a job (Sheely, 2020). This is because being in prison works to disrupt important factors relating to searching for work, such as the development of social networks (Lageson and Uggen, 2012). Where experience is important, prospective employers may also take note of gaps in work history and the lack of suitable recent referees (Apel and Sweeten, 2010).

There are various reasons why employers are reluctant to employ ex-offenders. For example, they can be perceived as not worth the risk, in terms of the possibility of criminal activity (Apel and Sweeten, 2010). Employers may also perceive ex-offenders as lazy and unreliable (Atherton and Buck, 2021) or as lacking work readiness skills such as time keeping or appropriate attitudes (Obastusin and Ritter-Williams, 2019). Their lack of work history and/or sporadic employment means that what they can offer to employers in terms of work experience is limited, and experience is sometimes very important in finding a job (Atherton and Buck, 2021).

Sheely (2020:974) terms this 'labour market exclusion', wherein 'due to employer reluctance to hire people with criminal records, as well as legal restrictions on the types of jobs they can acquire, people with criminal records searching for work may be unable to find it'. She also observes that such labour market exclusion may lead to 'labour market detachment', wherein

> people with histories of criminal justice involvement may drop out of the labour market because they do not believe they will be able to find employment ... searching for work takes time and effort. Given employer reticence to hire people with criminal records, as well as the occupational restrictions ... people who have been involved in the criminal justice system will have to engage in more extensive searches and apply for more jobs than people without a criminal record. (Sheely, 2020:977)

The key point to note is that labour market exclusion can cause labour market detachment. This is despite the fact that as Allison (2019) observes, most ex-offenders who find work do not reoffend, and yet many employers are reluctant to take this chance.

It is also important to note that ex-offenders can face legal requirements not only on the type of work they can do if Disclosure and Barring Service (DBS) requirements apply, but also what they need to declare to prospective employers, in relation to 'spent' and 'unspent' convictions as set out in the Rehabilitation of Offenders Act 1974. This is something that can actively exclude ex-offenders from sections of the labour market, as well as resulting in a reluctance on the part of employers to hire them (Sheely, 2020), both of which make it harder for potential employees to find work.

These barriers have a significant impact not just on individuals but also on society. For the individual, they make finding work in the legitimate labour market harder, thus increasing the chance of recidivism. They can also reinforce existing interconnected risk factors, such as mental illness and addiction (Cherney and Fitzgerald, 2016). For society, the consequences are a potential for increased crime and victimisation, as well as wasted productivity and human resources (Gana et al, 2021).

For those in prison, work and training programmes may be provided. There is some evidence that these improve employment outcomes post-release (Duwe and Clark, 2017). However, there is an irony in this evidence, in that the longer a person remains in prison, the better the outcomes, and vice versa. This is because the likelihood of participation in such programmes increases the longer a person is in prison (Duwe and Clark, 2017). For those on short sentences, a lack of access to such programmes increases their chances of recidivism.

It is important to note that evidence suggests it is not employment per se that is important to successful criminal justice outcomes, but it is the quality of the job that the offender has that is important (Lageson and Uggenn, 2012). Evidence shows that those who obtain high-quality jobs, particularly in terms of pay, benefits, stability and security, are less likely to reoffend than those who obtain lower quality jobs (Apel and Horney, 2017). The emphasis on 'a job is a job' that pervades many job programmes for offenders explains why so many fail, as 'such programmes are ineffective, as programmes rooted in a welfare to work philosophy are probably poor guides for prison work realities' (Apel and Horney, 2017:333). This is because high-quality jobs provide the opportunity to break from a criminal past, especially in terms of financial issues (Atherton and Buck, 2021). If jobs are poorly paid, offenders may return to criminality to supplement low wages (Apel and Sweeten, 2010). This highlights that it is job quality that is important, as a good job 'will make it easier to satisfy needs and desires through legitimate means' (Ramakers et al, 2018:1812).

Employment is used primarily as a rehabilitative tool by criminal justice practitioners. This means it is used principally when working with those who have already offended in order to positively change their behaviour. It is important to note that rehabilitation in any form still represents punishment, in that it is not generally something that the offender would freely choose to do (McNeill, 2014). McNeill (2014:15) distinguishes further between four forms of rehabilitation:

- *Psychological rehabilitation*: seeks to somehow change or restore the offender; to develop new skills or abilities, to address and resolve deficits or problems.
- *Judicial rehabilitation*: concerned with how and to what extent a criminal record and the formal stigma that it represents can ever be set aside, sealed or surpassed.
- *Moral rehabilitation*: where an offender has to 'pay back' or to 'make good' before s/he can 'trade up' to a restored social position as a citizen of good character.

- *Social rehabilitation*: entails both the restoration of the citizen's formal social status and the availability of the personal and social means to do so.

This distinction becomes relevant when we consider how employment is primarily used as a rehabilitation tool within the CJS. Employment is primarily used to encourage desistance. Its focus is largely on offenders and on changing individuals' behaviour, either so they develop new skills or resolve individual deficits. This orients employment in criminal justice practice as a form of psychological rehabilitation. Additionally, the legal requirements in terms of DBS checks and spent convictions for offenders trying to find work encapsulate judicial rehabilitation. Moral rehabilitation is something that is often evident when probation is at stake, as the offender is required to show that they have become a better person before they are able to be released, and employment can serve this purpose. It is primarily within these forms of psychological, judicial and moral rehabilitation that employment operates in the CJS. However, there is less focus on employment within a fourth form of rehabilitation, social rehabilitation, and this will be discussed later in more detail. This supports the point made earlier that employment in criminal justice practice is a form of punitive rehabilitation. Indeed, the emphasis on having a job per se as opposed to having a good-quality job supports this claim. The problematic nature of this becomes evident when we consider the significance of social policy in terms of employment.

What is the current social policy context of employment?

It is clear that employment conditions now are decisively different from those during the 'golden age' detailed earlier, and this has been the case particularly over the last 40 years. For example, the full employment of the post-war years no longer exists, and unemployment has been well above 3 per cent for most of the last 40 years. Indeed, in the aftermath of the financial crises of 2008, unemployment has been as high as over 8 per cent, which is equivalent to 2.7 million people. Had the unemployment rate been 3 per cent, there would have been just over 1 million people unemployed during this period, which is a significant difference. This high unemployment rate has meant that the possibility of having a job for life is no longer the reality for many, with employment being more insecure and frequently changing.

There have been a number of policy responses to these changes, and indeed a number of policy responses have driven these changes. In terms of the latter, the move away from nationalisation towards privatisation, meaning the selling off of nationalised industries such as energy, railways and manufacturing to private companies and individuals, has had an impact on the quality of jobs and led to significant changes in the income that people can expect. In effect, there has been a change from a high wage to a low wage economy, as exemplified by the huge shift from an economy with a majority of manufacturing jobs (including engineering and technology), to an economy with a majority of service sector jobs (such as retailing and hospitality) (Hine and Wright, 1998). This change in the type of jobs available has also affected their nature. While manufacturing jobs tend to be mainly full time, service sector jobs include higher levels of part-time work (OECD, 2001), and the increase in service sector jobs in the UK has seen an increase in part-time workers to over 8 million people (ONS, 2022a). Moreover, according to the Office for National Statistics (ONS, 2020), prior to COVID-19, self-employment was showing continuous growth, peaking at 5 million people in 2019, which is the highest number ever. The number of female workers also peaked in 2020, before falling slightly in 2021 (Buchanan et al, 2023). There has also been an increasing use of **zero hours contracts** (Key Learning Box 6.5).

KEY LEARNING BOX 6.5 ZERO HOURS CONTRACTS

A zero hours contract job is where a person is employed by a company with no guarantee of the hours that they will be required to work. In a standard contracted job, a person is given a set number of hours that they are expected to work each day, week or month. But with a zero hours contract, this is not the case. Instead, the employee is expected to be on call as and when the employer needs them, and is only paid when they work. Zero hours contracts do not normally include sick pay.

These contracts are a relatively new phenomenon. However, according to the ONS (2022), there are over 1 million people employed in this way, and their number is growing every year. Zero hours contracts are most evident in low-paid sectors, such as retailing and hospitality. For example, out of the 23,000 people that Sports Direct employs, 20,000 are on zero hours contacts. Similarly, 80 per cent of Wetherspoon's employees are on zero hours contracts.

Employees on these contracts do not have the same employment rights as contracted employees, principally because they are classified as self-employed. Moreover, because they do not have secure and guaranteed work hours, their income can be lower than other employees, and can vary from week to week.

In terms of policy responses to these changes, a key shift has been an increased emphasis on what are termed **Active Labour Market Policies** (ALMPs) (Key Learning Box 6.6). The ALMPs that government policy has focused on include measures such as 'placement services with stronger work incentives, time limits on recipiency, benefit reductions, and the use of sanctions – the so-called workfare approach' (Bonoli, 2010:439). To sum up this approach in a pithy way, if we were defining the approach in terms of a carrot or stick approach to increasing employment, the approach is more stick than carrot (Haapanala, 2021). As examples of the stick approach, the focus has been on measures such as time-limiting unemployment benefits, low unemployment benefit levels, mandatory job searching for receipt of unemployment benefits, and the whole or partial ending of unemployment benefits under certain conditions.

KEY LEARNING BOX 6.6 ACTIVE LABOUR MARKET POLICIES

ALMPs seek to improve the chances of individuals finding work or increasing what they earn by primarily focusing on improving their skills. The best example of this is job training schemes, but ALMPS can also include subsidised jobs and start-up grants. This approach is different from the full employment approach of the post-war period, when the focus was on creating jobs so that individuals could enter the labour market. The key points about ALMPs are that they are usually aimed at the unemployed and are mandatory for those wishing to receive unemployment benefits.

An example of this approach is the expansion of higher education as a route into work, albeit a circuitous, lengthy and increasingly expensive route. For those not minded to proceed with higher education, there is the possibility of gaining Level 3 (equivalent to A level) qualifications through the National Careers Service (NCS), although the beneficial outcomes for those who use this are not clear (Lane et al, 2017). There is also the opportunity for a range of work training, through Skills for Life, some of which is free and some of which is self-funded, and also through the Job Centre. This includes apprenticeships, skills bootcamps, and training in numeracy and literacy skills.

Apprenticeships in particular are reminiscent of the Youth Training Scheme (YTS) that was introduced in the 1980s and lasted in its original form for ten years. The YTS was geared towards young people aged 16–17 at a time of high unemployment among young people. Negative long-term experiences of the YTS (Goodwin et al, 2020) led some to question the motives behind it, with it being regarded as a way to either massage unemployment figures or to regulate young people's behaviour (Finn, 1987). The YTS's failures highlight important points for employment training schemes, namely that they have to be properly funded, providing real life work experience as opposed to providing cheap or free labour, paying a proper rate of pay with a proper work and/or educational outcome.

A specific feature of this changed emphasis in social policy on work has been a focus on having a job per se, meaning that any job is seen as better than no job (Tomlinson et al, 2016). This means that for those without work, policy has been focused on getting them into a job, any job. This means that issues such as under-employment, which can refer not only to a lack of hours, but also to 'being employed in a job that requires less education, skills and experience than they possess, being employed in a job that does not relate to their area of education, or in a job that offers inferior pay and conditions when compared to a previous employment' (Heyes et al, 2017:73) is not considered to be a policy concern.

This is despite the fact that such issues can have a significant negative impact on well-being (Heyes et al, 2017).

These changes have altered the nature of employment for many people in terms of its beneficial outcomes. As detailed earlier, employment is rationalised as providing both economic and social benefits to the individual. This is dependent on work providing a level of income that enables these benefits to be met. However, it has become apparent that the income that a significant majority receive from employment has not kept up with the cost of living, owing to the entrenching of low pay and insecure employment (Grady, 2017). Consequently, these changes mean that 'work does not pay' (Standing, 2021), meaning that economic and social benefits ascribed to work are limited or non-existent.

How can a social policy focus on employment improve criminal justice practice?

In this regard, criminal justice practice can learn from the changes that have occurred in social policy over the last 40 years, which have seen a change in the labour market from 'the golden age' of employment to a period characterised by a focus on having any job, leading to low pay, low skills, high unemployment and high under-employment. The outcome has been the entrenchment of a negative impact on well-being. The relevance to criminal justice practice is that where employment rehabilitation schemes are similarly focused on a job per se, as many schemes are, the benefits are limited, which in turn limits the rehabilitative potential of employment. For example, van der Geest et al (2011) outline that offenders engaged in job reintegration schemes need full-time permanent jobs as opposed to temporary jobs, because the latter do not provide the beneficial outcomes of the former, particularly in terms of opportunities for personal development and growth within the community. This point is reinforced by Skardhammer and Savolainen's (2014) observation that having a job that lasts less than six months does not contribute to desistance from crime. In addition, van der Geest et al (2011) observe that the effects of employment on desistance increased with the hours worked, and also that regular employment stimulates desistance more quickly than irregular employment. Berg and Huebner (2011) note that high-quality jobs diminish the likelihood of recidivism among ex-offenders, and McNeely (2021:3) writes that 'recidivism is lower among those who find stable high-quality employment ... especially [when] individuals work in "career jobs" rather than "survival jobs"'. Similarly, Cherney and Fitzgerald (2016) state that finding stable employment is one of the best predictors of post-release success among offenders. Aspects such as job satisfaction and a sense of fulfilment are also important to desistance (Adeling-Judge, 2021). This means that criminal justice practice programmes need to provide training in high-value and enduring work. However, it is often the case that such programmes provide training in areas that are 'overcrowded and low-paying, using outmoded equipment and instructional materials', which lead to job roles in low-paid and menial jobs, and so 'discourage their efforts to participate in the legal labour market' (Duwe and Clark, 2017:659). All these factors suggest that for employment to be as effective as possible in terms of criminal justice practice, it should move away from the stick approach that has been experienced and exemplified by social policy since the 1980s.

Another key social policy change that has occurred is a focus on employment as an individual rather than a structural problem. Whereas in the past social policy emphasised full employment and measures that encouraged it such as work generation schemes, today the responsibility for finding employment lies squarely with the individual. Similarly, within criminal justice practice, emphasis is wholly on the individual to find work, not on its provision. This is an important distinction, because it means that the CJS treats offenders almost like anyone else, leaving them to the vagaries of the labour market. The exception are schemes such as the **New Futures Network** (NFN, Key Learning Box 6.7), which provides incentives to employers such as National Insurance holidays if they take on ex-prisoners. This is as far as the incentives go, and for the most part ex-offenders are on their own, despite the fact that evidence shows they need more help than most to find a job because of the entrenched stigma and inequalities that they face. The experience of high unemployment over the last 40 years or so shows that from a social policy perspective it is hard enough for non-offenders to find a job without specific help, which suggests that it is counterintuitive for criminal justice practitioners to expect ex-offenders to be able to do so. Rather, employment programmes need to take place over a significant period of time, not just when offenders are in prison but also for a time after they have been released (Savolainen et al, 2018; McNeeley, 2021). Programmes also need to address practical barriers to obtaining and maintaining employment, such as interview-appropriate clothing and transportation (McNeeley, 2021).

KEY LEARNING BOX 6.7 NEW FUTURES NETWORK

The NFN is part of HM Prison and Probation Service (HMPPS). Its aim is to build partnerships between prisons and employers so businesses can fill skills gaps and prison leavers can find employment. This is done either through employers setting up commercial businesses in prisons and employing prisoners, providing work for serving prisoners on day release or offering employment to ex-prisoners on release. See https://newfuturesnetwork.gov.uk/.

In a wider sense, it is worth discussing the ultimate aim of employment for criminal justice practice. We have seen that a key but often overlooked beneficial outcome that employment can have on criminal justice practice is the prevention of crime through the provision of a social and economic lifestyle that avoids the need to commit crime in the first place. This outcome is also beneficial for social policy, as it means less need to deal with other issues directly and indirectly related to crime, such as unemployment and treatment programmes respectively. In an ideal world, employment would be used as a tool to prevent crime, but this is not really something that is foregrounded in criminal justice practice, as employment is rarely something that criminal justice practice uses as a tool to actively prevent crime. Rather, the focus of employment is primarily on responding to crime through rehabilitation.

This brings us to the fourth of McNeill's meanings of rehabilitation, that of social rehabilitation, which refers to an individual feeling a valued part of the community. Employment has been shown to be important in preventing crime from happening in the first place, simply by enabling people to pay their bills, which limits the economic incentives to crime and enables them to develop networks that tie them to the community they live, thus limiting the social incentives to crime (Berg and Huebner, 2011). For example, Sheely (2020:973) notes that employment in the paid labour market is 'linked to multiple positive life outcomes, such as increased income, access to broader social networks, better mental health outcomes, improving family functioning as well as higher self-esteem'. In relation to those who have already offended, employment can help with reintegration by providing 'pro-social' roles that are important to identity, through provision of the financial and social resources to fulfil these roles, such as partner, parent, friend and colleague (Cherney and Fitzgerald, 2016). It is clear that such social rehabilitation cannot occur where employment functions to limit the potential of the individual or where they are not happy in what they are doing. As an example, Apel and Horney (2017) observe that the more committed an offender is to a job, the less likely it is that they will become involved in criminal activity. Atherton and Buck (2021:187) argue that job stability promotes desistance by 'creating new social bonds, reducing criminal opportunities, informal social control and nurturing a pro-social identity ... facilitat[ing] increased self-confidence, personal autonomy, and the ability to demonstrate steps towards "going straight"'. In other words, just as good-quality employment is important for the physical health, well-being, life satisfaction, personal autonomy and human capital development of those outside the CJS, so it is important for those inside the CJS.

Summary

This chapter has presented evidence that employment is key to good criminal justice practice outcomes. In particular, there is good evidence that employment not only increases desistance from crime, but also reduces recidivism, notwithstanding some key issues that can limit this effectiveness. These are very significant criminal justice practice considerations.

However, the chapter has outlined that within criminal justice practice employment is used as a form of punitive rehabilitation, with the focus primarily on responding to crime, through rehabilitation. It has been argued that this focus is problematic in terms of criminal justice practice because it limits the effectiveness of employment in a number of key ways, as seen in relation to changes in social policy over the last 40 years or so. For example, the focus on having a job per se limits the rehabilitative potential of employment. Additionally, the focus on employment as an individual rather than a structural problem ignores the evidence that shows ex-prisoners need more help than most to find a job because they face entrenched stigma and inequalities.

These limitations lead to a consideration of what the ultimate aim of employment is for criminal justice practice. In an ideal world, employment would be used as a tool to prevent crime, but this is not something that is foregrounded in criminal justice practice, despite the fact that employment has been shown to be important in preventing crime from happening in the first place. Employment can prevent crime occurring because it can provide a social and economic lifestyle that avoids the need to commit crime. This can only occur, though, when criminal justice practice foregrounds good-quality employment that leads to good physical health, well-being, life satisfaction, personal autonomy and human capital development.

References

Adeling-Judge, D. (2021) 'Social opportunities and controls: Revisiting the desistance effect of employment', *Deviant Behaviour*, 42(9): 1177–1193.

Allison, E. (2019) 'The message is clear: Give ex-prisoners a job to stop them returning to crime', *The Guardian*. Available from: https://www.theguard ian.com/society/2019/oct/29/ex-prisoners-job-return-crime-reoffending [Accessed 29 April 2022].

Apel, R. and Horney, J. (2017) 'How and why does work matter? Employment conditions, routine activities, and crime among adult male offenders', *Criminology*, 55(2): 307–343.

Apel, R. and Sweeten, G. (2010) 'The impact of incarceration on employment during the transition to adulthood', *Social Problems*, 57(3): 448–479.

Atherton, P. and Buck G. (2021) 'Employing with conviction: The experiences of employers who actively recruit criminalised people', *Probation Journal*, 68(2): 186–205.

Berg, M. and Huebner, B. (2011) 'Reentry and the ties that bind: An examination of social ties, employment, and recidivism', *Justice Quarterly*, 28(2): 382–410.

Bonoli, G. (2010) 'The political economy of active labor-market policy', *Politics and Society*, 38(4): 435–457.

Buchanan, I., Pratt, A. and Francis-Devine, B. (2023) 'Women and the UK economy'. Research Briefing SN06838. London: House of Commons Library. Available at: https://researchbriefings.files.parliament.uk/documents/SN06838/SN06838.pdf [Accessed 10 March 2023].

Cherney, A. and Fitzgerald, R. (2016) 'Finding and keeping a job: The value and meaning of employment for parolees', *International Journal of Offender Therapy and Comparative Criminology*, 60(1): 21–37.

Duwe, G. and Clark, V. (2017) 'Nothing will work unless you did: The predictors of postprison employment', *Criminal Justice and Behaviour*, 44(5): 657–677.

Finn, D. (1987) *Training without Jobs. New Deals and Broken Promises.* Basingstoke: Macmillan Education.

Gana, O., Saeed, K. and Halid, H. (2021) 'Reintegration after prison: Encouraging employers to hire ex-offenders to be a part of the society', *Albukhary Social Business Journal*, 2(2): 1–9.

Gilbert, J. (1998) "A job for life" into "a life of jobs", *Empowerment in Organisations*, 6(6): 165–174.

Goodwin, J., O'Connor, H., Droy, L. and Holmes, S. (2020) 'Returning to YTS: The long-term impact of Youth Training Scheme participation', *Journal of Youth Studies*, 23(1): 28–43.

Grady, J. (2017) 'The state, employment, and regulation: Making work not pay', *Employee Relations*, 39(3): 274–290.

Haapanala, H. (2021) 'Carrots or sticks? A multilevel analysis of Active Labour Market Policies and non-standard employment in Europe', *Social Policy and Administration*. https://doi.org/10.1111/spol.12770.

Hatton, T. and Boyer, G. (2005). 'Unemployment and the UK labour market before, during and after the golden age', *European Review of Economic History*, 9: 35–60.

Heyes, J., Tomlinson, M. and Whitworth, A. (2017) 'Underemployment and well-being in the UK before and after the Great Recession', *Work, Employment and Society*, 31(1): 71–89.

Hine, R.C. and Wright, P.W. (1998) 'Trade with low wage economies, employment and productivity in UK manufacturing', *The Economic Journal*, 108(450): 1500–1510.

Howard League for Penal Reform (2021) 'Written evidence from Howard League for Penal Reform'. Available from: https://committees.parliament.uk/writtenevidence/36424/html/ [Accessed 28 July 2022].

ILO (International Labour Organisation) (1988) *ILO Glossary of Statistical Terms*, ILO: Geneva. Available from: https://www.ilo.org/ilostat-files/Documents/Statistical%20Glossary.pdf [Accessed 29 April 2022].

Kelf-Cohen, R. (1973) *British Nationalisation 1945–1973*. Basingstoke: Palgrave Macmillan

Lageson, S. and Uggen, S. (2012) 'How work affects crime – and crime affects work – over the life course', in C.L. Gibson and M.D. Krohn (eds) *Handbook of Life-Course Criminology: Emerging Trends and Directions for Future Research*. New York: Springer, pp. 201–212. https://doi.org/10.1007/978-1-4614-5113-6_12.

Lane, V., Conlon, G., Peycheva, V., Mantovani, I. and Chan, S. (2017) *An Economic Evaluation of the National Careers Service*, DFE-RR672, London: Department of Education.

Lochner, L. (2008) 'Education and crime', in P. Peterson, E. Baker and B. McGaw (eds) *International Encyclopaedia of Education*, 3rd edition, Philadelphia: Elsevier, pp. 239–244.

Marginson, S. (2019) 'Limitations of human capital theory', *Studies in Higher Education*, 44(2): 287–301.

McDowell, L. (2002) 'Transitions to work: Masculine identities, youth inequality and labour market change', *Gender, Place and Culture: A Journal of Feminist Geography*, 9(1): 39–59.

McNeeley, S. (2021) 'A long-term follow-up evaluation of an employment assistance re-entry programme', *Justice Evaluation Journal*. https://doi.org/10.1080/24751979.2021.1965494.

McNeill, F. (2014) 'Punishment as rehabilitation', in G. Bruinsma, and D. Weisburd, D. (eds) *Encyclopaedia of Criminology and Criminal Justice*. New York: Springer, pp. 4195–4206.

Mesters, G., van der Geest, V. and Bijleveld, C. (2014) 'Crime, employment and social welfare: An individual-level study on disadvantaged males', *Tinbergen Institute Discussion Paper, No. 14–091/III*, Amsterdam and Rotterdam: Tinbergen Institute.

Millward, R. (1997) 'The 1940s nationalizations in Britain: Means to an end or the means of production?', *Economic History Review*, 50(2): 209–234.

Ministry of Justice (2013) *Transforming Rehabilitation: A Summary of Evidence on Reducing Reoffending*. London: Ministry of Justice.

Obastusin, O. and Ritter-Williams, D. (2019) 'A phenomenological study of employer perspectives on hiring ex-offenders', *Cogent Social Sciences*, 5(1): 1571730.

OECD (Organisation for Economic Co-operation and Development) (2001) *OECD Employment Outlook 2001: June*. OECD Publishing. https://doi.org/10.1787/empl_outlook-2001-en.

ONS (Office for National Statistics) (2020) 'Coronavirus and self-employment in the UK'. Available from: https://www.ons.gov.uk/employmentandlabourmarket/peopleinwork/employmentandemployeetypes/articles/coronavirusandselfemploymentintheuk/2020-04-24 [Accessed 29 April 2022].

ONS (Office for National Statistics) (2022) 'EMP17: People in employment on zero hours contracts'. Available from: https://www.ons.gov.uk/employmentandlabourmarket/peopleinwork/employmentandemployemploymentypes/datasets/emp17peopleinemploymentonzerohourscontracts [Accessed 24 March 2022].

ONS (Office for National Statistics) (2022a) 'EMP01 SA: Full-time, part-time and temporary workers (seasonally adjusted)'. Available from: https://www.ons.gov.uk/employmentandlabourmarket/peopleinwork/employmentandemployemploymentypes/datasets/fulltimeparttimeandtemporaryworkersseasonallyadjustedemp01sa [Accessed 7 April 2022].

Poinasamy, K. (2013) *The True Cost of Austerity and Inequality. UK Case Study*. Oxford: Oxfam.

Prisoner Learning Alliance (2020) 'Prisoner Learning Alliance (PLA) submission to education committee inquiry on adult skills and lifelong learning'. Available from: https://committees.parliament.uk/writtenevidence/9597/html [Accessed 29 April 2022].

Ramakers, A., Nieuwbeerta, P., Wilsem, J. and Dirkzwager, A. (2017) 'Not just any job will do: A study on employment characteristics and recidivism risks after release', *International Journal of Offender Therapy and Comparative Criminology*, 61(16): 1795–1818.

Sage, D. (2015) 'Do Active Labour Market Policies promote the well-being, health and social capital of the unemployed? Evidence from the UK', *Social Indicators Research*, 124: 319–337.

Savolainen, J., Aaltonen, M. and Skardhamar, T. (2018). 'Employment, crime, and the life course', in D.P. Farrington, L. Kazemian and A.R. Piquero (eds) *The Oxford Handbook of Developmental and Life-Course Criminology*. New York: Oxford University Press, pp. 495–514.

Sheely, A. (2020) 'Criminal justice involvement and employment outcomes among women', *Crime and Delinquency*, 66(6–7): 973–994.

Skardhamer, T. and Savolainen, J. (2014) 'Changes in criminal offending around the time of job entry: A study of employment and desistance', *Criminology*, 52(2): 263–291.

Standing, G. (2021) *The Corruption of Capital: Why Rentiers Thrive and Work Does Not Pay*. Hull: Biteback Publishing.

Tomlinson, M., Walker, A. and Foster, L. (2016) 'Social quality and work: What impact does low pay have on social quality?', *Journal of Social Policy*, 45(2): 345–371.

Van der Geest, V., Bijleveld, C. and Blokland, A. (2011) 'The effects of employment on longitudinal trajectories of offending: A follow-up of high-risk youth from 18 to 32 years of age', *Criminology*, 49(4): 1195–1233.

Wang, Y. and Wui, S. (2016) 'Education, human capital and economic growth: Empirical research on 55 countries and regions (1960–2009)', *Theoretical Economic Letters*, 6: 347–355.

7

Physical health/mental health, criminal justice practice and social policy

This chapter aims to:

- detail evidence for the importance of physical and mental health conditions to criminal justice outcomes;

- analyse the current approaches of the Criminal Justice System (CJS) in dealing with physical and mental health conditions;

- outline ways in which a social policy approach could improve criminal justice practice outcomes for those with physical and mental health conditions.

Introduction

It has only been relatively recently that there has been a realisation that physical and mental health are significant to criminal justice practice, the evidence having mounted that they have substantial consequences for crime and vice versa in two main ways. First, there is evidence that differences in health can lead to significantly different experiences of crime, meaning that some health conditions are linked to increased crime (Weisburd and White, 2019). Secondly, there is evidence that crime has a significant impact on the health of victims, which in turn affects the demands placed on health services (Robinson and Keithley, 2000). And thirdly, there is evidence that mental health may be the biggest contributory factor to murders in the UK (Gadenne et al, 2022). Consequently, there has been growing evidence that there may be benefits for the CJS if it put in place measures to deal with health conditions.

The chapter's key focus is on detailing why and how criminal justice practice currently deals with physical and mental health conditions and how this could be improved. The chapter opens with an outline of the current context of physical and mental health in relation to the CJS, discussing the evidence of a criminogenic link between physical and mental health and criminal justice outcomes, and also the factors that contribute to increase the likelihood of CJS involvement, such as comorbidity, dual diagnosis and Adverse Childhood Experiences (ACEs). An analysis of how the CJS manages those with physical and mental health conditions follows, with a particular focus on the cost of prison, but also the wider costs to the CJS. The chapter outlines measures that have been identified as ways to improve the outcomes for those with physical and mental health conditions in the CJS. Finally, there is a summary of how a social policy approach to dealing with physical and mental health, focused on universalism, citizenship, equivalence and integration, could improve the outcomes for criminal justice practice.

What is the current context for physical and mental health in the CJS?

The most widely used definition of health is still the one provided in 1948 by the World Health Organization (WHO): 'Health is a state of complete physical, mental, and social well-being and not merely the absence of disease or infirmity' (WHO, 1948). The key point about this definition is the focus on health as a state of well-being, meaning that determining someone's health does not narrowly rely on the condition that they have, but is also defined more broadly by *both* what someone can do *and* how they feel about themselves. In practical terms, this means that while a person may have a health condition that means they cannot do some things, it is also important to determine what they can do and the way that they feel about themselves, as these may be factors that can both limit and improve measures geared towards making the life of the individual better. As an example, consider a person living with a long-term physical disability. While there may be limitations on what that person can do physically, focusing solely on that ignores the fact that they may still be mentally agile and therefore able to do lots of things that improve not only their life, but also the lives of others, such as working, social activities and family interactions, as evident from the example of Stephen Hawking in Key Learning Box 4.4.

Of the three types of health listed in the WHO definition (physical, mental and social well-being), physical and mental health are the two most frequently discussed, and for this reason they will be the focus of this chapter. It is therefore important to define these further. In this chapter, physical health refers not just to the physical conditions that a person has, but also to the living conditions that they experience. Mental health refers to the emotional, psychological and social factors that affect how people think, feel and act, and which either limit their mental health or enable them to improve it. Using these basic definitions enables us to outline how the CJS views them and the measures that are in place to deal with them.

At a simple level, physical and mental health conditions can impact on a person's social or work activities, such as going out, employment, personal care, ability to exercise or simply walking (Weisburd and White, 2019). This may impact on the ability of individuals to interact in their community and with other organisations and people who may be able to assist them in improving their health. For example, someone with a physical health condition that restricts their mobility can be limited in their ability to attend health appointments and/or other interventions that may be beneficial. These health effects may be reinforced if the fear of crime means that a person limits when and where they go outside, resulting in not accessing services and interventions that may improve their health. Limiting social interaction in this way may result in an increase in the fear of crime, a so-called feedback loop that further affects what they do (Lorenc et al, 2014). For example, it may limit the ability to participate in crime reduction schemes such as Neighbourhood Watch.

Physical health can be affected in the short term by a temporary injury such as a broken arm, or by longer-term physical health conditions, those for which there is currently no cure and require management through drugs or other treatment, such as arthritis, asthma and a number of cardiovascular diseases. It is hard to estimate the extent of short-term physical health conditions, but according to Naylor et al (2012), 15 million people, or 30 per cent of the population, have a long-term physical health condition. Some of these have been linked to negative criminal justice outcomes, with individuals who engage in increased levels of delinquency being at greater risk of heart attack, stroke, diabetes, insulin resistance and non-alcoholic fatty liver disease (Schwartz et al, 2020). Schwartz et al argue further that 'The link between these exposures and physiological dysfunction is relatively unsurprising, as one would expect repeated victimization, childhood trauma, or living in a constant fear of victimization, to contribute to psychological stress and ultimately, physiological dysfunction' (Schwartz et al, 2020:1348).

This highlights the fact that it is important to understand that short-term physical health conditions occurring as a result of crime can have important longer-term consequences on wider health. For example, aside from leading to premature death, repeated exposure to violence can lead to significant non-fatal injuries that cause long-term physical health conditions, such as paralysis. Evidence also shows that residents living in areas with higher crime rates have worse physical health (Lovasi et al, 2014). For women in particular, the total crime rate, violent crime rate and crime at night are significantly associated with lower physical health (Lovasi et al, 2014), and domestic violence, which predominantly affects women, is known to lead to a wide range of physical and mental health problems (Robinson and Keithley, 2000). The link between ill health and crime is also exemplified by considering the physical health profile of people involved in crime. Research shows that people in prison have a health profile that is ten years above their chronological age, meaning that they are in general less physically and mentally healthy (Department of Health and Social Care, 2021).

It is also important to note that it is not just violent crime that leads to negative physical health outcomes. The recent rise in cybercrime in particular has highlighted how experiencing this can lead to negative outcomes, such as less engagement in social or physical activity. Additionally, when people fear crime in their communities, they may engage in less social or physical activity (Naylor et al, 2012). The longer-term health effect of this may include, for example, a higher level of obesity owing to reduced physical activity. Crime or the fear of crime may lead to other stresses such as sleep deprivation or coping behaviours such as tobacco or alcohol use, all of which are known to have negative consequences on long-term health.

Research suggests that mental health is a growing problem in the UK as a whole, evidenced not only by a rise in anxiety among young people in particular, but also the increased use of prescription medication such as antidepressants, which is contrary to similar trends in other countries (Clark and Wenham, 2022). It is important to distinguish between severe mental health illness (SMI) and common mental health illness (CMI). SMI refers to conditions such as psychosis, schizophrenia and eating disorders that cause serious functional impairment substantially interfering with or limiting one or more major life activities. CMI refers to conditions such as stress, anxiety and phobias that affect the whole population but do not have the severity of SMI (although it is important to acknowledge that a CMI can be an early sign of and lead on to a more serious SMI). To highlight the difference between these two terms more specifically, while about 2 per cent of the adult population are estimated to live with SMI (Hardoon et al, 2013), about 16 per cent of the adult population are estimated to live with CMI (McManus et al, 2016).

The significance of mental health to the CJS is exemplified by the fact that it is estimated that up to 40 per cent of police time involves a mental health element (Home Affairs Select Committee, 2015). More recently, research by Gadenne et al (2022) outlined that mental health is the most prevalent factor in murder cases, with this being identified as a feature in more than half of all cases in the study. While it is important to note, as Knapp and Iemmi (2014) state, that 'most people with mental illness are not violent and most people who are violent are not mentally ill', at the same time it is relevant to comment that people with mental health problems are more likely to find themselves in the CJS, either as perpetrators or victims of crime. In relation to perpetration of crime, research shows that poor mental health and other vulnerabilities are exceptionally common within the prison population (Centre for Mental Health, 2021). Additionally, according to the Howard League for Penal Reform (2021), most people in prison have current or previous mental health needs, with more than half of incarcerated adults having had contact with mental health services. In relation to CMI, research has shown that 42.5 per cent of ex-prisoners have a CMI, which is a rate about three times that of the rest of the population (Bebington et al, 2021), as detailed earlier. Similarly, in relation to an SMI such as psychosis, prisoners display a prevalence rate of around 10 per cent, which is much higher than the general population (Bebington et al, 2021). More specifically, it is estimated that 25 per cent of prisoners meet the diagnosis criteria for attention deficit/ hyperactive disorder (ADHD), when within the wider population it is 5.3 per cent of children and 2.5 per cent of adults (Young et al, 2018).

In relation to people with mental illness being more likely to be victims of crime, this occurs because, as Varshney et al (2016:223) observe, 'symptoms associated with severe mental illness such as impaired reality testing, disorganised thought processes, impulsivity and poor planning and problem solving, can compromise one's ability to perceive risks and protect oneself and make them vulnerable to physical assault'.

In these paragraphs, physical health and mental health have been detailed as separate, but in the real world this distinction is not so clear cut. It is known that physical health conditions are often linked to mental health conditions, which is an aspect of what is known as **comorbidity** (Key Learning Box 7.1). This means that people with long-term physical health conditions are two to three times more likely to experience mental health problems than the general population. In particular, there is evidence of higher than usual levels of mental health problems among people with other conditions, including asthma, arthritis, cancer and HIV/AIDS (McManus et al, 2016). More specifically, even where there is experience of a low level of CMI, this is known to be associated with higher rates of chronic physical conditions, suggesting that physical health can affect mental health and vice versa in multiple and significant ways.

KEY LEARNING BOX 7.1 COMORBIDITY

In simple terms, comorbidity is when one medical condition has a negative effect on another condition. For example, having asthma can increase the effect of allergic irritants to things such as pollen, dust or mould. More specifically, it refers to how one major condition is being directly made worse by one or more additional conditions. For example, type 2 diabetes is a major condition on its own; however, type 2 diabetes can be made worse by having other health conditions that occur independently of it, such as high blood pressure. In relation to mental health, comorbidity between a mental health and physical health condition refers to a physical health condition negatively affecting a person's mental health. For example, a diagnosis of cancer can lead to increased depression.

The context of physical and mental health for the CJS is perhaps revealed most clearly by the suicide rate. Morbidity is used as a proxy for health, meaning that a higher death rate within a population indicates a less healthy population. In England and Wales, male prisoners are 3.7 times more likely to die from suicide than men in the general population (ONS, 2019), and the suicide rate per 10,000 inmates in England and Wales is double the European suicide rate (5.2 compared with 10.1) (Robinson, 2021). More recently, the suicide rate has been increasing (Ministry of Justice, 2022). If we take the suicide rate as a proxy for health, it suggests that those in the CJS experience significantly worse health, both physical and mental, than the general population.

In addition, those experiencing SMI in prisons often experience more than one mental health condition at the same time (McManus et al, 2016), which is known as **dual diagnosis** (Key Learning Box 7.2). For example, they may experience psychosis and schizophrenia or anxiety and depression together. This means that their condition is more complex and therefore more difficult to manage effectively.

KEY LEARNING BOX 7.2 DUAL DIAGNOSIS

Dual diagnosis refers to someone who is suffering from an SMI also having drug or alcohol problems. The research shows that having a SMI significantly increases the chances of misusing alcohol and drugs (NICE, 2016). The key point about dual diagnosis is not just that someone is affected by the specific negative individual effects of the SMI and also the misuse of alcohol or drugs, but that together these conditions can make their effects worse and last longer than they would singularly.

Does having physical and mental health conditions make people more criminogenic?

The previous section outlines evidence that those with physical and mental health conditions are not only more likely to be victims of crime, but also more likely to be perpetrators of crime. This implies that physical and mental health conditions can specifically lead to crime, and if this is the case, it is important to understand how the relationship can occur. In this context, it has been observed that some physical and mental health conditions are more susceptible to being affected by crime.

There are two simple reasons for this link between health and crime. The first is what Lorenc et al (2014) term 'perceived vulnerability', meaning that people with some health conditions are regarded as more vulnerable by criminals and therefore are targeted by them. Perceived vulnerability also works to limit the activities of those who are vulnerable because of their increased fear of crime. This means they are less likely to take part in activities that may improve their health and also reduce their susceptibility to crime. It should be noted that this perceived vulnerability from having a health condition can be more than perceived but can actually be a reality, such as the fact that a person with severe mental health problems is three times more likely to be a victim of crime than someone without (HMICFRS, 2018).

However, it is also important to consider why people with poor physical and mental health are more likely to end up in prison, which suggests they are more criminogenic in nature than other individuals. We can begin to answer this question by considering some of the other factors that are strongly associated with criminality – which include sexual abuse, emotional abuse, living in a high crime neighbourhood, experiencing neglect, substance abuse in the home, having mentally ill family members and growing up with parents in prison (Bjorkenstam et al, 2019). These factors can all be related to lifetime adversities, meaning negative factors that are experienced while growing up. Adverse Childhood Experiences (ACEs) (Key Learning Box 7.3) are perhaps the best known of these. Evidence suggests that when these negative factors occur, they not only lead to negative physical and mental health outcomes in later life, but also to 'maladaptive' personality traits that lead to crime (Bjorkenstam et al, 2019). For example, those who experience four or more ACEs are 20 times more likely to be imprisoned during their lifetime (Bellis et al, 2015).

KEY LEARNING BOX 7.3 ADVERSE CHILDHOOD EXPERIENCES

These are events in the life of a child that can result in negative outcomes later in childhood or in adulthood. They include experiencing or witnessing violence, child abuse, neglect or the death of a family member. Growing up in and experiencing negative environments such as substance abuse, mental health and parental separation are also defined as ACEs. It is important to note that while some of these ACEs are factors that are criminal in nature, such as child abuse and neglect, others are not, such as divorce and parental death, meaning that it is the negative experience that is important, not whether it is criminal in nature. This is due to the negative effect that such ACEs can have on individuals.

The key point is that experiencing such ACEs 'can set individuals on a health-harming life course; increasing their risks of adopting health-harming behaviours … [leading] to individuals developing anti-social behaviours, including a propensity for aggressive and violent behaviour and ultimately problems with criminal justice services' (Bellis et al, 2015:6).

To answer the question as to whether people with poor physical and mental health are more criminogenic than those with good health, evidence suggests that poor health is one of many factors that can be linked to criminality, but is not a cause of crime on its own. Rather, poor health is a likely to be an artefact of other factors that cause crime, meaning that those in the CJS with poor health have very likely experienced factors that have not only caused their poor health, but also caused their criminal behaviour. Poor health is therefore not specifically criminogenic in nature, but is strongly linked to other factors that are criminogenic, such as substance misuse, abuse and neglect, which are health harming in nature. This has significant implications for criminal justice practice.

How effectively does the CJS treat those with physical and mental health conditions?

People with physical and mental health conditions can access care at various times when they are involved with the CJS. This can be when in contact with the police, when in prison or when on probation.

The first point of contact is typically with the police. Evidence suggests that both poor physical and mental health are significant for those in police custody (Sondhi and Williams, 2018). However, the high levels of morbidity among detainees in police custody compared with the general population suggests an inability to adequately manage these conditions (Sondhi and Williams, 2018).

Police use screening mechanisms to identify those with physical and mental health conditions in custody, but evidence suggests this is limited and inadequate (Antunes et al, 2021), and there are particular problems concerning how those with dual diagnosis conditions are dealt with (Sondhi and Williams, 2018).

Prisons have also been observed to lead to increased negative health outcomes, Clinks (2021) detailing how unsatisfactory conditions lead to and exacerbate poor mental and physical health, with long-lasting and traumatising effects. As with the police, there is an initial screening process for physical and mental health conditions when entering prison, but this is a self-referral process, which means that many first-time prisoners in particular are either too traumatised or too dazed to understand and participate in the process (House of Commons Justice Committee, 2021). Indeed, the limitations of this approach are exemplified by the fact that many diagnoses of mental health conditions occur well after the screening process (Slade et al, 2016). Additionally, the Department of Health and Social Care (2021) has observed that factors such as noise and overcrowding, fear of violence, bullying and other abuse, access to substances (including other people's prescription medicines), prolonged solitude and lack of privacy, limited meaningful activity, lack of choices, isolation from social networks, insecurity and perceived lack of control over current and future prospects increase the risk of suicide in prisons. Consequently, as Bebington et al (2021:2084) state, 'It has long been accepted that the prison environment is detrimental to the rehabilitation of prisoners with serious mental health problems … imprisonment seems virtually guaranteed to exacerbate mental ill-health and to put prisoners at particular risk following release.' This is because prisons are traumatising environments, especially for those who have previously experienced traumatic events and are then retraumatised by prison (Centre for Mental Health, 2021). Even when someone does not have a pre-existing condition, the impact of imprisonment can still lead to anxiety and depression (Leese et al, 2021).

This means that, as the Howard League for Penal Reform (2018:2) states, 'Prisons are having a detrimental impact on the physical, mental, intellectual, moral and social wellbeing of prisoners and staff. Overcrowding, staff shortages, high levels of violence, poorly maintained buildings and infestations in prisons are damaging to health and wellbeing.' Factors such as restrictions on physical activity, social interaction, visits and phone calls all contribute negatively to health and well-being. One of the reasons for this is that there are more people in prison than the system was built to hold, meaning that overcrowding is a significant problem, one that has important implications for the conditions people experience (Davies et al, 2020).

The negative effects of prison continue to some degree when individuals are released. For example, ex-prisoners exhibit greater levels of psychiatric problems compared with the rest of the population, including both CMI and SMI (Brooker et al, 2012). Perhaps not surprisingly, recidivism in prisoners is strikingly high: '51% of the people released from custody in England in 2016 received a further custodial sentence within a year. This recidivism seems likely to be linked to the mental health and social situations characteristic of released prisoners' (Bebbington et al, 2021:2084). One reason for this is because while release is a point of particular risk that demands effective liaison between prison mental health services and the community services that assume responsibility after release, in reality the quality of transition and release planning is often poor, with little attention paid to psychological needs that can be significant outside prison (Howard League for Penal Reform, 2021). People released and in contact with probation already have a higher prevalence of health problems than the general population, and the inadequate level of care provided post-release can result in their health conditions getting worse, leading to other negative social determinants of health such as unemployment and homelessness, which increases the risk of recidivism (Brooker et al, 2020).

There is also evidence that mental health conditions can lead to increased contact with the CJS owing to the stigma that is associated with them. This occurs through 'labelling', a criminological theory that argues there are negative social reactions to being labelled as 'deviant' or 'bad', as a consequence of the label being internalised by the individual to the point that he or she assumes a deviant identity (Schwartz et al, 2020). Perhaps the best example of this is in relation to the stigma that surrounds schizophrenia, with the labelling of those who suffer from the condition as dangerous and psychopathic (Anglin et al, 2014). This can colour interactions between an individual and criminal justice practitioners, leading to outcomes such as greater use of force, more arrests and longer prison sentences (Walsh and Yun, 2017). In the context of stigma, it is also important to note that individuals with mental health conditions such as schizophrenia are also much more vulnerable than the average person as victims of crime, and this is also because of stigma (Varshney et al, 2016). Stigma therefore works to increase involvement in the CJS both as perpetrator and victim.

Stigma and shame can also mean that individuals do not report health conditions, and so do not get the help they need (House of Commons Justice Committee, 2021), which indicates there are many unmet physical and mental health needs in the CJS.

What are the wider impacts on the CJS of poor physical and mental health?

There are direct costs to the CJS associated with poor physical and mental health outcomes, involving prolonged use of police, courts, prisons and probation, for example. The estimated financial cost of arresting, convicting, imprisoning and supervising people with mental health conditions in the CJS is £1.6 billion per year (Bird and Shemilt, 2019). The cost for those with physical health conditions is less clear, but is likely to be close to this figure. Victims of crime also incur direct costs such as lost wages and property damage and indirect costs such as reduced quality of life.

These poor outcomes also have implications for the wider community and society as a whole. The cost of dealing, or not dealing, with health issues is felt much more widely than within the CJS. For example, health issues can impact negatively on the lifetime trajectories of individuals, which affects a range of services such as health, housing, social care and employment. Poor access to healthcare for prisoners is likely to mean that certain diseases are identified late on, resulting in longer and more complex treatments, greater suffering and higher costs. In the case of failure to proactively manage a long-term condition such as diabetes, the result can be serious but avoidable complications (including amputation), which carry high costs not just for the CJS, but also for the National Health Service (NHS) and for social care, and likely other services (Davies et al, 2020).

What measures have been identified as ways to improve physical and mental health outcomes in the CJS?

The limitations of the CJS in dealing with physical and mental health conditions has led to specific attempts to improve the situation. The most consistent of these is limiting the use of prisons for those with health conditions, particularly mental health conditions. This is because they are not appropriate places to house those with such needs, as they are by definition places of punishment, not places of treatment (Ismael, 2021). Limiting the impact of prison on mental health was addressed in the Bradley Report (2009), which made a number of recommendations to improve the CJS for those with mental health conditions. Two key suggestions were the consideration of alternatives to prison and improvement in the care of those leaving prison, through, for example, **Community Sentence Treatment Requirements** (CSTRs, Key Learning Box 7.4). More recently, the importance of alternatives to prison has been highlighted by the government (HM Government, 2019).

> **KEY LEARNING BOX 7.4** COMMUNITY SENTENCE
> TREATMENT REQUIREMENTS
> CSTRs aim to use substance misuse and mental health treatments to reduce reoffending. The focus is on a requirement to access treatment to deal with the substance misuse and mental health problems that caused offending in the first place. This is done by adding treatment requirements to community or suspended sentences. Crucially, treatments are provided in the community, not in prison, so to be granted a CSTR involves a mandatory requirement to undertake mental health or substance misuse treatment.

It has been argued that if an individual is in prison this can provide an opportunity for early intervention, in that there is an opportunity for diagnosis and treatment that might not be taken in the community (Davies et al, 2020). For example, prison may provide the opportunity to identify and support individuals who may be at risk of mental illness, self-harm or a suicide attempt and can also help to identify where preventative work should be directed (Ford et al, 2020:2). However, the use of prisons in this way is limited by the issues previously highlighted, such as inadequate screening and poor conditions. The key limitation of focusing on prisons is that, as detailed earlier, the majority of health conditions that prisoners exhibit occur before they reach prison, meaning that by the time that an individual is imprisoned, most of the damage from the health conditions they have has already occurred. This means that a focus on prisons alone would not deal with these issues before they occur, and so a sole reliance on prisons to improve the health of prisoners would be both late and futile.

How could the social policy approach to physical and mental health improve outcomes for criminal justice practice?

The primary focus of the CJS is to punish and deter offenders principally through imprisonment and probation, regardless of their physical and mental health status. While compassion is sometimes provided by the CJS in relation to healthcare needs, punishment is the primary focus of criminal justice practice, which restricts prisoners' access to healthcare and can contribute to worsening health outcomes for a variety of reasons. This means there is an additional health penalty paid by those in the CJS, in terms of diminished access to healthcare and worsened health needs, which compounds their already adverse situation before they enter the CJS. This penalty can be indirectly imposed, such as poor conditions that enable diseases to thrive, or directly imposed, such as limiting contact with family and friends, both of which can affect physical and mental health.

However, it is important to note that, as Edge et al (2021:1) state, 'There is an international consensus that restriction of access to appropriate healthcare should not be part of the deprivation of liberty imposed as punishment.' The current state of healthcare provision in the CJS breaches this consensus, and, indeed, it is acknowledged by the government that 'governments have a special duty of care for those in places of detention which should cover safety basic needs and recognition of human rights, including the right to health' (HM Government, 2019:9). At this point, it is important to state that individuals within the CJS have the same legal rights to healthcare as individuals in the general population. Despite this, those in the CJS tend to be of poorer health than the general population and have more complex healthcare needs. This suggests there are issues in the CJS in relation to accessing care and the quality of care provided.

It is therefore important for criminal justice practice to regard the healthcare needs of those in the CJS as a right and not as a privilege. The emphasis in UK social policy is on healthcare as a universal right, which was set out in the founding principles of the NHS in 1948 and remains today in its Constitution. Universality in this context means that entitlement to healthcare is available for the whole target population on the principle of equal access. This means that regardless of income level or status, entitlement is available. The NHS is the purest form of universalism for social policy benefits, as it is available to all regardless of need (Beland et al, 2014). This links to Marshall's ([1950] 1973) conceptualisation of citizenship as set out in Chapter 4, which argues that to be a complete citizen, not only are civil and political rights necessary, but also social rights to ensure that these rights are attainable. Marshall defines social rights as rights to provision such as health, housing, social security and education, meaning social policy services and benefits, and argues that such social rights are as important as civil and political rights, as 'the right to freedom of speech has little real substance if, from a lack of education, you have nothing to say that is worth saying, and no means of making yourself heard if you have to say it' (Marshall, [1950] 1973:151).

This notion can also be applied to health, as without the right to access to good healthcare, it is very hard to participate in political and civil society. For example, it is very likely that someone with a mental health condition will find it much harder to completely exercise their right to freedom of speech. From a criminal justice perspective, this means that without rights to healthcare, access to justice becomes less possible if not impossible.

It is also important to note that Marshall's conception of rights is positive rather than negative, meaning that there is an obligation on the state to take action to ensure that it meets the rights that the individual has. In relation to criminal justice practice, this means that healthcare should be seen as essential, not optional. More specifically, it is relevant to note that the notion of 'right to health' as set out by the WHO Constitution (WHO, 1948) refers to 'the enjoyment of the highest attainable standard of health is one of the fundamental rights of every human being'. This means that adherence to the notion of healthcare as a universal right entails that criminal justice practice should provide healthcare that is of 'equivalence' to the healthcare provided for the rest of the population, meaning that each should be as good as the other (HM Government and NHS England, 2019). This means that 'the restriction of access to appropriate healthcare should not be part of the deprivation of liberty imposed as punishment' (Edge et al, 2020:1). Healthcare should be broad in its focus and provide the widest range of health services, as detailed in Table 7.1.

As can be seen in Table 7.1, a narrow health focus is concerned merely with the absence of illness, meaning that only if a person is evidently physically ill are they seen as having health needs. A comprehensive health outcome is concerned with physical, mental and social well-being as well, meaning that health is seen as wider than just physical illness and considers the ability

Table 7.1 Differences between narrow and broad health outcomes

Narrow health focus	Broad health focus
Having the absence of illness: not having cancer, heart disease, etc	Having complete physical, mental and social well-being: good physical and mental health

of individuals to participate in society. An example of this is obesity, which affects individuals' ability to participate in society in particular ways over the long term.

The importance of such a broad approach is exemplified, from a social policy perspective, by considering that if we define health only in narrow terms to limit treatment to those illnesses with immediate necessity such as cancer, there are numerous other health conditions that would not be eligible for treatment. Denying treatment for these non-immediate conditions would save the NHS money in the short term. However, obesity, for example, limits individuals' welfare over the longer term, increasing the risk of heart attacks, diabetes, high blood pressure and mental illness. Because of these long-term impacts, the cost of obesity in the UK is growing and is predicted to reach £50 billion by 2050 (National Obesity Forum, 2014). Limiting health resources so they only meet needs in a narrow way can have longer-term costs for social policy that are above and beyond the initial cost of dealing with broader conditions. The clear implication of this for social policy is that unless the focus is on ensuring that both narrow and broad healthcare needs are met as fully as possible, individuals will not reach their full potential. If this does not happen, the effectiveness of social policy is limited in terms of its overall aims of improving individuals' welfare. For criminal justice practice, this requires a focus on integrated care, meaning provision of healthcare that meets both physical and mental health needs. As detailed earlier, comorbidity of health needs is an important issue for those in the CJS, but is something that is often overlooked. This is made worse by the lack of integration between different parts of the care system, for example primary care and mental healthcare. The move towards integrated care in the NHS has not been replicated in the CJS, despite the opportunities to improve healthcare that it provides (House of Commons Justice Committee, 2021).

In this context, a key issue is the conditions in prisons that make them inadequate not only for providing healthcare, but also for improving health in general. As the Howard League for Penal Reform (2018:3.1) outlines:

> Prisons need to look at health in a holistic way and address the entire spectrum of health and wellbeing needs. This requires a shift in focus and scope. Prison health is not merely about providing medical treatment for individual prisoners who are unwell, important though that is. Prisons must provide conditions which enable people to thrive, to stay healthy, improve their health and wellbeing and prevent the deterioration of their health.

Finally, while health in itself is not specifically criminogenic, it is strongly linked to other factors that are health harming and are typically the cause of crime. This may suggest to criminal justice practitioners that dealing with health conditions should be secondary to dealing with the latter conditions. However, there are a number of problems with such a narrow approach.

The main problem is that, as previously noted, health conditions may be linked to a range of non-health issues that cause criminal behaviour. For example, a short-term health injury that an individual in the CJS has experienced, such as a broken arm, may be an indicator of other issues that cause criminality, such as gang violence. Similarly, a long-term health condition such as asthma may be symptomatic of drug use and/or involvement in drug-related crime. A holistic understanding of an individual's health can allow us to understand the wider context in which they live.

This may suggest that dealing with a health condition may provide a cure for criminality that is occurring. However, a health condition that appears to be the main cause of criminality may not be so. For example, mental health is often causatively linked to violent behaviour, but it is often other factors such as substance abuse that are the cause of the violence (Varshney et al, 2016).

Additionally, as noted earlier, while health conditions rarely lead directly to crime, they can contribute significantly to other factors that do. For example, having a mental health condition increases the risk of being both a victim and a perpetrator of crime. There are clearly key benefits in providing health interventions before an individual has contact with the CJS. This suggests that a narrow criminal justice approach to health is inadequate and a reason for evident failures. Rather, a broader social policy approach that focuses on preventing crime through preventing physical and mental health issues may be more effective.

It is important to note that the NHS took over responsibility for healthcare in prisons in April 2005, over concerns at the time that the care being provided by prisons was inadequate. However, the evidence suggest that these concerns persist. This means that the issues related to health and crime are more fundamental than simply changing providers, and that a wholesale change in approach is needed as detailed above. For example, it is important to acknowledge that the negative outcomes of the CJS in general and prisons in particular have been exacerbated recently by funding cuts which have reduced services and mean that many health needs are no longer being met (HMICFRS, 2018).

Summary

The chapter has detailed how and why criminal justice practice currently deals with physical and mental health conditions, and how this could be improved. Poor physical and mental health are key areas of concern for criminal justice practice, as these factors create substantial risks of crime and vice versa. The current evidence suggests that poor physical and mental health is not only associated with more contact with the CJS, but also the likelihood of being a crime victim.

However, it is important to understand that poor health is not specifically criminogenic in nature, but is strongly linked to other factors that are, such as substance misuse, abuse and neglect, which are health harming in nature. This has significant negative implications for criminal justice practice.

Despite this, it is evident that the way in which criminal justice practice currently treats those with physical and mental health conditions is inadequate. The CJS is poor at identifying these conditions, and also treating them. The nature of prisons does not lend them to positive outcomes for physical and mental health conditions, and this negatively impacts criminal justice practice in many ways, directly and indirectly.

A number of measures have been identified and enacted to try to improve outcomes for those with physical and mental health conditions, but these have either not been fully enacted or are limited in nature. This means that it is highly unlikely that problems will be dealt with before they become serious.

The focus of the CJS is primarily on punishment. While relevant to its overall aims, this can increase the health penalty already experienced by those with physical and mental health conditions. However, understanding that even those in prison have a right to adequate healthcare can point a way towards improving outcomes. A social policy focus on criminal justice practice, so that healthcare is provided as a universal right, increases the possibility that outcomes will improve for criminal justice practice in various ways. It also orients criminal justice practice towards an approach that focuses on preventing crime through preventing physical and mental health problems, notwithstanding current funding issues.

References

Anglin, D.M., Greenspoon, M.I., Lighty, Q., Corcoran, C.M. and Yang, L.H. (2014) 'Spontaneous labelling and stigma associated with clinical characteristics of peers "at-risk" for psychosis: Labelling of psychosis risk', *Early Intervention in Psychiatry*, 8(3): 247–252. https://doi.org/10.1111/eip.12047.

Antunes, O.S., Wainwright, V. and Gredecki, N. (2021) 'Suicide prevention across the UK Criminal Justice System: An overview of current provision and future directions', *The Journal of Forensic Practice*, 23(1): 53–62. https://doi.org/10.1108/JFP-07-2020-0029.

Bebbington, P.E., McManus, S., Coid, J.W., Garside, R. and Brugha, T. (2021) 'The mental health of ex-prisoners: Analysis of the 2014 English National Survey of Psychiatric Morbidity', *Social Psychiatry and Psychiatric Epidemiology*, 56(11): 2083–2093. https://doi.org/10.1007/s00127-021-02066-0.

Béland, D., Blomqvist, P., Andersen, J.G., Palme, J. and Waddan, A. (2014) 'The universal decline of universality? Social policy change in Canada, Denmark, Sweden and the UK', *Social Policy & Administration*, 48(7): 739–756. https://doi.org/10.1111/spol.12064.

Bellis, M.A., Ashton, K., Hughes, K., Ford, K., Bishop, J. and Paranjothy, S. (2015) *Adverse Childhood Experiences and Their Impact on Health-harming Behaviours in the Welsh Adult Population: Alcohol Use, Drug Use, Violence, Sexual Behaviour, Incarceration, Smoking and Poor Diet*. Cardiff: Public Health Wales.

Björkenstam, E., Burström, B., Hjern, A., Vinnerljung, B., Kosidou, K. and Berg, L. (2019) 'Cumulative childhood adversity, adolescent psychiatric disorder and violent offending in young adulthood', *European Journal of Public Health*, 29(5): 855–861. https://doi.org/10.1093/eurpub/ckz089.

Brooker, C., Sirdifield, C., Blizard, R., Denney, D. and Pluck, G. (2012) 'Probation and mental illness', *Journal of Forensic Psychiatry & Psychology*, 23(4): 522–537. https://doi.org/10.1080/14789949.2012.704640.

Centre for Mental Health (2021) 'Written evidence from Centre for Mental Health, May 2021'. Centre for Mental Health. Available from: https://committees.parliament.uk/writtenevidence/36325/pdf/ [Accessed 28 July 2022].

Clark, T. and Wenham, A. (2022) *Anxiety Nation? Economic Insecurity and Mental Distress in 2020s Britain*. York: Joseph Rowntree Foundation. Available from: https://www.jrf.org.uk/file/59328/download?token=9iDQ_G2Z&filetype=full-report [Accessed 26 January 2023].

Clinks (2021) 'Written evidence from Clinks'. Available from: https://committees.parliament.uk/writtenevidence/36351/html/ [Accessed 28 July 2022].

Davies, M., Rolewicz, L., Schlepper, L. and Fagunwa, F. (2020) *Locked Out? Prisoners' Use of Hospital Care*. London: Nuffield Trust. Available from: https://www.nuffieldtrust.org.uk/research/locked-out-prisoners-use-of-hospital-care [Accessed 28 July 2022].

Department of Health and Social Care (2021) 'Joint written evidence from Department of Health and Social Care and NHS England and NHS Improvement'. Available from: https://committees.parliament.uk/writtenevidence/36697/html/ [Accessed 28 July 2022].

Edge, C., Stockley, M.R., Swabey, M.L., King, M.E., Decodts, M.F., Hard, D.J. and Black, D.G. (2020) 'Secondary care clinicians and staff have a key role in delivering equivalence of care for prisoners: A qualitative study of prisoners' experiences', *EClinicalMedicine*, 24: 100416. https://doi.org/10.1016/j.eclinm.2020.100416.

Ford, K., Bellis, M.A., Hughes, K., Barton, E.R. and Newbury, A. (2020) 'Adverse Childhood Experiences: A retrospective study to understand their associations with lifetime mental health diagnosis, self-harm or suicide attempt, and current low mental wellbeing in a male Welsh prison population', *Health & Justice*, 8(1): 13. https://doi.org/10.1186/s40352-020-00115-5.

Gadenne, V., Devereux, C., Mackinson, L., Holt, M., Stuijfzand, B., Moseley-Roberts, T. and Sugg, O. (2022) *Understanding Homicide: A Framework Analysis*. London: Mayor of London Violence Reduction Unit/The Behavioural Insights Team. Available from: https://www.london.gov.uk/media/98790/download [Accessed 26 January 2023].

Hardoon, S., Hayes, J.F., Blackburn, R., Petersen, I., Walters, K., Nazareth, I. and Osborn, D.P.J. (2013) 'Recording of severe mental illness in United Kingdom primary care, 2000–2010', *PLoS ONE*, 8(12): e82365, edited by K. Laws. https://doi.org/10.1371/journal.pone.0082365.

HM Government (2019) 'Government Response to the Health and Social Care Committee's Inquiry into Prison Health', London: Her Majesty's Stationery Office. Available at: https://assets.publishing.service.gov.uk/government/uploads/system/uploads/attachment_data/file/770805/Government_Response_to_the_Health_and_Social_Care_Committee_s_inquiry_into_prison_health.pdf [Accessed 30 December 2022].

HM Government and NHS England (2019) 'National Prison Healthcare Board principle of equivalence of care for prison healthcare in England'. Available from: https://assets.publishing.service.gov.uk/government/uploads/system/uploads/attachment_data/file/837882/NPHB_Equivalence_of_Care_principle.pdf [Accessed 28 July 2022].

HMICFRS (HM Inspectorate of Constabulary and Fire & Rescue Services) (2018) *Policing and Mental Health: Picking Up the Pieces*. Birmingham: HMICFRS. Available from: https://www.justiceinspectorates.gov.uk/hmicfrs/publications/policing-and-mental-health-picking-up-the-pieces/ [Accessed 28 July 2022].

Home Affairs Select Committee (2015) 'House of Commons – policing and mental health – home affairs'. Available from: https://publications.parliament.uk/pa/cm201415/cmselect/cmhaff/202/20203.htm [Accessed 28 July 2022].

House of Commons Justice Committee (2021) *Mental Health in Prison*. London: House of Commons Justice Committee. Available from: https://committees.parliament.uk/publications/7455/documents/78054/default/ [Accessed 28 July 2022].

Howard League for Penal Reform (2018) 'Howard League for Penal Reform response to the Health and Social Care Committee's inquiry on prison healthcare'. Available from: https://howardleague.org/wp-content/uploads/2018/06/Response-to-the-Health-and-Social-Care-Committee%E2%80%99s-inquiry-on-prison-healthcare.pdf [Accessed 28 July 2022].

Howard League for Penal Reform (2021) 'Written evidence from Howard League for Penal Reform'. Available from: https://committees.parliament.uk/writtenevidence/36424/html/ [Accessed 28 July 2022].

Ismail, N. (2021) 'Written evidence submitted by Nasrul Ismail, lecturer in criminology, University of Bristol executive summary'. Available from: https://committees.parliament.uk/writtenevidence/36321/pdf/ [Accessed 28 July 2022].

Knapp, M. and Iemmi, V. (2014) 'The economic case for better mental health', in S. Davies (ed.) *Annual Report of the Chief Medical Officer 2013, Public Mental Health Priorities: Investing in the Evidence*. London: Department of Health, pp. 147–156.

Leese, M., Thomas, S. and Snow, L. (2006) 'An ecological study of factors associated with rates of self-inflicted death in prisons in England and Wales', *International Journal of Law and Psychiatry*, 29(5): 355–360. https://doi.org/10.1016/j.ijlp.2005.10.004.

Lorenc, T., Petticrew, M., Whitehead, M., Neary, D., Clayton, S., Wright, K., Thomson, H., Cummins, S., Sowden, A. and Renton, A. (2014) 'Crime, fear of crime and mental health: Synthesis of theory and systematic reviews of interventions and qualitative evidence', *Public Health Research*, 2(2): 1–398. https://doi.org/10.3310/phr02020.

Lovasi, G.S., Goh, C.E., Pearson, A.L. and Breetzke, G. (2014) 'The independent associations of recorded crime and perceived safety with physical health in a nationally representative cross-sectional survey of men and women in New Zealand', *BMJ Open*, 4(3): e004058. https://doi.org/10.1136/bmjopen-2013-004058.

Marshall, T.H. (1973) *Class, Citizenship, and Social Development: Essays*. Westport, CT: Greenwood Press.

McManus, S., Bebbington, P., Jenkins, R. and Brugha, T. (2016) *Adult Psychiatric Morbidity Survey: Survey of Mental Health and Wellbeing, England, 2014*. Leeds: NHS Digital. Available from: https://digital.nhs.uk/data-and-informat ion/publications/statistical/adult-psychiatric-morbidity-survey/adult-psychiat ric-morbidity-survey-survey-of-mental-health-and-wellbeing-england-2014 [Accessed 28 July 2022].

Ministry of Justice (2022) 'Safety in custody statistics, England and Wales: Deaths in prison custody to December 2021, assaults and self-harm to September 2021'. Available from: https://www.gov.uk/government/statistics/safety-in-custody-quarterly-update-to-september-2021/safety-in-custody-statistics-engl and-and-wales-deaths-in-prison-custody-to-december-2021-assaults-and-self-harm-to-september-2021 [Accessed 25 July 2022].

National Obesity Forum (2014) 'State of the nation's waistline. Obesity in the UK: Analysis and expectations'. Available from: http://www.nationalobesityfo rum.org.uk/media/PDFs/StateOfTheNationsWaistlineObesityintheUKAnal ysisandExpectations.pdf [Accessed 28 July 2022].

Naylor, C., Galea, A., Parsonage, M., McDaid, M., Knapp, M. and Fossey, M. (2012) *Long-term Conditions and Mental Health*. London: Kinks Fund. Available from: https://www.kingsfund.org.uk/publications/long-term-conditions-and-mental-health [Accessed 28 July 2022].

NICE (National Institute for Health and Care Excellence) (2016) 'Coexisting severe mental illness and substance misuse: Community health and social care services'. NICE guideline [NG58]. Available from: https://www.nice.org.uk/guidance/ng58 [Accessed 21 April 2023].

ONS (Office for National Statistics) (2019) 'Male prisoners are 3.7 times more likely to die from suicide than the public – Office for National Statistics'. Available from: https://www.ons.gov.uk/news/news/maleprisonersare37timesmorelikelytodiefromsuicidethanthepublic [Accessed 28 July 2022].

Robinson, F. and Keithley, J. (2000) 'The impacts of crime on health and health services: A literature review', *Health, Risk & Society*, 2(3): 253–266. https://doi.org/10.1080/713670168.

Robinson, N. (2021) 'UK prison population third highest in Europe and suicide rate twice the average – The Justice Gap', The Justice Gap. Available from: https://www.thejusticegap.com/uk-prison-population-third-highest-in-europe-and-suicide-rate-twice-the-average/ [Accessed 28 July 2022].

Schucan Bird, K. and Shemilt, I. (2019) 'The crime, mental health, and economic impacts of prearrest diversion of people with mental health problems: A systematic review', Criminal Behaviour and Mental Health, 29(3): 142–156. https://doi.org/10.1002/cbm.2112.

Schwartz, J.A., Savolainen, J., Granger, D.A. and Calvi, J.L. (2020) 'Is crime bad for your health? The link between delinquent offending and cardiometabolic risk', Crime & Delinquency, 66(10): 1347–1368. https://doi.org/10.1177/0011128720903048.

Slade, K., Samele, C., Valmaggia, L. and Forrester, A. (2016) 'Pathways through the Criminal Justice System for prisoners with acute and serious mental illness', Journal of Forensic and Legal Medicine, 44: 162–168. https://doi.org/10.1016/j.jflm.2016.10.007.

Sondhi, A. and Williams, E. (2018) 'Health needs and co-morbidity among detainees in contact with healthcare professionals within police custody across the London Metropolitan Police Service area', Journal of Forensic and Legal Medicine, 57: 96–100. https://doi.org/10.1016/j.jflm.2017.07.012.

Varshney, M., Mahapatra, A., Krishnan, V., Gupta, R. and Deb, K.S. (2016) 'Violence and mental illness: What is the true story?', Journal of Epidemiology and Community Health, 70(3): 223–225. https://doi.org/10.1136/jech-2015-205546.

Walsh, A. and Yun, I. (2013) 'Schizophrenia: Causes, crime, and implications for criminology and criminal justice', International Journal of Law, Crime and Justice, 41(2): 188–202. https://doi.org/10.1016/j.ijlcj.2013.04.003.

Weisburd, D. and White, C. (2019) 'Hot spots of crime are not just hot spots of crime: Examining health outcomes at street segments', Journal of Contemporary Criminal Justice, 35(2): 142–160. https://doi.org/10.1177/1043986219832132.

WHO (World Health Organization) (1948) 'Constitution of the World Health Organization'. Available from: https://www.who.int/about/governance/constitution [Accessed 28 July 2022].

Young, S., Gudjonsson, G., Chitsabesan, P., Colley, B., Farrag, E., Forrester, A., Hollingdale, J., Kim, K., Lewis, A., Maginn, S., Mason, P., Ryan, S., Smith, J., Woodhouse, E. and Asherson, P. (2018) 'Identification and treatment of offenders with attention–deficit/hyperactivity disorder in the prison population: A practical approach based upon expert consensus', BMC Psychiatry, 18(1): 281. https://doi.org/10.1186/s12888-018-1858-9.

8

Substance abuse, criminal justice practice and social policy

This chapter aims to:

- outline the context of substance abuse in the Criminal Justice System (CJS);

- detail evidence for the link between substance abuse and crime;

- outline how the social policy approach could improve criminal justice practice outcomes.

Introduction

This chapter focuses on the criminal justice practice approach to substance abuse. It begins by highlighting the high rate of substance abuse in the CJS, despite the general trend in society since the mid–1990s towards a decrease. This high rate together with the criminogenic nature of substance abuse makes it a particular concern for criminal justice practice. The punitive approach of the CJS in dealing with substance abuse is considered alongside alternative approaches, such as harm reduction, decriminalisation and regulation of the drug market. This leads to an analysis of how a social policy focus could improve the current context of criminal justice practice. This details the need for criminal justice practice to move away from an individualised and narrow approach to risk management towards an approach that focuses on social harm and the comprehensive causes of substance abuse, including personal, social, financial and emotional causes, and that seeks to provide as broad a range of measures and services as possible to prevent and break the cycle of substance abuse.

What is substance abuse?

While the seven pathways to reducing reoffending specifies substance abuse as a key issue that impacts on reoffending, it does not define what substance abuse is. The World Health Organization (WHO, 2021) defines substance abuse as 'the harmful or hazardous use of psychoactive substances including alcohol or illicit drugs'. From this definition, it is important to note that a 'substance' can be either illegal or legal, and therefore includes a wide range of substances. However, it is important to distinguish substance abuse, which refers to someone taking a substance specifically for its psychoactive effect, from substance misuse, which refers to someone taking a substance to treat a medical ailment but, for example, overusing it to get an enhanced medical effect. It is relevant to note that substance abuse and substance misuse can both refer to legal and illegal substances. For example, alcohol is legal and can be both abused and misused. For the purposes of this chapter, the focus is on substance abuse – that is, the use of a wide range of substances specifically for their psychoactive effect – while acknowledging that this is a limited focus that ignores the many negative issues related to substance misuse. Additionally, it is important to state at the outset that while many people use substances on a regular basis without abuse and without harmful effects, the concern here is where substance abuse causes issues for criminal justice practice.

How widespread is substance abuse in the general population?

According to the Black Report (Black, 2020), 3 million people took drugs in England and Wales in the previous year. However, the general trend in illegal drug use since the mid-1990s has been downward, according to the Home Office (2019), meaning that fewer people are using illegal drugs. In more recent years, though, the trend has been slightly upwards, and drug use among children aged 11 to 15 is an area that has seen significant growth, up 40 per cent since 2014 (Black, 2020).

Graph 8.1 details police-recorded drug offences for the period between 2002 and 2021. It shows that these peaked in 2008–2009 at close to 250,000 offences, then dropped consistently for a decade until 2019 when they began to rise again. This data supports the point already made that, notwithstanding recent increases, the trend in substance abuse is downwards. It is important to note, however, that the data do not record all drug offences and so may be an under-representation of the true level.

One way of identifying the level of substance abuse is to look at deaths related to drug poisoning. According to the Office for National Statistics (ONS, 2021) in 2020 there were 4,561 deaths related to drug poisoning in England and Wales, which was an increase on 2019 and the highest number

Graph 8.1 Police-recorded drug offences (England and Wales, April to March 2002–2021)

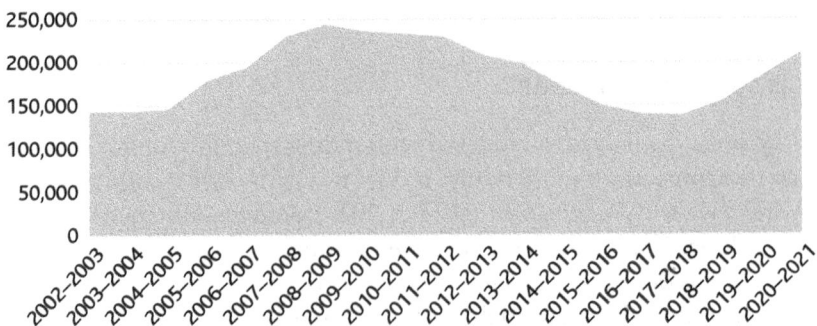

Source: ONS (2022), table A4

since records began. Additionally, drugs-related poisoning has increased, and has been increasing since 2012. In relation to alcohol, 2020 saw the highest year-on-year increase in total deaths since records began (ONS, 2021a), and the death rate also increased in England and Wales from 2019 to 2020 during the period of COVID-19, despite the number of non-drinkers increasing during this period (OHID, 2022). These may seem somewhat contradictory findings, of decreased substance abuse but increased deaths, despite improvements in medical technology in dealing with abuse. However, the rise in deaths can be accounted for by a rise in in the use of Class A drugs (Home Office, 2019), which according to the **UK Drug Classification System** (Key Learning Box 8.1) are the most dangerous. In short, while the absolute number of people exposed to harm from drug abuse has decreased, the level of harm for those who do abuse drugs has significantly increased. Similarly, the data for alcohol shows that as the number of drinkers has decreased, so the number of units of alcohol consumed by drinkers has increased (OHID, 2022), which would account for the increased harm. What these data suggest is that while the number of substance abusers in the general population may be falling, the risk of harm for those who do abuse substances is rising owing to riskier behaviours.

KEY LEARNING BOX 8.1 UK DRUG CLASSIFICATION SYSTEM

Drugs that are deemed illegal are classified according to the risk or harm caused by their use. The stated aim of this classification system is to control the availability of and access to drugs, in order to reduce the harm from their use. The classification also specifies the criminal penalties that occur from the use or possession of particular drugs, as well as trying to supply them to others. Drugs in the UK are classified as A, B or C, although in other countries there are more than three classes. Class A is for those drugs deemed the most harmful, such as heroin, cocaine and ecstasy, and so they have the highest penalties for possession, use or supply. Class B includes drugs such as amphetamines, barbiturates and codeine. Class C includes cannabis, anabolic steroids and ketamine, and has the least punishment for possession, use or supply.

How widespread is substance abuse in the CJS?

A relevant way to look at how widespread substance abuse is in the CJS is to consider the types of offences committed. According to the Black Report (Black, 2020), more than a third of people in prison are there owing to crimes related to drugs, and on a given day nearly one in four prisoners are in prison because they committed crimes related to their substance abuse. Drug offences are the third most common type of offence committed by those aged over 18 (Sturge, 2021), which suggests that drug offences are highly significant to criminal justice. It should also be remembered that there is the possibility that other crimes, such as violence and robbery, may not be allocated as drug crimes but may be specifically linked to drugs.

Therefore, a more relevant way to consider the prevalence of substance abuse in the CJS is by looking at its incidence among those in the system. These data have their limitations, such as the fact that some prisoners only begin substance abuse when in prison, but it nevertheless provides an indication of how widespread substance abuse is.

According to ONS (2020), an estimated 1 in 11 adults in England and Wales aged 16 to 59 years had taken a drug in the previous year, representing 9.4 per cent of the population and an increase over the previous decade. More specifically, drug use was related to age, as around one in five (20 per cent) people aged 16 to 24 years had taken a drug in the previous year. In comparison, according to the Ministry of Justice (2019), approximately 45 per cent of prisoners in custody in England and Wales had drugs misuse needs and 17 per cent had alcohol misuse needs. Both of these figures suggest significantly higher substance abuse in the prison population than in the population at large. These figures are in line with various studies (e.g. Walters, 2017; Kooistra, 2021). In particular, they support McKeganey et al's (2016) observation that nearly two-thirds of a sample of prisoners in England and Wales had used illicit drugs in the month before entering custody and that a similarly high proportion of prisoners reported past heavy use of alcohol. More specifically, Kolind and Duke (2016) observe that studies in many countries, including in the UK, report that drug users are over-represented in prisons, and that prisoners have higher rates of lifetime drug use, injecting drug use and problematic drug use than the general population.

In summary, all the evidence shows that substance abuse is much more widespread for those in the CJS than among the rest of the population.

What is the evidence for a link between substance abuse and crime?

In Chapter 7, it is established that although physical and mental health are strongly linked with crime, they are not criminogenic in that they do not directly lead to crime. Substance abuse, however, is wholly different and there is a wealth of evidence to suggest that it is criminogenic. As Welte et al (2005:268) state, 'It has been demonstrated in hundreds of studies that persons who abuse alcohol or other drugs are also prone to criminal offending. This positive correlation is one of the most reliable results obtainable in criminology.'

Overall, evidence suggests that those who abuse substances are those who are most likely to become involved in crime. Statistically, there is evidence that the odds of someone committing a crime is between 2.8 to 3.8 greater for users of some drugs than for non-users (Bennett et al, 2008), meaning that someone who uses particular drugs is between 70 to 80 per cent more likely to go to prison than someone who does not use drugs. As a comparison, this is higher than the odds of getting cancer, which is approximately 50 per cent.

As detailed in the Black Report (Black, 2020), illegal drugs are a major driver for the increases in serious violence since 2013, as well as gang culture and an increase in the **county lines drug trade** (Key Learning Box 8.2). Additionally, research also shows a strong association between using illegal drugs at an early age and criminal activity in later life (Stenbacka and Stattin, 2007). Specifically, Welte et al (2005) report that the earlier substance abuse occurs in young people, the greater the length and level of criminal activity will be in later life. In other words, the more the substance abuse, the more crime they commit. This suggests that the relationship between crime and substance abuse may be reciprocal, meaning that involvement in substance abuse increases the likelihood of involvement in crime and vice versa (Chen, 2018).

KEY LEARNING BOX 8.2 COUNTY LINES DRUG TRADE

The county lines drug trade has recently come to prominence as a method by which criminal gangs supply drugs to individuals. The gangs take orders for drugs over the phone, then supply the drugs via vulnerable people with physical or mental health issues, or children. This is because vulnerable individuals and children are more likely to be treated leniently by the CJS if caught. Often, drugs are ordered in one area and supplied in another, with the term county lines referring to the use of a phone line as well as the supply of drugs across county boundaries. These two key features are recent phenomena, as is the recruitment and use of vulnerable people and children.

In terms of rehabilitation, evidence suggests that substance abuse has a negative effect on recidivism. Belenko et al (2013:1) argue that illegal drug use in particular increases the likelihood of continued involvement in criminal activity, with 'high rates of relapse and recidivism found among drug-involved offenders'. Additionally, Wooditch et al (2014:293) observe that a reduction in substance abuse is likely to decrease recidivism.

As discussed in Chapter 7, comorbidity, referring to the occurrence of physical and mental health conditions at the same time, is highly relevant to the incidence of crime, and it is also relevant in relation to substance abuse. As Chen (2018) observes, where mental health problems and substance abuse co–occur, the risk of offending and reoffending increases, and higher levels of future offending may be predicted. In relation to young people, the evidence is that comorbidity is evident in a significant proportion of juvenile offenders (DeLisi et al, 2019). For example, Walters (2015) has put forward the 'worst of both worlds' hypothesis, which argues that substance abuse and crime compound each other in significant ways, meaning that those who experience substance abuse and crime together are likely to have worse outcomes than those who experience only substance abuse or only crime or neither. This supports the point that comorbidity in relation to substance abuse and crime is a compounding negative outcome.

As previously noted, the occurrence of substance abuse in prisons is well above levels in the general population. One reason for this is because prisons are 'high-risk environments for initiation into drug use or starting to use drugs again after a period of abstinence' (Kolind and Duke, 2016:89). And although the extent of drugs use in prison is not specifically known, evidence suggests that it is 'rife' (O'Hagan and Hardwick, 2017). For example, one study reported that 75 per cent of prisoners had taken illegal drugs while in prison, and that 60 per cent of prisoners reported they had used cannabis and heroin in prison (O'Hagan and Hardwick, 2017).

It should be noted here that there are many people for whom substance abuse is an issue but who do not commit crime. However, the evidence is that overall substance abuse is highly criminogenic.

How does substance abuse lead to crime?

The main theories that try to account for the link between substance abuse and crime are summarised below:

- substance abuse leads to crime;
- crime leads to substance abuse;
- substance abuse and crime have common causes. (Kooistra, 2021)

In relation to the first of these theories, this refers to where people commit crimes in order to sustain their substance abuse, meaning that crime occurs primarily out of economic necessity through the need to pay for their substance abuse. Evidence for this is found in Bennet at al (2008), who observe a significant relationship between some types of drug use and prostitution, burglary, robbery and shoplifting. This leads them to argue that expensive drug use (such as heroin, crack and cocaine) is associated with income-generating crimes. Additionally, McKeganey et al (2016) note that 41 per cent of prisoners reported having committed offences in order to pay for drugs, and DeLisi et al (2019) outline the existence of 'drug exclusive offenders', meaning those whose criminal activity is nearly or entirely exclusive to drug crimes. More specifically, while just 40 per cent of people in prison for a drug-related crime are there for a specific drug offence, such as drug trafficking, 60 per cent are there for crimes related to drug addiction, such as theft (Black, 2020).

The second theory refers to people finding themselves surrounded by criminal peers and illegal substances, and consequently beginning to experiment with drugs, which leads to substance abuse. The age of adolescence is typically highlighted as a period when the influence of criminal peers is of significance. For example, Stenbacka and Stattin (2007) highlight how adolescent use of drugs at 18 is a significant predictor of adult criminality, and also that considerable drug use in adolescence is strongly associated with the frequency of committing crimes in adulthood. Moreover, Walters (2020) has outlined how negative peer influence in the form of delinquency has been shown to lead to illicit drug use.

The third theory refers to substance abuse and crime occurring as responses to traumatic experiences, such as bullying and growing up in a violent household. In this view, crime and substance abuse are the results of other issues. For example, Smith (2017) details how childhood abuse is emphasised as a significant risk for drug use and subsequent offending. This refers to the Adverse Childhood Experiences (ACEs) discussed in Chapter 7. Additionally, Valdebenito et al (2015) observe a specific link between being a victim of bullying and substance abuse, suggesting that the use of drugs functions as an important coping mechanism for trauma in this and possibly other circumstances.

It is possible to provide evidence for all three theories, but it is important to note that they all have limitations. The first two orient crime and drug use as somewhat deterministic, assuming that one thing leads to another – despite the fact that this often does not happen. They also fail to adequately explain either prior substance abuse or prior criminal activity. The third, by focusing on other common causes, may ignore the active role that individuals' actions may play in their criminality and/or substance abuse.

The debate can be expanded by looking at what happens in prison. A key reason given for continued drug abuse in prison is prison itself, as abuse is a way to deal with issues such as boredom, violence, loss of liberty and lack of social relations. It is for this reason that drugs such as heroin and cannabis are used so highly, as their analgesic effects relieve the 'pains of imprisonment' (Kolind and Duke, 2016:90). This provides support for the third of these theories, that substance abuse and criminality have common causes such as trauma.

What are the costs to society of substance abuse and crime?

For the CJS, the most obvious outcome of substance abuse is its strong criminogenic nature, which has both economic and social costs for society. The economic costs are shown in Graph 8.2.

As shown in Graph 8.2, the total cost to society of illegal drugs is estimated to be £20 billion per year (Black, 2020), which includes health harms, costs of crime and wider impacts on society. That so many prisoners are imprisoned for crimes linked to drugs means that the cost is very high economically. For example, according to the Ministry of Justice (2022), the average cost of holding a prisoner for a year is £32,716. If we consider that drugs crimes are a third of all crimes, this means that they directly account for approximately £800 million per year just in prison costs. However, this figure is very likely an underestimation, as it does not take into account that other crimes, such as violence and robbery, may not be regarded specifically as drugs crimes but may be linked to drugs. Additionally, dealing with drugs in prisons also incurs other significant costs, such as healthcare and drug abuse treatment (O'Hagan and Hardwick, 2017), while supervision and monitoring outside

Graph 8.2 Costs associated with illicit drug use (£billions)

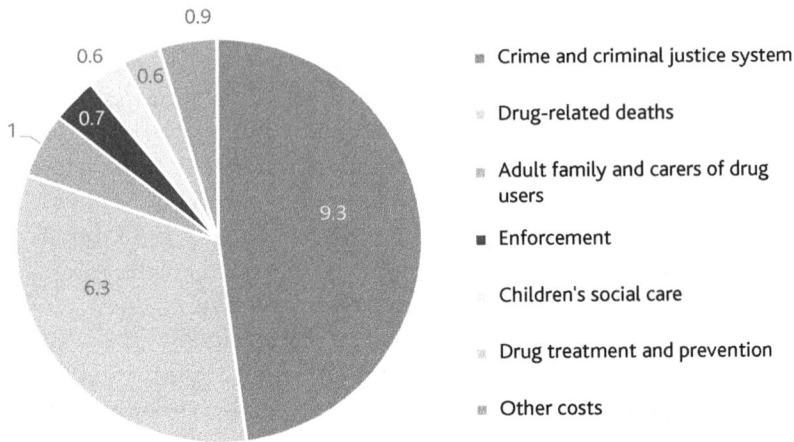

Source: Black (2021)

prison such as through HM Prison and Probation Service (HMPPS) can also accrue considerable costs.

In terms of social costs, this relates to the increase in victims of crime that are linked to substance abuse. So as we saw above, crimes like prostitution, robbery, burglary and shoplifting are all linked to substance abuse, although not exclusively, which means an increase in victims of these crimes. These crimes can be devastating to victims, and have long-term psychological effects such as increasing the fear of crime.

These social costs are also felt by those who have been in prison with substance abuse issues. For example, O'Hagan and Hardwick (2017:5) state that 'a horrifying statistic is that in the week after release from prison, prisoners are approximately 40 times more likely to die than in the general public, and more than 90% of deaths are drug related'. What this shows is that the social costs of substance abuse can be serious for a wide range of people, including victims, perpetrators and their families.

This makes it evident that substance abuse not only has a significant economic cost, but it also causes and exacerbates social and emotional harms and misery for individuals, communities and society.

What is the current CJS approach to substance abuse and crime?

The CJS deals with substance abuse and crime in a punitive manner, meaning that successive governments have focused on punishment, and this has become an increasingly salient problem (Kolind and Duke, 2016). A punitive approach relates to harsher, longer and more punishments, as detailed by Carvalho et al (2020:266):

- harsher – stricter prison regime, mandatory work, criminalisation of minor offences related to, for example, drugs, trespass, treatment of minors;
- longer – longer prison sentences for offences such as child sexual offences and crimes against emergency services;
- more punishments – a wider variety of punishments including prison + electronic tagging, fines + probation.

This emphasis on a punitive approach is exemplified by the Psychoactive Substances Act 2016 legislation, which criminalised the selling of substances that were previously legal. A relevant observation here is that of 175,000 drug crimes recorded in England and Wales in 2019–2020, 63 per cent were for cannabis possession (*The Guardian*, 2021), suggesting that a lot of resources are directed towards what in criminal justice terms is a relatively minor offence, as cannabis is a Class C drug. Additionally, the notion of 'cracking down' on drugs exemplifies the punitive approach to substance abuse, and this is something that Prime Minister Boris Johnson emphasised as a priority of the government's ten-year drugs plan that was published in 2022 (Johnson, 2022).

This punitive approach is rationalised on the grounds that crimes from substance abuse cause numerous harms to individuals, communities and society, such as through organised crime, addiction that leads to broken families, crime as addicts seek to feed their habits, shoplifting and antisocial behaviour that affects businesses as well as the lives of illicit drug users. The emphasis is on punishment, and particularly punishment as a deterrent, meaning that it is so severe that it makes the offender reconsider committing the crime.

A number of arguments against this approach are set out by Holland (2020). The first is that making some substances illegal but not others is illogical, as exemplified by the fact that alcohol is implicated in many deaths but is not illegal, even though it unnecessarily increases costs to the CJS. The enactment of the 'legally flawed, scientifically problematic, potentially harmful' (Stevens et al, 2015) Psychoactive Substances Act 2016 can be seen as an example of this.

The second is that criminalising substances can lead to further, much more harmful outcomes to those who are thus deemed criminal. For instance, contact with and/or prosecution by the CJS leads to further harms such as the inability to get a job as well as psychological distress, meaning that 'for the vast majority who use drugs, the negative impact of a criminal record would be much more significant than the negative impacts of continued infrequent drug use' (Holland, 2020:3). This can be exemplified in relation to the CJS by the observation made by Stover and Hariga (2016) that when people are arrested and imprisoned, they are often put in an environment that puts them at higher risk not only of exposure to drug use, but also to diseases such as HIV and hepatitis B, hepatitis C, syphilis and tuberculosis.

Thirdly, the fear of punishment from using drugs can lead to people using drugs in riskier ways and refusing to engage with services that could help them, which they would do if they were less fearful, and this leads to the possibility of much more harm and further negative outcomes. This can be exemplified in relation to the CJS by Kolind et al's (2016) observation that prisoners sometimes switch from using cannabis, a Class C drug, to heroin, a Class A drug, because cannabis is traceable through a mandatory urine test for longer than other drugs, and therefore changing the drug of choice makes it less likely that drug use will be traced by testing.

The current punitive approach to substance abuse can therefore be seen to have specific limitations for criminal justice practice, the main one being that there is very little evidence, either nationally or internationally, that it works. The fundamental basis of the approach is that punishment acts as a deterrence. However, crime linked to substance abuse is still prevalent despite the increasingly punitive approach, clearly evident from the number of people in prison with substance abuse issues and the number of crimes recorded that are directly linked to substance abuse. Rather, the evidence is that a punitive approach can present barriers to effective treatment and harm reduction (Windle, 2015).

What alternative approaches to substance abuse and crime could criminal justice practice employ?

It should be noted that the punitive approach is not the only approach that could be taken in relation to substance abuse by the CJS. There are three other main approaches that could be taken, as detailed below.

Decriminalising drug use and possession for personal use

Decriminalisation refers to where something is no longer deemed a crime, and so the decriminalisation of drug use and possession for personal use would mean that these would no longer be considered criminal acts. Czechia, the Netherlands, Portugal and Switzerland are four countries that have taken this approach, and the state of Oregon in the US has made possession of small amounts of hard drugs a civil rather than a criminal matter. Making possession and/or use of drugs no longer a criminal offence is the key focus of decriminalisation, although there may be other civil penalties that can be incurred. Decriminalisation is a primarily criminal justice approach to tackling substance abuse.

The key limitation of this approach is the potential harm that it can cause owing to the increased exposure to drugs that occurs, as substance abuse becomes viewed as a normal activity, especially by young people, and this can lead to drug use in later life (Coelho, 2015).

However, a key benefit of decriminalisation is that it reduces the stigma and discrimination that hampers access to healthcare, and this has the effect of reducing transmission of diseases such as HIV (UNAIDS, 2020). A more specific analysis of the decriminalisation of drugs in Portugal since 2001 (Slade, 2021:1) shows that:

- drug-related deaths fell, and have remained below the EU average;
- the proportion of the prison population sentenced for drug offences has fallen from over 40 per cent to 15 per cent;
- rates of drug use have remained consistently below the EU average.

Also in Portugal, the social costs of drugs have been shown to have fallen as a consequence of the reduction in drug-related deaths, a 'significant reduction' in costs associated with criminal proceedings for drug offences and reduction in the lost income of individuals who would previously have been imprisoned (Slade, 2021:7).

The regulation of the drug market

A second alternative approach is the regulation of the drug market, wherein the control of drugs is overseen by government agencies. This means that the government oversees the licensing, price, strength and availability of drugs, as well as who can sell and access them. The key difference between decriminalisation and regulation is that the former means the act of possessing the substance is no longer illegal but the substance itself can still remain illegal, while the latter means both the substance and the act of possessing it become legal. As an example, in Uruguay where the emphasis is on regulation it is legal to grow up to six cannabis plants, as long as users are registered with the correct government body. However, in Portugal, where the emphasis is on decriminalisation, the cannabis plants would be destroyed but the person would not receive a criminal record. Regulation is primarily an economic approach to tackling substance abuse.

The rationale for regulation is that drugs are harmful but regulation can reduce the harm that they cause, as evident in the regulation of other harmful substances such as tobacco and alcohol (Global Commission on Drug Policy, 2018). Various states in the US have regulated their drugs market, such as Washington, Colorado, Alaska and Oregon, and in 2013 Uruguay became the first country to legalise the production, distribution and use of cannabis for non-medical and non-scientific purposes, while Jamaica has also done so but in a more limited manner.

The key limitation of the regulation approach is evident with alcohol and tobacco, namely that it does not reduce potential individual harm, as despite regulation, these substances are still highly harmful. A key stated benefit from regulation is financial, as the money that would have been given to criminals passes to the government instead, and this has been observed in Uruguay, with the state now serving 20 per cent of the cannabis market (Fiore and Pereira, 2021). Another key argument is that regulation is a way to tackle crime, as it removes the control of drugs from criminals, resulting in particular in less violent crime.

While the evidence for this in Uruguay is less clear, it has not made the country more violent (Fiore and Pereira, 2021).

Harm reduction

Harm reduction refers to lessening or minimising the health and social harms of drug use through a range of treatments and measures, without necessarily requiring complete abstention from the behaviour that is being treated. A simple example of this is nicotine patches, with the aim being to lessen the harm from nicotine in cigarettes, without requiring the cessation of nicotine intake. Harm reduction in relation to illegal drugs can include supplying sterile injection materials, needle exchanges and overdose prevention sites. The simple rationale is that as people will use harmful substances, they should be enabled to do this in a respectful, safe and informed way. This is a health approach to dealing with substance abuse, as opposed to a criminal justice approach. Harm reduction strategies operate all over the world.

The key limitation of the harm reduction approach is that it views substance abuse as 'a treatable health condition', akin to diabetes for example. In doing so, it has the potential to result in 'treatment' that does not cure a condition but can sustain abuse for a long time (Coelho, 2015), rather than leading to a substance-free existence.

Evidence in support of harm reduction can be found in relation to beneficial outcomes for infection and overdose prevention (Peckham and Young, 2020), and it has been shown to lead to a decrease in recidivism (International Drug Policy Consortium, 2016). As noted earlier, a key issue is the prevalence of the use of drugs in prison, and harm reduction strategies in that setting have been shown to improve prisoners' health and make the environment safer for both prisoners and staff (Collier, 2016).

The various alternative ways to tackling substance abuse detailed here approach the issues around substance abuse from different criminal, economic and health angles. They all have significant beneficial outcomes in comparison with the punitive approach, but they also all have significant limitations.

How could a social policy approach to substance abuse improve criminal justice practice?

This section outlines the possibility of a social policy approach to dealing with substance abuse as a way to improve criminal justice practice.

The first key point to make is that it is evident that the punitive approach of the CJS has some serious limitations, which in some instances has arguably made the problem worse. An example of this is in relation to the punitive approach in prisons, which in some cases not only leads to initiating substance abuse, but also makes it worse by leading to the use of even more harmful substances. This goes beyond prison acting as 'warehousing' for crime (Forrest, 2017) towards prisons acting as an incubator for substance abuse, which at the very least makes the possibility of rehabilitation harder for criminal justice practitioners and at the worst leads to further and more dangerous criminality. For example, while 72 per cent of people who go to prison for theft are repeat offenders, the figure is 91 per cent for those who go to prison for drug offences (Cuthbertson, 2017). This is an example of how criminal punishment, and by extension criminal justice practice, contribute to the production and entrenchment of disadvantage (Coverdale, 2018).

On a more individual level, there is the case of Child Q in 2022. This relates to a 15-year-old Black girl who was strip-searched at her East London school by police, who knew she was menstruating, after teachers called them because they wrongly suspected her of carrying cannabis. This exemplifies the serious harm that the punitive approach can cause, as it negatively affected the relationships between the child, her family, the local community, the police, the school and wider society (Nickolls, 2022). It is unlikely that such an incident would have occurred in a less punitive criminal justice practice context.

The key focus of the CJS is on punishing an individual for committing a crime and ensuring that the punishment acts as a deterrent, hence the move towards harsher deterrents. There is a limited focus on the circumstances surrounding the crime and the contribution that these circumstances may make to it. The focus in criminal justice practice, as it has been in many public services, has been on managing the risks to the individual (Raynor, 2019). By risk is meant the chance that any activity or action could cause harm. The Offender and Assessment System (OASys) tool that prison and probation services use is an example of this, as it requires staff to complete a risk and needs assessment towards prioritising interventions targeting criminogenic risk factors. This approach can be defined as a form of 'personal rehabilitation', with its focus on seeking to change, improve or develop the person who has offended (Burke et al, 2018). It is the most influential form of rehabilitation, and one that locates the problem to be solved within the offender and the solution as prison or probation treatment, with the key aim being behavioural compliance with the law (Burke et al, 2018). This chimes with the punitive focus of punishments that aim to deter criminal behaviour.

From a social policy perspective, there are two linked problems to this approach. The first is that the focus on specifically defined risk located within the offender may miss other issues that may be contributing to the problem or may miscategorise certain behaviour as 'noncompliant, risk-generative behaviour, rather than as evidencing support requirements' (Hannah-Moffat and Innocente, 2013:97). For example, evidence shows that social issues such as lack of accommodation, employment prospects and a lack of interpersonal relationships play a significant role in substance abuse (Elison et al, 2016). In particular, as McKeganey et al (2016:125) state, 'Whether drug or alcohol problems are the cause of the offending that has resulted in the individual's custody, or a co-occurring behaviour alongside their offending, what is clear is that effective treatment and support will need to address much more than the individual's drug and alcohol use.' However, these issues are often underplayed or ignored in criminal justice practice, to the extent that such behaviour is seen as an individual failing. Consequently, the effectiveness of the specific aims of criminal justice practice, such as rehabilitation and desistance, are limited. However, a shift to focus on the pre-existing disadvantage of many offenders would move criminal justice practice away from a concern with meeting just the basic subsistence needs of individuals towards their wider participatory needs (Sealey, 2015). Rather than managing risk, those with substance abuse would be enabled to meet their own care needs (Coverdale, 2018), thereby enabling them not merely to survive but to survive and thrive (Sealey, 2015).

The other linked key limitation of the focus on risk is that this narrow approach that emphasises the individual dictates a similarly narrow provision of service. As an example of this, the Black Report (Black, 2020) identifies that expenditure on adult drug and alcohol prevention and treatment has decreased significantly since 2010, with related falls in services and the connected workforce. This decrease should not be seen as incidental or accidental but as a specific feature of the specific notion about risk, which has as its focus a concern for economy, efficiency and effectiveness (Metcalf, 2004). As an example of this, risk in criminology means the prioritisation of services and provision selectively rather than universally, meaning a focus on those identified as most at risk rather those least at risk. This is also evident in the primary focus on personal rehabilitation, rather than the societal level. Not surprisingly, criminal justice practice resources and services have become limited and constrained, which in turn limits and constrains outcomes. In this context, it is important for criminal justice practitioners to be aware and acknowledge that a significant consequence is that there is little time available for them to understand the wider social context of criminal justice practice itself, meaning understanding the connection between what they do and the social context and theories that govern these actions. In such contexts, it is hard for criminal justice practice to provide practice that values the quality of relationships, a deficiency that should be seen as highly consequential to beneficial practice in various ways (Sealey et al, 2022).

The limitations highlighted here reflect the need for criminal justice practice to move away from its individualised and narrow approach to risk that reflects the punitive emphasis in substance abuse policy towards one that embraces the concept of comprehensiveness as defined in social policy. In this context, this refers to criminal justice practice that rather than focusing primarily on individual failings seeks to provide a comprehensive account of the causes of substance abuse, including personal, social, financial and emotional. It also refers to criminal justice practice that seeks to provide a broad range of measures and services in order to prevent and break the cycle of substance abuse. This focus has the potential to overcome the limitations of current criminal justice practice around substance abuse.

Summary

Substance abuse presents specific problems for criminal justice practice in terms of its prevalence and effect. On the one hand, while the general trend since the mid-1990s has been towards a reduction in substance abuse, the harm that it does has not abated; if anything it has got worse. Harm here refers to not just to financial harm but to social harm, which is considerable. Also considerable is the high occurrence of substance abuse in the CJS, not just in terms of those committing crimes but also regarding prisoners, suggesting that prisons function as warehouses for substance abuse, and more detrimentally as incubators.

The strong evidence of a link between substance abuse and crime, as well as theories of how substance abuse leads to crime, suggests that the current criminal justice approach is actively creating crime as opposed to stopping it. This approach is underpinned by punitive measures, and this has severe limitations – not least of which is that the harm from substance abuse has not been reduced. This suggests that an alternative approach is needed, as followed by other countries and indeed in the UK for other substances, such as alcohol.

There is a need for a comprehensive approach to substance abuse rather than this punitive approach. From a social policy perspective, this refers to providing a comprehensive account of the causes of substance abuse, including personal, social, financial and emotional causes, and criminal justice practice that seeks to provide as broad a range of measures and services as possible to prevent and break the cycle of substance abuse. A focus on comprehensiveness has the potential to overcome the limitations of current criminal justice practice relating to substance abuse.

References

Belenko, S., Hiller, M. and Hamilton, L. (2013) 'Treating substance use disorders in the Criminal Justice System', *Current Psychiatry Reports*, 15(11): 414. https://doi.org/10.1007/s11920-013-0414-z.

Bennett, T., Holloway, K. and Farrington, D. (2008) 'The statistical association between drug misuse and crime: A meta-analysis', *Aggression and Violent Behavior*, 13(2): 107–118. https://doi.org/10.1016/j.avb.2008.02.001.

Black, Dame Carol (2020) *Review of Drugs: Executive Summary*. London: Home Office.

Black, Dame Carol (2021) *Review of Drugs Part Two: Prevention, Treatment, and Recovery*. London: Home Office. Available from: https://www.gov.uk/government/publications/review-of-drugs-phase-two-report/review-of-drugs-part-two-prevention-treatment-and-recovery [Accessed 1 August 2022].

Burke, L., Collett, S. and McNeill, F. (2018) *Reimagining Rehabilitation: Beyond the Individual*. First edition. New York: Routledge. https://doi.org/10.4324/9781315310176.

Carvalho, H., Chamberlen, A. and Lewis, R. (2019) 'Punitiveness beyond criminal justice: Punishable and punitive subjects in an era of prevention, anti-migration and austerity', *The British Journal of Criminology*, 60(2): 265–284. https://doi.org/10.1093/bjc/azz061.

Chen, G. (2018) 'Building recovery capital: The role of "hitting bottom" in desistance and recovery from substance abuse and crime', *Journal of Psychoactive Drugs*, 50(5): 420–429. https://doi.org/10.1080/02791072.2018.1517909.

Coelho, M.P. (2015) 'Drugs: The Portuguese fallacy and the absurd medicalization of Europe', *Motricidade*, 11(2): 3–15. https://doi.org/10.6063/MOTRICIDADE.7188.

Collier, R. (2016) 'Optimism for prison syringe programs', *CMAJ*, 188(11): E249–E249. https://doi.org/10.1503/cmaj.109-5294.

Coverdale, H.B. (2018) 'Punishment and welfare: Defending offender's inclusion as subjects of state care', *Ethics and Social Welfare*, 12(2): 117–132. https://doi.org/10.1080/17496535.2017.1364398.

Cuthbertson, P. (2017) *Who Goes to Prison? An Overview of the Prison Population of England and Wales*. London: Civitas.

DeLisi, M., Drury, A.J. and Elbert, M.J. (2019) 'Parent exposure to drugs: A "new" Adverse Childhood Experience with devastating behavioral consequences', *Journal of Drug Issues*, 49(1): 91–105. https://doi.org/10.1177/0022042618805738.

Elison, S., Weston, S., Davies, G., Dugdale, S. and Ward, J. (2016) 'Findings from mixed-methods feasibility and effectiveness evaluations of the "Breaking Free Online" treatment and recovery programme for substance misuse in prisons', *Drugs: Education, Prevention and Policy*, 23(2): 176–185. https://doi.org/10.3109/09687637.2015.1090397.

Fiore, M. and Pereira, P. (2021) 'The politics of evaluating cannabis regulation in Uruguay', *Novos Estudos – CEBRAP*, 40(1): 103–124. https://doi.org/10.25091/s01013300202100010005.

Forrest, A. (2017) 'Prisons are merely "warehousing" offenders, says peer'. *Big Issue*. Available from: https://www.bigissue.com/news/prison-estate-merely-warehousing-offenders-says-peer/ [Accessed 1 August 2022].

Global Commission on Drug Policy (2018) *Regulation – The Responsible Control of Drugs*. Geneva: Global Commission on Drug Policy. Available from: https://www.globalcommissionondrugs.org/reports/regulation-the-responsible-control-of-drugs [Accessed 1 August 2022].

The Guardian (2021) 'The Guardian view on poverty and crime: Speaking truth to Priti Patel', *The Guardian*, 22 April. Available from: https://www.theguardian.com/commentisfree/2021/apr/22/the-guardian-view-on-poverty-and-speaking-truth-to-priti-patel [Accessed 1 August 2022].

Hannah-Moffat, K. and Innocente, N. (2013) 'To thrive or simply survive: Parole and the post-release needs of Canadian women exiting prison', in B. Carlton and M. Segrave (eds) *Women Exiting Prison: Critical Essays on Gender, Post-Release Support and Survival*. London; New York: Routledge, pp. 77–97.

Holland, A. (2020) 'An ethical analysis of UK drug policy as an example of a criminal justice approach to drugs: A commentary on the short film *Putting UK Drug Policy into Focus*', *Harm Reduction Journal*, 17(1): 97. https://doi.org/10.1186/s12954-020-00434-8.

Home Office (2019) *Drugs Misuse: Findings from the 2018/19 Crime Survey for England and Wales*. London: Home Office.

International Drug Policy Consortium (2016) *IDPC Drug Policy Guide 3rd Edition*. Available from: https://idpc.net/publications/2016/03/idpc-drug-policy-guide-3rd-edition [Accessed 1 August 2022].

Johnson, B. (2022) *From Harm to Hope: A 10-Year Drugs Plan to Cut Crime and Save Lives*, GOV.UK. Available from: https://www.gov.uk/government/publications/from-harm-to-hope-a-10-year-drugs-plan-to-cut-crime-and-save-lives [Accessed 1 August 2022].

Kolind, T. and Duke, K. (2016) 'Drugs in prisons: Exploring use, control, treatment and policy', *Drugs: Education, Prevention and Policy*, 23(2): 89–92. https://doi.org/10.3109/09687637.2016.1153604.

Kolind, T., Holm, K., Duff, C. and Frank, V.A. (2016) 'Three enactments of drugs in Danish prison drug treatment: Illegal drugs, medicine and constrainers', *Drugs: Education, Prevention and Policy*, 23(2): 135–143. https://doi.org/10.3109/09687637.2015.1109608.

Kooistra, E.B. (2021) 'Substance abuse, self-control and crime', in B. van Rooij and D.D. Sokol (eds) *The Cambridge Handbook of Compliance*. First edition. Cambridge: Cambridge University Press, pp. 499–515. https://doi.org/10.1017/9781108759458.034.

McKeganey, N., Russell, C., Hamilton-Barclay, T., Barnard, M., Page, G., Lloyd, C., Grace, S.E., Templeton, L. and Bain, C. (2016) 'Meeting the needs of prisoners with a drug or alcohol problem: No mean feat', *Drugs: Education, Prevention and Policy*, 23(2): 120–126. https://doi.org/10.3109/09687637.2016.1150965.

Metcalf, C. (2004) 'Managing risk and the causes of crime', *Criminal Justice Matters*, 55(1): 8–42. https://doi.org/10.1080/09627250408553585.

Ministry of Justice (2019) *Identified Needs of Offenders in Custody and the Community from OASys*. London: Ministry of Justice. Available from: https://www.gov.uk/government/statistics/identified-needs-of-offenders-in-custody-and-the-community-from-oasys [Accessed 1 August 2022].

Ministry of Justice (2022) *Costs per Place and Costs per Prisoner by Individual Prison*. London: Ministry of Justice. Available from: https://assets.publishing.service.gov.uk/government/uploads/system/uploads/attachment_data/file/1050046/costs-per-place-costs-per-prisoner-2020_-2021.pdf [Accessed 1 August 2022].

Nickolls, L. (2022) 'Child Q and the law on strip search'. Available from: https://commonslibrary.parliament.uk/child-q-and-the-law-on-strip-search/ [Accessed 26 January 2023].

O'Hagan, A. and Hardwick, R. (2017) 'Behind bars: The truth about drugs in prisons', *Forensic Research & Criminology International Journal*, 5(3). https://doi.org/10.15406/frcij.2017.05.00158.

OHID (Office for Health Improvement and Disparities) (2022) 'Wider impacts of COVID-19'. Available from: https://analytics.phe.gov.uk/apps/covid-19-indirect-effects/# [Accessed 1 August 2022].

ONS (Office for National Statistics) (2020) *Drug Misuse in England and Wales – Office for National Statistics*. London: ONS. Available from: https://www.ons.gov.uk/peoplepopulationandcommunity/crimeandjustice/articles/drugmisusein englandandwales/yearendingmarch2020 [Accessed 1 August 2022].

ONS (Office for National Statistics) (2021) *Deaths Related to Drug Poisoning in England and Wales: 2020 Registrations*. London: ONS.

ONS (Office for National Statistics) (2021a) *Alcohol-Specific Deaths in the UK: Registered in 2020*. London: ONS.

ONS (Office for National Statistics) (2022) 'Crime in England and Wales: Appendix tables'. Available from: https://www.ons.gov.uk/file?uri=%2fpeoplepopulationa ndcommunity%2fcrimeandjustice%2fdatasets%2fcrimeinenglandandwalesapp endixtables%2fyearendingdecember2021/appendixtablesdec21.xlsx [Accessed 26 June 2022].

Peckham, A.M. and Young, E.H. (2020) 'Opportunities to offer harm reduction to people who inject drugs during infectious disease encounters: Narrative review', *Open Forum Infectious Diseases*, 7(11): ofaa503. https://doi.org/10.1093/ofid/ofaa503.

Raynor, P. (2019) 'Risk and need assessment development, critics, and a realist approach', in P. Ugwudike et al (eds) *The Routledge Companion to Rehabilitative Work in Criminal Justice*. Abingdon; New York: Routledge.

Sealey, C. (2015) *Social Policy Simplified: Connecting Theory with People's Lives*. London; New York: Palgrave Macmillan.

Sealey, C., Fillingham, J., and Unwin, P. (eds) (2022) *Social Policy, Service Users and Carers: Lived Experiences and Perspectives*. Zurich: Springer Nature Switzerland AG.

Slade, H. (2021) *Drug Decriminalisation in Portugal: Setting the Record Straight*. London: Transform Drug Policy Foundation. Available from: https://transfo rmdrugs.org/blog/drug-decriminalisation-in-portugal-setting-the-record-strai ght [Accessed 1 August 2022].

Smith, V.C. (2017) 'Substance-abusing female offenders as victims: Chronological sequencing of pathways into the Criminal Justice System', *Victims & Offenders*, 12(1): 113–137. https://doi.org/10.1080/15564886.2015.1017131.

Stenbacka, M. and Stattin, H. (2007) 'Adolescent use of illicit drugs and adult offending: A Swedish longitudinal study', *Drug and Alcohol Review*, 26(4): 397–403. https://doi.org/10.1080/09595230701373875.

Stevens, A., Fortson, R., Measham, F. and Sumnall, H. (2015) 'Legally flawed, scientifically problematic, potentially harmful: The UK Psychoactive Substance Bill', *International Journal of Drug Policy*, 26(12): 1167–1170. https://doi.org/10.1016/j.drugpo.2015.10.005.

Stöver, H. and Hariga, F. (2016) 'Prison-based needle and syringe programmes (PNSP) – still highly controversial after all these years', *Drugs: Education, Prevention and Policy*, 23(2): 103–112. https://doi.org/10.3109/09687637.2016.1148117.

Sturge, G. (2021) *UK Prison Population Statistics*. London: House of Commons Library. Available from: https://commonslibrary.parliament.uk/research-briefings/sn04334/ [Accessed 1 August 2022].

UNAIDS (Joint United Nations Programme on HIV and AIDS) (2020) 'Decriminalization works, but too few countries are taking the bold step'. Available from: https://www.unaids.org/en/resources/presscentre/featurestories/2020/march/20200303_drugs [Accessed 1 August 2022].

Valdebenito, S., Ttofi, M. and Eisner, M. (2015) 'Prevalence rates of drug use among school bullies and victims: A systematic review and meta-analysis of cross-sectional studies', *Aggression and Violent Behavior*, 23: 137–146. https://doi.org/10.1016/j.avb.2015.05.004.

Walters, G.D. (2015) 'Recidivism and the "worst of both worlds" hypothesis: Do substance misuse and crime interact or accumulate?', *Criminal Justice and Behavior*, 42(4): 435–451. https://doi.org/10.1177/0093854814551018.

Walters, G.D. (2017) 'The drug–crime connection in adolescent and adult respondents: Interaction versus addition', *Journal of Drug Issues*, 47(2): 205–216. https://doi.org/10.1177/0022042616681274.

Walters, G.D. (2020) 'Prosocial peers as risk, protective, and promotive factors for the prevention of delinquency and drug use', *Journal of Youth and Adolescence*, 49(3): 618–630. https://doi.org/10.1007/s10964-019-01058-3.

Welte, J., Barnes, G., Hoffman, J., Wieczorek, W. and Zhang, L. (2005) 'Substance involvement and the trajectory of criminal offending in young males', *The American Journal of Drug and Alcohol Abuse*, 31(2): 267–284. https://doi.org/10.1081/ADA-200047934.

WHO (World Health Organization) (2021) 'Substance abuse'. WHO, African Region. Available from: https://www.afro.who.int/health-topics/substance-abuse [Accessed 1 August 2022].

Windle, J. (2015) 'A slow march from social evil to harm reduction: Drugs and drug policy in Vietnam', *Journal of Drug Policy Analysis*, 10(2): 20150011. https://doi.org/10.1515/jdpa-2015-0011.

Wooditch, A., Tang, L.L. and Taxman, F.S. (2014) 'Which criminogenic need changes are most important in promoting desistance from crime and substance use?', *Criminal Justice and Behavior*, 41(3): 276–299. https://doi.org/10.1177/0093854813503543.

9

Low income and poverty, criminal justice practice and social policy

This chapter aims to:

- outline the context of low income and poverty in the UK;
- detail evidence for and against a link between poverty and crime;
- outline how the social policy focus on the social problems leading to poverty can improve criminal justice practice.

Introduction

In this chapter, the focus is on low income and poverty and their links to crime. There are a number of criminological and non-criminological theories that make an explicit link between crime and poverty. The chapter starts by distinguishing between absolute low income and poverty, and then rationalises the rest of the chapter's focus solely on poverty. It then analyses the evidence for and against a link between poverty and crime. This shows that crime and its effects hurt those living in poverty the most, something that should lead to a primary focus on what should be done to stop people living in poverty being victims of crime. However, criminal justice practice strongly emphasises crime prevention through what is typically referred to as crime reduction strategies, particularly situational crime prevention. The chapter analyses the limitations of this approach, and this leads to a discussion of how a social policy focus on the social problems leading to poverty, particularly a lack of power, can improve outcomes for criminal justice practice.

What are low income and poverty?

Low income and poverty are two terms that are often used to mean the same thing, and as they both imply that a person is living below some standard that means they are disadvantaged in some way, it may seem they are referring to the same thing. However, there is a crucial difference between the two terms.

The fundamental distinction is that low income does not necessarily indicate poverty, as it is possible to have a low income but not be in poverty, and vice versa. For example, while a student may have a low income, they may not necessarily be living in poverty because they have few responsibilities and therefore lower living costs. However, a family with two children attempting to live on the student's income would very likely be in poverty as their living costs and responsibilities would be so much greater. Conversely, it is possible to be in poverty but not have a low income. For example, someone with an income of £20,000 would not be considered to have a low income, but if they were disabled and incurred costs from this so they were not able to afford resources that others expected, this would mean that they were living in poverty.

This highlights that low income and poverty capture different things. Low income is essentially concerned with how much money a person earns, and poverty with what they are able to do with the resources they have. Despite these differences, it is poverty that is usually used as a general catch-all term to describe someone living below a set standard, and accordingly this is the term that will be mainly used in this chapter, notwithstanding the differences highlighted here. To clarify what this means in more detail, we can categorise poverty into two main types: absolute poverty and relative poverty.

The difference between absolute and relative poverty

Absolute poverty is a measurement based on the absolute minimum a person requires for biological survival. This means that someone is only defined as living in poverty if they lack the resources to meet biological necessities such as:

- food
- water
- warmth
- clothing
- shelter

The key point about these necessities, and therefore the notion of absolute low income and poverty, is that their absence quickly results in serious harm or death.

In contrast, relative poverty refers to an individual lacking the resources to maintain a standard of living compared to those around them or what others might reasonably be expected to have, not a set absolute minimum. It is based on the notion that an individual should have a life beyond an existence on the absolute minimum level, to live a life that is at least similar to what would be considered as acceptable within a society. This includes aspects such as good-quality housing, material possessions, the internet and access to social opportunities. In contrast to a focus on the absolute biological minimum that a person needs, relative poverty's focus is more on how the living standards of an individual compares to the living standards within a group or society. This means that if an individual's living standards are below the average living standards within the society that they live in, then they are considered as living in relative poverty.

To clarify the distinction further, an income level of $1.90 a day, which at the time of writing is equivalent to approximately £1.50, is often used as a reference point when referring to absolute poverty in emerging countries. This is an absolute measure of poverty because it is concerned with the level of income that is required to provide the minimum necessities. However, an income level of £10.90 an hour for work, the current Real Living Wage in the UK (www.livingwage.org.uk), is a relative measure of poverty, as it is designed to provide an income that meets needs beyond the absolute minimum, such as good-quality food and good-quality housing.

An important point to note is that absolute measures of poverty will always lead to a lower number of people being defined as living in poverty. This is because they determine that fewer resources are required than relative measures. So an absolute measure limits the number of people defined as living in poverty, while a relative measure leads to more people being defined as living in poverty.

How is poverty defined in the UK?

It is important to note that the UK government does not measure poverty but measures low income, and talks about low-income households. Low-income households are defined as **households** with **income below 60 per cent of the median**, as reported in the Households Below Average Income statistics. The two emboldened points are key to understanding the government's definition, as they refer to the following:

- **Households**: The measurement of low income is at household and not individual level. A household can consist of one or more people, and where it consists of more than one person, all incomes are added together. This means that the whole income of the household is taken into consideration when deciding if a person is living in low income. This is important because someone could have an income below the low-income level, but because they live in a household where someone else earns considerably above the level, they would not be considered to be living in low income. An example of this is someone aged under 18 or working as an apprentice earning the current National Minimum Wage of £5.28/hour, which would very likely mean an income below the low-income level after housing costs have been paid. However, if they are living at home, then the income of the rest of the household could mean they do not live in a low-income household.
- **Income below 60 per cent of the median income**: Low income for the government is defined in terms of income, or specifically the lack thereof. Note that income can include earnings from employment, benefits (such as tax credits, pensions, Universal Credit), investments and any other forms of income. In simple terms, someone is defined as living in low income if their income reflects the income of the lowest 30 per cent of the population. The median income is used because it 'provides a good indication of the standard of living of the "typical" individual in terms of income' (ONS, 2020:7). So, for example, in 2020 the median income after paying housing costs was £24,856

(Watson, 2022), meaning that 50 per cent of the population earned more than this and 50 per cent of the population earned less than this. As 60 per cent of the median income (meaning 60 per cent of £24,856) is £14,913, if a household income was below this after their housing costs had been paid, then depending on the number of people who lived in the household, they could be deemed to be living on a low income (note that this is a very simplified account of how low income is measured; for a more detailed account, refer to Sealey, 2015, chapter 6). The important point is that this is the definition referred to when talking about the UK government's definition of low income.

Using the government's definition of low income, there are an estimated 9.2 million people living in absolute low income, which represents 14 per cent of the population (DWP, 2021). To reinforce the point made earlier about how differences between absolute and relative poverty lead to differences in the number of people described as living in poverty, it is estimated that 14.4 million people live in relative low income, which represents 22 per cent of the population (DWP, 2021). This latter definition is referred to as a relative measure of low income by the government because to some extent the level of existence that it enables is above the basic subsistence levels described for absolute low income. This means that, for example, instances of individuals starving are rare, although this is sometimes thanks to the additional support that is provided by social policy benefits, such as Tax Credits. This threshold for low income is also modified year by year as income levels change, meaning there is some relative relationship between the income of the population and those below the low income threshold.

As noted, the government definition defines low income, not poverty. However, the Social Metrics Commission (2020:17) provides a widely used definition of poverty in the UK as 'the extent to which the material resources that someone has available to them now are sufficient to meet the material needs that they currently have'. This includes a consideration of other assets that individuals and families may hold other than income, such as savings, which moves the focus away from a solely income-based metric towards other resources. The key point of difference between this definition of poverty and the government's definition of low income is that whereas the government defines low income from a set percentage of the population's income, the Social Metrics Commission focuses on the actual living costs that individuals and families experience, and whether these cause them to experience poverty. This means poverty is defined from individual income, not population income.

If we contrast the way in which the government defines low income with the way the Social Metrics Commission defines poverty, there are several reasons why we could describe the government's definition as reflecting an absolute rather than a relative measure. The first is that the government's figure does not reflect the average income in any sense, but a figure well below the average. This means that anyone earning less than the low-income figure has a living standard that is significantly below that of the average person in the population. In other words, the government's low-income figure does not reflect the 'typical' standard of living for the rest of the population, while the Social Metrics Commission does to a greater degree.

The second reason is the cut-off point for the low-income figure. Using this suggests that someone is in low income if their income is below £14,913 per year, but not in low income if their income is at or above £14,914 per year. This suggests that poverty can be clearly defined in terms of an absolute level of income that is required to exist, with little consideration for the quality of life that such an income could provide.

Overall, the fact that the government's low-income level is well below the median income of the population leans it towards an absolute rather than a relative measurement of poverty. This is in contrast with the Social Metrics Commission definition, which because of its focus on material needs is a relative rather than an absolute definition of poverty. It is important, though, to acknowledge that poverty, whether defined as relative or absolute, is experienced as stressful by people in their daily lives, with stress-related consequences (Breitenbach et al, 2021).

Having discussed the important differences between low income and poverty, the focus of this chapter is on poverty for two key reasons. Firstly, low income, however defined, is essentially an absolute measure of living standards, as it does not capture the actual resources required by individuals, whereas poverty as defined by the Social Metrics Commission is a relative measure of poverty, as it provides a more accurate measure of the actual resources required by individuals. Secondly, it is poverty that is generally used and understood as a catch all term for to describe someone living below a set standard, and accordingly this is the term that will be used here. Having clarified this focus, we can now begin to explore the evidence for a link between poverty and crime.

What is the link between poverty and crime?

Poverty, however defined, has a long history of being linked to crime in order to explain why particular individuals become involved in criminal activity. As Newburn (2016:326) argues, 'it is as close to an established criminological "fact" as exists that the vast majority of crimes dealt with by the criminal courts are committed by people of relatively impoverished means'. Indeed, a number of criminological and non-criminological theories make an explicit theoretical link between crime and poverty, as detailed in Table 9.1.

These theories articulate an explicit relationship between poverty and crime, but do so in four different ways. The first, as per economic theory, sees crime as the only response to the situation of those living in poverty, an example of which is someone stealing something to feed themselves or their family because they are hungry and have no other way to eat. This is referred to as instrumental crime. The second, as per strain theory, is that crime occurs as it is the best of a bad set of options (De Courson and Nettle, 2020), an example being when someone steals an item that is more expensive than the one they already possess. The third,

Table 9.1 Theories linking poverty and crime

Theory	Explanation
Marxist/Conflict theory	Crime is a response aimed at a reorganisation of the unequal distribution of resources in a more equitable manner
Powerlessness theory	Crime and criminal acts are an attempt by those without power, such as the poor, to make a mark on the world, to be noticed, to get identity feedback, a desperate effort to make things happen, to assert control
Economic theory	Inequality leads to crime by placing low-income individuals who have low returns from market activity in proximity to high-income individuals who have things that are worth taking
Strain theory	Crime occurs when there is a gap between the cultural goals of a society (such as material wealth, status) and the structural means to achieve these (such as education, employment), and this strain puts pressure on individual citizens to commit crime
Underclass theory	Crime is caused by an underclass of people permanently separated from the normal standards of the rest of society and who have deviant behavioural norms, for example the unemployed, single parents, benefit recipients
Criminal motivation theory	Economic stress (such as increased unemployment) may increase the incentive for individuals to engage in illicit behaviours

as per Marxist theory/powerlessness theory, is crime as a response to the lack of power of those living in poverty, meaning that crime occurs when those with low income or in poverty feel their position is unjust and so commit crime, an example of this is social and economic riots. The fourth, as per underclass theory, is that crime occurs because of the individual characteristics of those living in poverty, and specifically negative characteristics that are learned and reproduced.

It should be noted that there are other theories that link poverty and crime, these are just some of the main ones. What is evident from them is that there is no theoretical consensus on the link between poverty and crime, thereby alerting us to the fact that the link is disputed in many ways, and this is also evident if we consider the evidence for and against the link. More significantly, if these theories linking poverty and crime are true, we would expect there to be strong evidence to support them.

What is the specific evidence of a link between low income/poverty and crime?

There is some evidence to support the theories that there is a link between poverty and crime. For example, according to the Prison Reform Trust (2014), 48 per cent of people in prison have a history of debt, and more than 50 per cent of short sentenced prisoners reported that having enough money was a key factor in stopping them reoffending.

Data from crime in London also provide evidence of a link. According to Trust for London (2022), there are several factors that link crime with poverty, such as:

- overall, 80 per cent more crimes were recorded in the most income-deprived areas;
- violence, robbery and sexual offences are 2.6 times more prevalent in the most income-deprived 10 per cent of areas compared with the least income-deprived 10 per cent; and
- drugs and weapons offences are 2.3 times more prevalent in the most income-deprived 10 per cent of areas compared with the least income-deprived 10 per cent.

This is supported by the observation that three-quarters of London boroughs with the highest levels of violent offending are also in the top ten of the most deprived, and the same boroughs also have higher proportions of children under 20 living in poverty than the London average (Khan, 2019).

Some strong evidence for this link occurred in the 2011 English riots, which caused extensive damage. In the aftermath of the riots, confidential interviews were carried out with 270 people who had taken part (see Key Learning Box 4.1). Despite the fact that the initial cause was the police shooting of an individual named Mark Duggan, those who took part in the survey stated that poverty was the most important reason for the riots. This was supported by an opinion poll among the general population (Lewis et al, 2011), wherein 'at heart of what the rioters talked about was a pervasive sense of injustice. For some this was economic – the lack of a job, money or opportunity. For others it was more broadly social, not just the absence of material things, but how they felt they were treated compared with others' (Lewis et al, 2011:24). Moreover, the evidence from two major longitudinal studies of adolescent crime and delinquency, **the Cambridge Study in Delinquent Development and the Pittsburgh Youth Study** (Key Learning Box 9.1), specifically shows that delinquency and crime could be linked to family poverty and that low family income is a childhood risk factor for future offending (Farrington, 2003).

KEY LEARNING BOX 9.1 THE CAMBRIDGE STUDY IN DELINQUENT DEVELOPMENT AND THE PITTSBURGH YOUTH STUDY

The Cambridge Study in Delinquent Development and the Pittsburgh Youth Study are two of the most well-known studies of crime in relation to young people. They were carried out in very similar ways, studying a group of youths over a relatively long period of time, and their aims were the same, to study the causes and development of delinquent behaviour. The key differences are that the Cambridge study took place in the UK and began in the 1960s, with participants aged from 8 to 48. In contrast, the Pittsburgh study took place in America, with participants aged 6 to 35. Despite these differences, both studies suggested important findings in relation to youth delinquency.

Further evidence is observed by Webster and Kingston (2014:6), who note:

> The steepest rises in the rate of property crime occurred during the 1980s and early 1990s, coinciding with sharp increases in the level of unemployment and inequality. For example, as unemployment rose steeply from 1979, peaking in the mid-80s and mid-90s, it had immediate and long-term effects on the property crime rate.

Low income and poverty are also more strongly associated with some types of crime than others, with low income associated with higher property crime and poverty linked with a surge in aggression and violent crime (Papaioannou, 2017). This last point is supported by McAra and McVeigh's (2016) observation that young people are significantly more likely to engage in violence if they are living in a family where the head of household is unemployed or in low status manual employment, or growing up in communities scarred by high levels of deprivation.

Additionally, Graph 9.1 shows the proportion of people living in poverty in and the trends in crime 1995–2020. There are three important caveats to the data that are represented in Graph 9.1.

First, it should be noted that the data do not refer to **recorded crime data** (Key Learning Box 9.2) but are from **crime survey data** (Key Learning Box 9.2) only, which means the figures do not represent actual recorded crime. Secondly, while the data for crime are for England and Wales, the data for poverty are for the UK, meaning that they are not figures from the same locality. Thirdly, the data for crime do not include fraud and computer misuse, to enable the data to be compared. However, the data suggest there is a link between poverty and crime, as it shows that as poverty has fallen, so has crime, although at a much faster rate, which supports the claim that there is a link between poverty and crime. In a wider context, Malby and Davis (2012) observe that there is a link between

Graph 9.1 Trends in crime versus poverty, 1995–2020

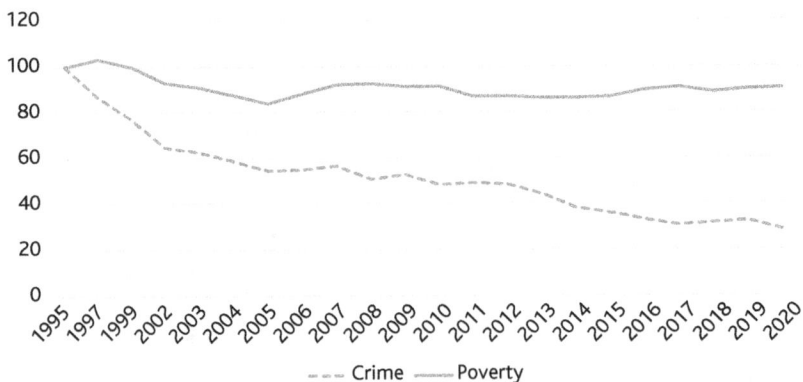

Source: Author's own calculations from ONS (2019) and DWP (2021)

economic crises and crime, with economic factors such as reduced economic growth acting as a predictor of crime for at least one crime type in the majority of countries analysed, particularly violent and property crime, suggesting some overall association between economic changes and crime.

> **KEY LEARNING BOX 9.2** RECORDED CRIME DATA VERSUS CRIME SURVEY DATA
>
> There are two main ways in which data on crime can be collected. The first is recorded crime data, which looks at crime that has been reported and uses this as the basis for the crime level. The main advantage of this is that it seems to provide a factual account of crime. The second is crime survey data, which is to ask people whether they have experienced crime, regardless of whether they have reported it. The main advantage of this is that it can include crime that goes unreported, which is a significant issue for criminal justice practice. For this reason, crime survey data usually show a higher level of crime than recorded crime data. Usually, the data from these two sources are combined, to provide a more accurate picture of crime.

Another relevant piece of evidence for a link between poverty and crime is provided by the observations of criminal justice practitioners themselves, such as senior police chiefs. For example, Patricia Gallan, the Metropolitan Police Assistant Commissioner, stated in 2018 that:

> I think there are lots of causes of crime. This is a very personal view. If you start looking at where crime impacts, it happens in the poorest areas of society. Those that end up in the criminal justice system tend to be the people who have less money and less opportunity in our society … I think if you are a young person and you haven't got opportunity necessarily – and this isn't an excuse for it, it is explanation – what's your risk? You've got a sense of belonging if you are in a group or a gang … and you get the material aspects that you would like, so that's part of the challenge. (Dodd, 2018)

Similarly, Andy Cooke, Chief Constable of Merseyside Police, stated in 2021 that:

> The best crime prevention is increased opportunity and reduced poverty. That's the best way to reduce crime. So there needs to be substantial funding into the infrastructure of our inner cities and our more deprived areas. Why do people get involved in crime and serious crime? It's because the opportunities to make money elsewhere aren't there for them. And never more so than in our inner cities and in our more difficult to police areas. We need to reduce that deprivation and the scale of deprivation that we see in some of our communities,

because if you give people a viable alternative, not all but a lot will take it. (Dodd, 2021)

These pronouncements are significant not just because of what is being said but also because who is saying it. The fact that those at the top of policing, with their extensive experience of crime, are explicit in their acknowledgement of a link between poverty and crime suggests that this cannot be discounted.

Linked to poverty is inequality, which refers to the unequal way in which resources are distributed in a society, and so is linked to low income/poverty. As with poverty, there is evidence that a more unequal distribution of economic resources is related to crime, as countries with such inequality tend to have higher crime rates (De Courson and Nettle, 2021), and, more specifically, both property crime and murder are higher in more unequal societies (Wilkinson and Pickett, 2017).

In summary, there is evidence to support the claim that there is a link between poverty and crime, both in terms of incidence and types of crime.

What is the evidence against a link between poverty and crime?

The key evidence against this link is the fact that the vast majority of people who are living in poverty never engage in criminal activity, whether poverty occurs suddenly or over a long period of time. Considering the figure of 14.4 million people living in poverty outlined earlier, if there was strong evidence for a link between poverty and crime, a much higher crime rate than there currently is would be expected. To exemplify this point further, the rates of poverty among different groups are shown in Table 9.2.

The term 'rate of poverty' in Table 9.2 refers to the percentage of people within that group who are living with poverty, for example, 31 per cent of children are living in poverty. What the table shows is that certain groups, such as lone parents, working households and children, have a higher poverty rate than the general population. If there was strong evidence of a link between poverty and crime, then these are the groups that we could expect to be committing large

Table 9.2 Rates of poverty among different groups

Group	Rate of poverty %
General population	22
Lone parents	45
Working household	42
Children	31
Disabled	27
Single pensioners	26
Working age females	21

Source: Created using data from Barry et al (2022)

numbers of crimes. However, this is not the case. As a simple example, Table 9.2 shows that lone parents are the group that have the highest rate of poverty. As around 90 per cent of lone parents are women (Gingerbread, 2019), we would expect women, and particularly single parents, to make up a significant majority of those in the Criminal Justice System (CJS) if the link between poverty and crime was strong. However, women account for just 4 per cent of the prison population (NAO, 2022). This anomaly is supported by the fact that the rate of poverty for working age females (21 per cent) is higher than the rate of poverty for working age males (19 per cent), which again is counter to what we should expect. Similarly, it is hard to equate the rate of poverty for children, disabled people and single pensioners with their rate of involvement in the CJS.

It is the rate of poverty for working households, though, which severely undermines the claim of a link between poverty and crime. As shown in Table 9.2, this is 42 per cent, which means that nearly half of people who work are living in poverty. With such a high rate, if there was a link between low income/poverty and crime, there would be an expectation that the crime rate would be much higher than it is. This reinforces the point that the vast majority of people experiencing poverty do not commit crime, which is the key limitation on the claim that poverty and crime are linked.

The second key argument against a link between poverty and crime is that evidence shows that people living in poverty are more likely to be victims of crime than its perpetrators. As Cuthbertson (2018) observes, the 'law abiding majority of the poor' are:

- considerably more likely to be attacked by someone they know and far more likely to be attacked by a stranger;
- twice as likely to suffer violence with injury;
- twice as likely to be burgled;
- three times as likely to be robbed and mugged;
- three times as likely to suffer rape or attempted rape;
- six times as likely to be a victim of domestic violence.

Additionally, those on the lowest incomes experience 62 per cent more personal crime and 73 per cent more violent crime (Cuthbertson, 2018), and 48 per cent of all burglaries happen to 1 per cent of all homes in England and Wales, principally those belonging to the poor and/or single parents (Webster, 2015). In this context, one way in which poverty and crime may be linked is that those who are better off are able to afford preventative measures and take steps to limit their exposure to crime, such as moving to a lower crime neighbourhood (Dong et al, 2020), but those living in poverty are not able to do so, and this increases their chance of being a victim of crime. This to some extent explains why crime is more prevalent in higher poverty localities, wherein it is easier to commit in such poorer communities than in richer but better protected communities. The outcome is that those living in a poorer area are more likely to be victims of crime than to be its perpetrators.

Linked to this, it has been observed that there is strong evidence to show that poverty increases the fear of crime in both individuals and communities. As observed by Elliott and Fagan (2017) the fear of crime is twice as likely among those earning low incomes compared with those on higher incomes. Additionally, according to the Social Metrics Commission (2020), people living in poverty are more likely to feel unsafe in their neighbourhood or worry about being affected by crime than those not living in poverty. This fear of crime can have significant consequences on health and well-being, such as restricting where people go, what they do and who they meet, which can lead to further neighbourhood isolation as well as worsened physical and mental health, as detailed in Chapter 7.

The third limitation when claiming a link relates to the nature of crime itself, and how it is defined. As detailed earlier, most of the evidence of a link between poverty and crime relates to crimes such as burglary and violence, while ignoring a range of others. As Newburn (2016:327) states, 'the gaze of the state, and that of academic criminologists, tends to focus on the crimes of the powerless, rather than the powerful, despite the very great harms caused by the latter'. More specifically, according to Webster and Kingston (2014:4), some laws 'may codify the interest of the influential, powerful and rich, and therefore are biased against the interest and wishes of the poor, the powerlessness and those without a voice'. What this means is that, on the one hand, evidence for a link is limited by the fact that the focus is skewed, meaning that the claim that there is a largely economic basis for crime is underpinned by an incomplete picture of the economic basis of all crime, not just the crime that affects the poor. On the other hand, the claimed link between poverty and crime does not really explain the occurrence of **white-collar crime** (Key Learning Box 9.3) or crimes perpetrated by the wealthy, which tend to be more financial in nature and have the potential to affect more people than crimes associated with poverty. For example, a single bank clerk stealing money from the accounts of customers over a long period of time will affect many more people than a single robbery committed by an individual. What white-collar crime highlights is that the assumption that poverty and crime are linked only makes sense if the focus is primarily on the crimes of those in poverty and not on the crimes of those who are not in poverty. This also relates back to the discussion in Chapter 3 of the importance of power in determining why some things become crimes and other do not.

KEY LEARNING BOX 9.3 WHITE-COLLAR CRIME

This term refers to non-violent crimes that are committed by a person of relatively high stature and social status. They can include crimes such as fraud, identity theft, money laundering and tax evasion. The term originated in America to describe the types of crimes mostly committed by those who worked in offices where people wore white-collared shirts, as opposed to those who worked in blue-collared shirts and worked in manual jobs. A key point about white-collar crime is that it is often viewed as less serious than other types of crime, and so sentencing is less severe

(Perri, 2011). The evidence is that white-collar crimes such as fraud, bribery and money laundering are increasing in the UK, particularly because of the increased use of the internet and the ease with which this facilitates such crimes (Bennett and Shalchi, 2022).

This point is reinforced if we consider how the prison population has increased at the same time that crime has ostensibly fallen, as shown in Graph 9.1. Since the end of World War Two (WW2), the prison population has increased by almost 400 per cent, from around 20,000 prisoners to around 80,000 prisoners (Sturge, 2021). During the same period, living standards have also improved significantly, by nearly 200 per cent (Milne, 2017). If there was a clear link between poverty and crime, there would be an expectation that this increase in living standards would be matched by a fall in the prison population, as a proxy for crime. However, the huge increase in the prison population despite the fall in crime suggests that it is the way that crime has been defined and redefined over the years that is the cause of the increased prison population, in which the 'gaze' is on crimes committed by those living in poverty rather than the better off.

These points indicate that while evidence shows that poverty can be important in understanding some aspects of crime, to state definitively that there is a direct link between poverty and crime is far from straightforward, and nowhere as clear as the evidence for the links between crime and substance abuse found in Chapter 8. If we consider the evidence for and against in totality, it can be seen that as Webster and Kingston (2014:5) observe, 'Poverty then might be a necessary, but it is not a sufficient, reason or condition why an individual engages in criminal activity. Living in poverty on its own is unlikely to lead to engagement in criminality.' One strong evidential link is that people living in poverty are more likely to be victims of crime and consequently more likely to live in fear of crime – as Cuthbertson (2018:2) states: 'Crime and its effects hurt the poor most.' This should lead to a focus on actions that stop people living in poverty being victims of crime.

How does criminal justice practice deal with the issues related to poverty and crime?

While there is some evidence of a link between poverty and crime, this is limited, and there is stronger evidence that those living in poverty are more likely to be victims of crime and also in fear of crime, which has important financial and psychological implications for them.

Also previously noted, one of the reasons why those living in poverty are more likely to be victims of crime is because they are less likely to be able to afford to take measures to limit their exposure to crime, such as moving home or taking security measures such as installing burglar alarms or security cameras, both of which have been shown to be effective in reducing neighbourhood crime (Tseloni et al, 2016). Living in a high crime neighbourhood can also incur extra

Table 9.3 Crime reduction strategies

Crime reduction strategy	Example of measures
Target Hardening – Making your property harder for an offender to access	Using window bars and grilles
Target Removal – Ensuring that a potential target is out of view	Removing valuables from sight
Reducing the Means – Removing items that may help commit an offence	Not leaving ladders lying about
Reducing the Payoff – Reducing the profit the criminal can make from the offence	Marking/registering property so it is harder to sell, such as bikes
Access Control – Looking at measures that will control access to a location, a person or object	Using window locks
Surveillance – Improving surveillance around homes, businesses or public places to deter criminals	Using CCTV
Environmental Change – Ensuring your property and wider community look cared for	Clearing away rubbish, graffiti and overgrowth
Rule Setting – Changing habits by setting rules and positioning signage in appropriate locations	Agreeing to leave lights on when going out
Increase the Chances of Being Caught – Increasing the likelihood that an offender will be caught prevents crime occurring	Using a burglar alarm
Deflecting Offenders – Deterring an offender or deflecting their intention	Using timer switches to make the home look occupied

Source: Created using data from Beckford (2023)

costs, such as higher insurance premiums or a lack of amenities, which can raise the cost of living. This can lead to a greater likelihood of further poverty and also of being a victim of crime. Within the CJS, there is a strong emphasis on crime prevention through what are typically referred to as crime reduction strategies, and also situational crime prevention, meaning that decreasing the number of criminal events that occur is the aim, through influencing an offender's decision or ability to commit crime at particular places or times. This approach is outlined in more detail in Table 9.3.

There is some evidence that crime reduction strategies can be effective in reducing crime (Levy et al, 2014:6). In particular, Tseloni et al (2016), in measuring the effectiveness of anti-burglary devices, argue that such crime reduction measures play an important role in the long-term decline of burglary rates. A specific advantage of this approach is that some of these measures can be easily understood by most people and can also be relatively easy and cheap to install.

However, there are significant limitations to this approach. The first is that it places the responsibility for reducing crime principally on the individual or on a community, in the absence of other agencies. Measures are primarily those that an individual takes, such as leaving lights on or using timer switches. Where such action is not taken and crime occurs, then there is the possibility that the victim will be blamed for not undertaking relevant action. This is relevant when considering that while some of these procedures may be cost free, such as clearing rubbish, others have financial implications, such as installing CCTV cameras or burglar alarms. The choice for some people living in poverty could literally be between food or security, which is not a choice anyone should have to make. In effect, those living in poverty can be blamed for being victims of crime, even when the very nature of their circumstances means that this is counter-intuitive.

Another limitation of this approach is that it can lead to crime displacement, meaning that rather than crime being prevented, it moves to another location, time or target, even becoming a different type of crime (Levy et al, 2014). This likely means that crime moves from one poor individual, house or neighbourhood where strategies have been put in place to another poor or poorer individual, house or neighbourhood where actions have not been taken. This emphasises the main limitation of the crime reduction approach, namely its focus is on limiting criminal behaviour, not on dealing with the underlying cause of crime. It does not prevent crime because it '[does] not examine factors such as poverty, inequality, discrimination, poor parenting, and so on, which are the root cause of crime. By focusing on the performance of criminal behaviour, [crime reduction] attacks symptoms and not underlying, systemic causes. It can at best provide a pragmatic, stop-gap solution to crime problems' (Wortley, 2010:2). In effect, crime reduction can only be seen as an approach to criminal justice practice that at best reduces crime in the short term but does not affect it in the longer term. This suggests that an alternative approach is required to deal with the impact and effects of poverty and crime.

How can a social policy approach improve criminal justice practice?

The limitations of the crime reduction approach suggest the need for an alternative approach to issues related to poverty and crime. Inherent within the crime reduction approach is a focus on the individual taking responsibility for reducing crime, meaning that the victim can be blamed which is wholly irrelevant to those living in poverty. While in some instances a crime reduction approach may have some utility, for it to be truly effective it needs to be underpinned by a focus on the social causes of crime (EUCPN, 2020). The comparable limitations observed when analysing the claim of a link between poverty and crime also point to the need for a more relevant approach by criminal justice practitioners, one that deals with the underlying causes of both poverty and crime.

What the evidence shows is that while the link between poverty and crime is weak, the link between poverty and being a victim of crime is strong. This means that those living in poverty are more likely to be victims of crime than its perpetrators, specifically because of their constrained circumstances. This is supported by the fact that there are specific circumstances that can lead to living in poverty. For example, from Table 9.2, it is evident that low pay is a significant cause of poverty. While this is something that occurs to individuals, it would be hard to argue that it is caused by individuals. Rather, low pay can be seen as something that is outside the control of the individual, as most people have no say over it.

As a simple example of how this related to criminal justice practice, at the time of writing the money given on release to prison leavers for immediate essentials, previously termed the discharge grant but now known as the one-off subsistence payment, totals approximately £83. This is very much below the government's own low-income threshold, and when linked to the fact that ex-prisoners can wait a significant amount of time before receiving relevant benefits, means that leaving prison can lead to living in absolute poverty, which increases the risk of further involvement in crime (McKeever, 2007). Similarly, there is an emphasis in criminal justice practice on ex-prisoners taking on chronically insecure work, which as shown earlier in this chapter and also in Chapter 6 is associated with a higher risk of poverty, and can lead to a return to reliance on informal criminal networks and recidivism (Fletcher and Flint, 2018). Again, such chronically insecure work can hardly be blamed on the individual, but when such work is lost it is typically blamed on the individual. This is an approach that can serve to increase the internalisation of social stigma and shame of individuals and communities, through its association with notions of people being responsible for their own individual failings (Bunting et al, 2017), thus leading to negative beliefs, assumptions and stereotypes about those in poverty (Bucelli et al, 2019). Consequently, the overall outcome from such an approach is to reinforce the poverty that such groups experience, thereby reinforcing negative crime outcomes. However, evidence suggests the need for criminal justice practitioners to focus on the root causes of crime, meaning the social problems that lead to poverty and crime (Unnever et al, 2008). From a social policy perspective, this can be done in two specific ways.

It is evident that it is the constrained circumstances of individuals and communities that makes crime more likely to happen to those living in poverty than to better-off individuals and communities. In simple terms, a lack of resources makes crime more of a reality. If those with more resources are less likely to be victims of crime, it does not take a great leap to conclude that improving the resources of those living in poverty will mean that they are less likely to be victims of crime. In social policy terms, the simplest way that this could be done is to improve the resources of those living in poverty so that fewer people live in poverty. For criminal justice practice, this can be done in a number of ways, for example by working to increase the wages that people earn so that fewer people earn 'poverty wages' or through working to ensure that work is secure. However, as should be evident, these are not changes that can be made at the individual level, but require a conceptualisation of poverty that is rooted in society's basic structure.

In order to have effective outcomes for criminal justice practice, there therefore needs to be a focus on the transformation of social relations within criminal justice practice, particularly on those factors that limit the ability of those living in poverty to escape from that situation. This is where a concern with the root processes that cause poverty has particular relevance, not only for those who are living in poverty, but also for those who believe in tackling inequality and social justice. It is only with such a focus on the root processes that cause poverty that the true nature of poverty as located within the society, not in the nature of the individual, becomes apparent, as evidence exists that dealing with the specific root cause of low income can reduce crime in specific ways (Noghani Behambari and Maden, 2021).

For those who are in a position to fight such poverty, attention should be drawn to the fact that it is only by working to enable those who are living in poverty to overcome deliberate and organised powerlessness that the possibility of social justice as discussed in Chapter 4 becomes apparent. Criminal justice practice therefore has to encompass the fact that poverty is created not by the individual but by specific facets of society, such as insecure work and low pay, which are outside the power of most people to influence but underpin their lack of power. This makes it evident that the conditions for poverty are caused by individuals' lack of power rather than their inadequacy or deviancy.

Summary

In this chapter, the concern has been with poverty and its links with crime. The first significant point to make is that even from the government's own 'absolute' definition of low income, there are estimated to be 9.2 million people living with an income below the government's low income threshold which is an astonishing figure in a rich and developed country. Poverty, however defined, has a long history of specifically being linked to crime as an explanation of why particular individuals become involved in criminal activity, and there are a number of criminological and non-criminological theories that make an explicit theoretical link between crime and poverty. Considering the actual evidence for this link, there is some support for the claim that there is a link between poverty and crime, both in terms of incidence and types of crime. However, the counter-evidence shows that while poverty can be important in understanding some aspects of crime, it is not possible to say that there is a direct link between poverty and crime if we consider the evidence for and against in its totality. One strong evidential link is that people living in poverty are more likely to be victims of crime and consequently more likely to live in fear of crime, meaning that in some ways crime and its effects hurt the poor most. This should lead to a primary focus on what can be done to stop people living in poverty being victims of crime.

Within criminal justice practice, there is a strong emphasis on crime prevention through what are typically referred to as crime reduction strategies, meaning that the concern is diminishing the number of criminal events that occur by influencing an offender's decision or ability to commit crimes at particular places or times. The limitations of the crime reduction approach suggest the need for an alternative approach to issues related to poverty and crime. In particular, inherent within the crime reduction approach is a focus on the individual taking responsibility for reducing crime, which has the potential to bring about victim blaming and is not relevant in the context of the constrained circumstances of those living in poverty. The comparable limitations observed when analysing the claim of a link between poverty and crime also point to the need for a more relevant approach for criminal justice practitioners, and the need for criminal justice practitioners to focus on the root causes of crime, meaning a focus on the social problems leading to poverty and crime. By this is meant a criminal justice practice that recognises the fact that poverty is created not by the individual but by specific facets of society, such as insecure work and low pay, which are outside the power of most people to influence and underpin their lack of power. This makes it evident that poverty is caused by individuals' lack of power rather than their inadequacy or deviancy.

References

Barry, A., Brook, P., Cebula, C., Collingwood, A., Drake, B., Elliott, J., Embleton, B., Leese, D., Matejic, P., Schwendel, G., Wenham, A. and Wincup, E. (2022) *UK Poverty 2022: The Essential Guide to Understanding Poverty in the UK*. York: Joseph Rowntree Foundation. Available from: https://www.jrf.org.uk/report/uk-poverty-2022 [Accessed 1 August 2022].

Beckford, I. (2023) *Ten Principles of Crime Prevention*. Available from: https://thecrimepreventionwebsite.com/police-guidance/720/ten-principles-of-crime-prevention/ [Accessed 26 January 2023].

Bennett, O. and Shalchi, A. (2022) *Economic Crime in the UK: A Multi-Billion Pound Problem*. London: House of Commons Library. Available from: https://researchbriefings.files.parliament.uk/documents/CBP-9013/CBP-9013.pdf [Accessed 26 January 2022].

Breitenbach, M., Kapferer, E. and Sedmak, C. (2021) *Stress and Poverty: A Cross-Disciplinary Investigation of Stress in Cells, Individuals, and Society*. Cham: Springer International Publishing. https://doi.org/10.1007/978-3-030-77738-8.

Bucelli, I., McKnight, A. and Summers, K. (2019) *Understanding the Relationship between Inequalities and Poverty: Policy Toolkit*. CASEreport 125. Centre for Analysis of Social Exclusion, LSE. Available from: https://sticerd.lse.ac.uk/CASE/_new/publications/abstract/?index=6845 [Accessed 1 August 2022].

Bunting, L., Webb, M.A. and Shannon, R. (2017) 'Looking again at troubled families: Parents' perspectives on multiple adversities', *Child & Family Social Work*, 22: 31–40. https://doi.org/10.1111/cfs.12232.

Cuthbertson, P. (2018) *Who Goes to Prison? An Overview of the Prison Population of England and Wales*. London: Civitas.

De Courson, B. and Nettle, D. (2021) 'Why do inequality and deprivation produce high crime and low trust?', *Scientific Reports*, 11(1): 1937. https://doi.org/10.1038/s41598-020-80897-8.

Dodd, V. (2018) 'Rising crime is symptom of inequality, says senior Met chief', *The Guardian*, 14 June. Available from: https://www.theguardian.com/uk-news/2018/jun/14/rising-is-symptom-of-inequality-says-senior-met-chief [Accessed 1 August 2022].

Dodd, V. (2021) 'Tackle poverty and inequality to reduce crime, says police chief', *The Guardian*, 18 April. Available from: https://www.theguardian.com/uk-news/2021/apr/18/tackle-poverty-and-inequality-to-reduce-says-police-chief [Accessed 1 August 2022].

Dong, B., Egger, P.H. and Guo, Y. (2020) 'Is poverty the mother of crime? Evidence from homicide rates in China', *PLoS ONE*, edited by S. Fu, 15(5): e0233034. https://doi.org/10.1371/journal.pone.0233034.

DWP (Department for Work and Pensions) (2021) 'Households below average income (HBAI) statistics'. Available from: https://www.gov.uk/government/collections/households-below-average-income-hbai--2 [Accessed 1 August 2022].

Elliott, D.S. and Fagan, A. (2017) *The Prevention of Crime*. Chichester: Wiley Blackwell.

EUCPN (European Crime Prevention Network) (2020) 'Toolbox – family-based crime'. Available from: https://eucpn.org/toolbox-familybasedcrime [Accessed 1 August 2022].

Farrington, D. (2003) 'Key results from the first forty years of the Cambridge Study in Delinquent Development', in T.P. Thornberry and M.D. Krohn (eds) *Taking Stock of Delinquency: An Overview of Findings from Contemporary Longitudinal Studies*. New York; Boston, MA; Dordrecht: Kluwer Academic/Plenum Publishers.

Fletcher, D.R. and Flint, J. (2018) 'Welfare conditionality and social marginality: The folly of the tutelary state?', *Critical Social Policy*, 38(4): 771–791. https://doi.org/10.1177/0261018317753088.

Gingerbread (2019) 'Single parents: Facts and figures'. Available from: https://www.gingerbread.org.uk/what-we-do/media-centre/single-parents-facts-figures/ [Accessed 1 August 2022].

Khan, S. (2019) *Mayor of London Speech on the Causes of Crime*. Available from: https://www.london.gov.uk//press-releases/mayoral/sadiq-khan-delivers-major-speech-on-violence [Accessed 1 August 2022].

Levy, L., Santhakumaran, D. and Whitecross, R.W. (2014) *What Works to Reduce Crime? A Summary of the Evidence*. Justice Analytical Services, Scottish Government. Social Research. Available from: http://www.nls.uk/scotgov/2014/9781784128241.pdf [Accessed 1 August 2022].

Lewis, P., Roberts, D. and Newburn, T. (2011) *Reading the Riots: Investigating England's Summer of Disorder*. First edition. London: Guardian Books.

Malby, S. and Davies, P. (2012) *Monitoring the Impact of Economic Crisis on Crime*. Office of Justice Programs. Available from: https://www.ojp.gov/ncjrs/virtual-library/abstracts/monitoring-impact-economic-crisis-crime [Accessed 1 August 2022].

McAra, L. and McVie, S. (2016) 'Understanding youth violence: The mediating effects of gender, poverty and vulnerability', *Journal of Criminal Justice*, 45: 71–77. https://doi.org/10.1016/j.jcrimjus.2016.02.011.

McKeever, G. (2007) 'Citizenship and social exclusion: The re-integration of political ex-prisoners in Northern Ireland', *British Journal of Criminology*, 47(3): 423–438. https://doi.org/10.1093/bjc/azl070.

Milne, C. (2017) *Is Wage Growth at the Same Level as during the Napoleonic Wars?* Available from: https://fullfact.org/economy/wage-growth-napoleonic-wars/ [Accessed 1 August 2022].

NAO (National Audit Office) (2022) 'Improving outcomes for women in the Criminal Justice System – National Audit Office (NAO) Report'. Available from: https://www.nao.org.uk/report/improving-outcomes-for-women-in-the-criminal-justice-system/ [Accessed 1 August 2022].

Newburn, T. (2016) 'Social disadvantage, crime, and punishment', in H. Dean and L. Platt (eds) *Social Advantage and Disadvantage*. Oxford: Oxford University Press, pp. 322–340. https://doi.org/10.1093/acprof:oso/9780198737070.003.0016.

Noghani Behambari, H. and Maden, B. (2021) 'Unemployment insurance generosity and crime', *Applied Economics Letters*, 28(13): 1076–1081. https://doi.org/10.1080/13504851.2020.1798337.

ONS (Office for National Statistics) (2019) 'Crime in England and Wales – Office for National Statistics'. Available from: https://www.ons.gov.uk/peoplepopulationandcommunity/crimeandjustice/bulletins/crimeinenglandandwales/yearendingdecember2021 [Accessed 1 August 2022].

ONS (Office for National Statistics) (2020) *Average Household Income, UK: Financial Year Ending 2020 (Provisional)*. London: ONS. Available from: https://www.ons.gov.uk/peoplepopulationandcommunity/personalandhouseholdfinances/incomeandwealth/bulletins/householddisposableincomeandinequality/financialyearending2020provisional#:~:text=The%20provisional%20estimate%20of%20median,30%2C100)%20shown%20in%20Figure%201 [Accessed 1 August 2022].

Papaioannou, K.J. (2017) '"Hunger makes a thief of any man": Poverty and crime in British Colonial Asia', *SSRN Electronic Journal* [Preprint]. https://doi.org/10.2139/ssrn.2780577.

Perri, F. (2011) 'White-collar crime punishment too much or not enough?', *Fraud Magazine*: 21–45.

Prison Reform Trust (2014) *Prison: The Facts*. Available from: https://www.choiceforum.org/docs/prf.pdf [Accessed 1 August 2022].

Sealey, C. (2015) *Social Policy Simplified: Connecting Theory with People's Lives*. London; New York: Palgrave Macmillan.

Social Metrics Commission (2020) 'Measuring poverty 2020'. Available from: https://socialmetricscommission.org.uk/measuring-poverty-2020/ [Accessed 1 August 2022].

Sturge, G. (2021) *UK Prison Population Statistics*. London: House of Commons Library. Available from: https://commonslibrary.parliament.uk/research-briefings/sn04334/ [Accessed 1 August 2022].

Trust for London (2022) 'Crime and income deprivation'. Available from: https://www.trustforlondon.org.uk/data/crime-and-income-deprivation/ [Accessed 1 August 2022].

Tseloni, A., Thompson, R., Grove, L., Tilley, N. and Farrell, G. (2016) 'The effectiveness of burglary security devices', *Security Journal*, 30(2): 646–664. Available at: https://doi.org/10.1057/sj.2014.30.

Unnever, J.D., Cullen, F.T. and Jones, J.D. (2008) 'Public support for attacking the "root causes" of crime: The impact of egalitarian and racial beliefs', *Sociological Focus*, 41(1): 1–33. https://doi.org/10.1080/00380237.2008.10571321.

Watson, B. (2022) *EARN06: Gross Weekly Earnings by Occupation – Office for National Statistics*. Available from: https://www.ons.gov.uk/employmentandlabourmarket/peopleinwork/earningsandworkinghours/datasets/grossweeklyearningsbyoccupationearn06 [Accessed 1 August 2022].

Webster, C. (2015) 'Poverty, inequality and justice', *Scottish Justice Matters*, 3(3). Available from: http://scottishjusticematters.com/wp-content/uploads/SJM_3-3_November2015-Complete.pdf [Accessed 1 August 2022].

Webster, C. and Kingston, S. (2014) *Anti-Poverty Strategies for the UK: Poverty and Crime Review*. York: Joseph Rowntree Foundation. Available from: https://ncvc.dspacedirect.org/handle/20.500.11990/858 [Accessed 1 August 2022].

Wilkinson, R.G. and Pickett, K.E. (2017) 'The enemy between us: The psychological and social costs of inequality', *European Journal of Social Psychology*, 47(1): 11–24. https://doi.org/10.1002/ejsp.2275.

Wortley, P. (2010) 'Critiques of situational crime prevention', in B. Fisher and S. Lab (eds) *Encyclopedia of Victimology and Crime Prevention (Vol. 1)*. Thousand Oaks, CA: SAGE Publications, pp. 880–884. Available from: https://discovery.ucl.ac.uk/id/eprint/1301877/1/Wortley_2010_SCP_criticisms.pdf [Accessed 1 August 2022].

10

Children and families, criminal justice practice and social policy

This chapter aims to:

- outline the Criminal Justice System (CJS) approach to children and families;

- analyse the evidence for and against the criminal justice approach to children and families;

- detail the contribution that a social policy approach can make to improving criminal justice practice for children and families.

Introduction

When talking about children and families, an obvious and uncontroversial point is that they are intimately linked – as Collier and Mears (2022:1) state, 'Families play a crucial role in childhood development. Research has found that family structure and characteristics can contribute to or inhibit success in a range of childhood, adolescent, and adulthood outcomes, including education, employment, mental health, and marital status.' Another uncontroversial point is that there are many different types of children and families, so when we talk about these we are actually talking about a variety of experiences and outcomes. It is arguable that no two childhoods are the same, and similarly that no two families are the same.

When considering how the CJS engages with children and families, it becomes evident that the emphasis is primarily negative, with a focus on their 'delinquent' and 'troublesome' nature (see Key Learning Box 7.1). This is perhaps most famously exemplified in the following quote from Prime Minister David Cameron in the immediate aftermath of the 2011 English riots:

> I don't doubt that many of the rioters out last week have no father at home. Perhaps they come from one of the neighbourhoods where it is normal for young men to grow up without a role model, looking to the street for their father figures. So if we want to have any hope of mending our broken society, family and parenting is where we've got to start. … We've known for years that a relatively small number of families are the source of a large proportions of problems in our society. Drug addiction. Alcohol abuse. Crime.

A culture of disruption and irresponsibility that cascades through generations. (Cameron, 2011)

It is clear from this that Cameron is laying the blame for the riots, and therefore criminality, specifically at the door of delinquent and problem children and families.

The chapter explores this focus of the CJS in detail. The chapter considers the evidence for and against this focus, and the wider implications of it. Finally, the chapter details the contribution that a social policy approach can make to improving criminal justice practice for children and families.

What are 'children' and 'families'?

In discussing the relevance of children and families to criminal justice practice, it is important to define and understand what is meant by these terms, as they can mean different things to different people. Defining these terms is also important as the nature of both children and families has changed significantly over time and continues to change.

There are specific legal definitions of children. In England and Wales, a child is defined as someone under the age of 18. However, this is less definitive when talking about the CJS. The minimum age of criminal responsibility in England and Wales in ten years old, meaning that children can be arrested, taken to court and given a custodial sentence for committing a crime at this age, although they will be treated differently from adults. The case of the murder of James Bulger in 1993 exemplifies the **alternative investigation, trial, sentencing and release of minors** (Key Learning Box 10.1). Actions committed before the age of ten cannot be charged as criminal in nature, although actions such as curfews, child safety orders and being taken into care can still occur. From the age of 18, young people are treated as adults in the CJS in England and Wales, although they are sent to a secure centre for young people until the age of 25, when they are sent to adult prison.

KEY LEARNING BOX 10.1 ALTERNATIVE INVESTIGATION, TRIAL, SENTENCING AND RELEASE OF MINORS

In 1993, two-year-old James Bulger was abducted, tortured and killed in Liverpool by Robert Thompson and Jon Venables, both aged ten. Owing to the age of Thompson and Venables, special measures were put in place during the investigation, trial, sentencing and release. During the investigation, while being questioned they were allowed to have their parents present as well as their lawyers, and during their trial a social worker sat with them in the dock. They were also given anonymity and an injunction was issued to stop the press releasing details about them that might reveal their identity. After sentencing, they were not sent to prison but to secure care units, and after they were released, they were provided with new identities and moved to new locations.

It should be noted that this minimum age of ten for criminal responsibility is low compared with other countries, and is the lowest in Europe (Kelly, 2019). For example, it is 12 in Scotland, 14 in Germany, 15 in Norway and 16 in Portugal. The key point about the minimum age of criminal responsibility is that provides an age at which a society sees 'children as fully rational and responsible beings – like "mini-adults"' (Haines et al, 2021). The lower the threshold, the earlier children become seen as mini-adults and therefore responsible for their behaviour. An obvious point to make is that in many other spheres of life, the age at which children become perceived as mini-adults is much later, at 16 (age of consent), 18 (age of marriage) or even 21 (leaving care). This difference between definitions of a child and the minimum age of criminal responsibility makes it hard to specifically define what a child is. However, as the focus in this book is on criminal justice practice, where the term 'child' or 'children' is used, it will refer to the minimum age of criminal responsibility definition for England and Wales, that is from ten onwards, unless specified otherwise.

When trying to define 'families', the first point to make is that, unlike children, there is no legal and/or criminal justice definition. What exists is policy that focuses on a certain type of family, one that was defined in the post-war *Beveridge Report*:

> In any measure of social policy in which regard is had to facts, the great majority of married women must be regarded as occupied on work which is vital though unpaid, without which their husbands could not do their paid work and without which the nation could not continue. (Beveridge, 1942:para 107)

This concept of family is one that clearly separates the roles that men and women play in society, with men functioning as breadwinners and women as stay-at-home carers for children. This family type derives from a **functionalist concept of the family** (Key Learning Box 10.2) and is known as the 'nuclear family'. This consists of parents and children, with the nucleus of the family being the man and the roles of the wife and children built around him. The key functionalist argument for this family type is that it is universalist in nature, meaning that it can be found in all cultures and that it serves to provide stability in a society through two key features. First, the nuclear family enables young people to be taught the rules of society, which is important for the socialisation of the young and therefore a stable society. Secondly, it enables the steadying of adult personalities, as it provides a place where the stresses of society can be dealt with, thus reducing societal conflict. It should be noted that there are strong counter-arguments against these explanations, especially from feminist perspectives (Jaspers et al, 2022).

KEY LEARNING BOX 10.2 FUNCTIONALIST CONCEPT OF THE FAMILY

Functionalism is a theory that argues society is made up of institutions and that each different institutional part serves a specific function within wider society. To exemplify, consider how a house is built. Functionalism specifies that this requires different occupations and skills to function together to design and construct it. Without one part of the system, say bricklayers, the house would not be built as efficiently as possible. Similarly, the functionalist concept of the family argues that family is part of a wider system that enables society to function. The crucial aspect of this concept is that it argues a specific type of family, the nuclear family, is the type that best enables society to function, as it provides specific roles for each part of the family. The role of the female is to provide care and nurturing, while the role of the male is to act as the breadwinner. Functionalism is therefore a theory that states that individuals within society have specific roles, and that these roles need to be followed for the benefit of society.

The key point here is that the *Beveridge Report* argued that the post-war welfare state should be built around the nuclear family for the simple reason that it was the dominant family type at the time. Beveridge thought it would remain the dominant family type in the future, and therefore the post-war welfare state constructed social policies around it. For example, social policy assumed that women would give up work when they became married to have children, and would become dependent on the earnings and/or benefits of their husband, regardless of the type of work that either did. This was despite the fact that during the war, many married women worked and contributed to the household.

Beveridge's assumption that the nuclear family type would continue to remain dominant was correct in the immediate period after World War Two (WW2), but more recently there have been some significant changes in family types, as shown in Graph 10.1. This shows that 'couple households with children', that is the nuclear family, were by far the main type of household in the immediate period after WW2. However, since then there has been a huge decline in this family type and correspondingly a great increase in others, to the extent that the nuclear family is no longer the most dominant. In fact, there are both more 'one person households' and 'couple households with no children' than the nuclear family type. There has also been an increase in lone parent households. There are various reasons for this, such as fewer people getting married, people getting married later, more people co-habiting and an increase in divorce. A significant effect of these changes is that 'becoming a parent is occurring at increasingly older ages and happening more frequently outside of marriage' (Kiernan et al, 2022:3). A particular trend that is almost exclusive to Britain is that of 'non-partnered motherhood', meaning children born to parents who do not live together, which stands at around 5 per cent or less in most western and northern European nations, but is 16 per cent for England and Wales (Kiernan et al, 2022).

Graph 10.1 Changes in household type in the UK, 1961—2010

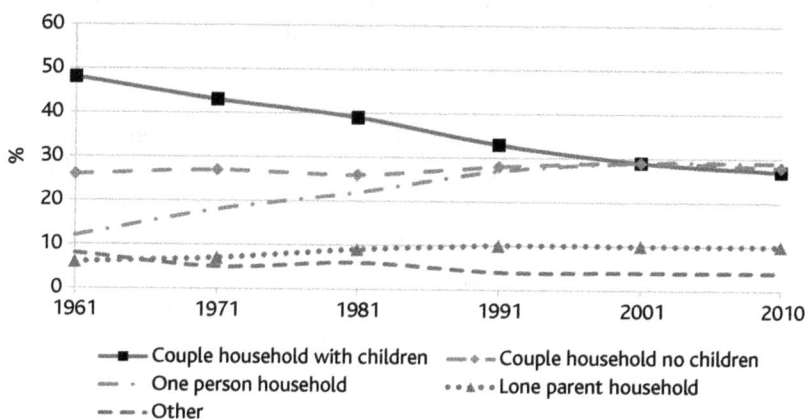

Couple household with children — Couple household no children — One person household — Lone parent household — Other

Source: ONS (2011), table 2

All these changes mean that the nuclear family type that Beveridge constructed the post-war welfare policy around has declined significantly, and other family types are now more predominant.

This means that over recent decades, defining 'the family' as the nuclear family is inaccurate. The reality as shown in Graph 10.1 means that the notion of 'the family' as a single type is no longer credible. Rather, it has been displaced by the notion of 'families', which reflects the reality that there is a vast array of different types. Referring to the quote from David Cameron above, this shift clearly has relevance for criminal justice practice.

The important observation to take from this brief attempt to define children and families is that they both mean different things according to context and time. While there are specific legal definitions of children, the fact that there is not just one indicates that the term is a social construction, meaning that it is 'an invention/ label that has been revised and reconstructed socio-historically within and between nation states' (Haines et al, 2021). The same applies to the term 'family'.

How does the CJS regard children and families in relation to crime?

The key starting point when analysing how children and families are considered by the CJS is set out in the European Crime Prevention Network (EUCPN, 2020:11), which states that 'there is no doubt that growing up in a family of criminals increases the likelihood that an individual becomes a criminal him or herself'. There is a high level of consensus about this among criminologists and criminal justice practitioners.

The key notion that underpins this is that crime occurs through intergenerational transmission. This means that where some members of a family have a criminal personality, they transmit this to other family members, in the same way that someone being close to someone with a cold can transmit that cold to you.

Such transmission may occur from direct exposure to criminal behaviours, or may occur through the communication of attitudes, beliefs and interactions (Coop et al, 2021). This means that when children live in a family with criminal tendencies, they will 'learn' to become criminals from family members. By living in such families, criminality becomes normalised, meaning that not only do they learn how to commit criminal acts, but they also learn to disregard social norms (EUCPN, 2020). This learning can occur either directly, through for example parents teaching their children the 'tricks of the trade', or indirectly and unintentionally through everyday interactions and behaviours such as a lack of emotional warmth or attachment.

The key factor that underpins this notion of intergenerational transmission is that of inadequate parenting, either intentionally or unintentionally (Anker and Andersen, 2021). More specifically, it sees this inadequate parenting as flowing down through the generations in an unbreakable cycle.

Charles Murray's description of the 'underclass theory' is a good example of this perspective, as outlined here: 'The underclass are defined by their behaviour. Their homes are littered and unkempt. The men in the family are unable to hold down a job. Drunkenness is common. The children grew up ill-schooled and ill-behaved and contribute to a disproportionate share of juvenile delinquents' (Murray, 1990:24). A key focus of this theory is the notion of absent fathers, as the lack of a positive role model results in children becoming delinquent as they turn to other role models who are criminal in nature.

Some theories point to the specific characteristics of some family types as causing criminality. For example, family size is frequently cited, with the claim that children from larger families engage in more delinquency and crime (Colliers and Mears, 2022). According to social control and social bond theories, in larger families there is less possibility that parents will form strong social bonds with all their children than in smaller families, which also means less social control. Consequently, children are less likely to respond to attempts at social control within the family, such as discipline, and are more likely to form social bonds outside the family home with less desirable individuals. These theories see family resources as a zero-sum game – that there is a finite amount of family resources, whether emotional, financial or social, to go around, so when one child gets access to a family resource, another child necessarily loses out. Another key point of this perspective is that those who commit crimes tend to prefer to associate with people they can trust, and this usually means people in their social network, which especially relates to family members (Hobbs, 2002). Therefore, according to these theories, the family provides a ready site of recruitment for criminal activity, through the bonds that already exist and are important to crime.

The notion of attachment plays an important role in these social control and social bond theories of intergenerational transmission of crime (Segeren et al, 2020). Attachment, as set out by Bowlby (1969), argues that children are programmed to form strong attachments to their primary caregiver, which is usually positive. However, where such a caregiver is criminal in nature, the opportunities for the transmission of crime are strong. However, Bowlby also argues that where there is no strong attachment this can lead to a variety of negative behaviours, all of which research has linked to criminality.

Social labelling theory is another significant theory that is relevant to children, families and crime (Rowe and Farrington, 1997). It argues that the children of families who are known to the police and other authorities for previous criminality are subject to bias from those agencies, simply from being children from such families. This works on two levels. At the level of experience, this means more contact with the CJS through the police and the courts, and therefore more socialisation into criminal ways. On a psychological level, knowing that you are being seen as a criminal simply by association can turn out to be a **self-fulfilling prophecy** (Key Learning Box 10.3), meaning that it leads to committing crimes. The key point here in relation to the family is that it is the criminality of the family as opposed to the individual that leads to such labelling and ultimately to crime.

KEY LEARNING BOX 10.3 SELF-FULFILLING PROPHECY

The notion of a self-fulfilling prophecy, as proposed by Merton (1948), argues that what someone believes in their mind becomes the reality they experience. A belief or expectation that something is true leads to that belief or expectation becoming true. As a simple example, if someone believes they will not pass a test, the outcome will be that they will not pass, but if someone believes they will pass, they will. Applied to criminal justice practice, this means that if someone is told negative things about themselves, they will believe and act out those negative things, and vice versa. A key point is that self-fulfilling prophecies can be both positive and negative.

More recently, genetic explanations for crime in families have emerged. This suggests that those with criminal parents are more likely to become criminal because criminality is passed through genes (Farrington et al, 2001). Linked to this is the notion that criminal individuals become part of criminal families as people choose partners who are similar to themselves in terms of personality and characteristics. The key point here is the claim that people actively seek out individuals who are similar to themselves genetically, which means there is greater likelihood of genetic inheritance of such characteristics by their children. This reflects the belief that criminality is inherent in the nature of individuals, as some people are born criminals, and this criminality is transmitted from generation to generation.

What evidence is there for a link between children and families and criminality?

There is some specific evidence to support these theories that reflect how the CJ regards children and families as outlined above. First, in relation to the notion that crime occurs within families, Farrington et al's (2001:582) research from the Pittsburgh Youth Study supports the notion of criminal families, meaning crimes are committed by a variety of family members. Their research observed that there was a concentration of offending in particular families, meaning that very few families were responsible for a large number of crimes. Not only were prisoners more likely to have family members who were imprisoned, but they were also more likely to have a family member who had been arrested: 'Arrested fathers tended to coincide with arrested mothers, arrested uncles tended to coincide with arrested aunts, and arrested grandfathers tended to coincide with arrested grandmothers' (Farrington et al, 2001:592). This is supported by more recent research from the Department for Communities and Local Government (DCLG, 2014:20), which shows that 'the presence of an adult in the household [who is] involved in crime makes it more likely that a child or young person in that family will also be involved in crime'. More recently, Copp et al (2021) have observed that the children of parents in prison are more likely to become involved in the CJS than those with parents not in prison. Interestingly, they relate this link as caused by stigma and labelling, whereby the families of those involved in crime are more likely to be under the close watch of criminal justice authorities than the families of those not involved in the CJS, which supports social labelling theory.

Collier and Mears (2022) observe that family size is a strong predictor of delinquency, as the larger the family the more likely that a child will be delinquent. Segeren et al (2020) also observe that in relation to juvenile delinquency, growing up in a 'dysfunctional family' is related to developing young adult violent crime behaviour. They argue that their research provides evidence for social learning as an explanation for the intergenerational transmission of criminal behaviour. Additionally, in relation to family type, Kroese et al (2021) detail that the evidence from a large body of studies is that there is a positive relation between single parent families and crime levels, as children who grow up in a single parent family are more likely to be involved in crime during adolescence.

The key emphasis in the CJS is the notion of intergenerational transmission of crime between children and families, and evidence for this would see children who live with criminal parents being more likely to engage in crimes compared with those who do not live with criminal parents. According to EUCPN (2020:9), there is evidence to support this. In particular, according to Anker and Andersen (2021:1269):

> One of the most well-established findings in studies on the intergenerational transmission of contact with the criminal justice system is that 'crime runs in families', that is, the consistent finding that children with convicted parents are much more likely to commence a criminal trajectory themselves compared to children of non-convicted parents.

For example, Rowe and Farrington (1997), from the Cambridge Study in Delinquent Development, observed that there was evidence of the 'familial transmission of convictions', meaning that if a parent was convicted of a crime, the likelihood that their child would also have a conviction significantly increased. It should also be noted that crime within a family is linked to other negative outcomes. For example, according to the DCLG (2014), having an adult in the household with a recent proven offence was associated with a range of other outcomes, such as having a child in care, a child with special needs and a young person who was not in education, employment or training, also referred to as NEET.

Bunting et al's (2017) research also provides some good evidence of the notion of intergenerational transmission. It focuses on families experiencing 'multiple adversities' – that is, a range of negative issues such as poverty, child abuse and crime. The research detailed how in many cases, the adversities experienced by participants in their childhood were replicated in their adulthood, as detailed by one of Bunting et al's (2017:34) research participants:

> The abuse … you know it was unbelievable because here you were, it was like a circle repeating itself, history. I was brought up in an abusive relationship and here I am in an abusive relationship. It is like a pattern, you know, and it is a true saying, you do go after fellas like your father. History is proving. (Lucy)

This suggests that problems experienced within childhood can transmit themselves from generation to generation, meaning that family plays an important role in the occurrence of crime.

What evidence is there against a link between children and families and criminality?

Evidence against the notion of this link is made by Anker and Andersen (2021), who highlight a significant flaw in the notion of intergenerational transmission that is related to the move away from the nuclear family. As they observe, the notion of intergenerational transmission by its nature implies a primarily biological connection between familial generations. However, as noted earlier, the nature of the family and family complexity has changed significantly, meaning that the important biological family type is significantly less dominant than in the past. Rather, the family is a concept that now includes a large proportion of non-biological parents and children living together. As Graph 10.1 shows, this is a change that has been in progress for over 50 years, thus meaning the possibility of biological familial contact that is essential for intergenerational transmission has diminished. Anker and Anderson argue instead that it is the presence of a stepfather that has most significance in the intergenerational transmission of crime, which suggests that it is not biology that is at the core of intergenerational transmission but the nature of individuals.

Colliers and Mears (2022) conclude that it is a myth that large family size is linked to delinquency. Rather, they argue that their research highlights the beneficial effects of larger families, such as the possibility of sibling supervision and contribution to the family income. They also observe a difference between large families with only biological siblings or non-biological siblings, with the former less likely to be linked to delinquency and the latter more likely. They suggest that where a link between family size and delinquency exists, it is more complicated than has previously been thought.

There is also an inherent contradiction in the accounts of intergenerational transmission. On the one hand, such theories argue that key to this is the family as a site of intimate contact, meaning being around people who are able to exert a considerable emotional influence, and hence transmit criminality through intimate bonds. On the other hand, however, there is the claim that it is the absence of such people that leads to the family functioning as a site of dysfunction, as what such families transmit is a lack of social bonds between families and communities, which leads to crime. Additionally, intergenerational transmission primarily refers to something that happens between father and sons. However, as noted earlier, the father–son dynamic has changed, as is evident in the increase in single parenthood, which is predominately female in nature and therefore limits the notion of father–son crime transmission. Therefore, the significant changes in the nature of the family undermine the essential biological basis of intergenerational transmission.

In accounts of the intergenerational transmission of crime, there is very little if any discussion of long-standing research that suggests crime is disproportionately committed by young people in general (Shulman et al, 2013). This is typically referred as the age–crime curve, and evidences that offending increases in adolescence and decreases in the transition to adulthood, as adolescents tend to show more delinquency and commit more crime than either younger children or adults. This 'points strongly to the conclusion that there is something about adolescence as a developmental period that inclines youth toward law-breaking behaviour' (Shulman et al, 2013:858). This age–crime curve highlights the importance of biology to crime, but in a way that is different from accounts of intergenerational transmission, as rather than biological links to the family being important, it is biology linked to age that is significant.

Within criminal justice accounts of children and families, the emphasis is almost exclusively on the negative impact that families have on crime. However, there is also evidence that the family plays a positive role in the CJS, especially in relation to recidivism and desistance. In relation to recidivism, families have been observed as providing important social control and social support to ex-prisoners and also helping to find employment, all of which serve to reduce the chances of recidivism (Berg and Huebner, 2011). Families are also important in providing financial and non-financial support to ex-prisoners, which is very important as most prisoners leave prison with minimal resources. Family support has been reported by ex-prisoners as the most important factor in keeping them out of prison (Gana et al, 2021).

In terms of desistance, Berg and Huebner (2011) observe how the relational ties of the family mean they are less likely to stigmatise ex-prisoner family members, which leads to a greater chance of full rehabilitation, and therefore desistance from crime. Similarly, Duwe and Clarke (2011) argue that the family can 'bond' an ex-prisoner to a more conventional lifestyle, meaning that they become more inclined to maintain it. As an example of this, Cherney and Fitzgerald (2016) highlight how when family members enable an ex-prisoner to find a job, this binds the prisoner to a normal life as they do not wish to let the family member down.

However, perhaps the most succinct evidence against notions of underclass and intergenerational transmission is provided by Gordon (2011:5–6), who states definitively that:

> These ideas are unsupported by any substantial body of evidence. Despite almost 150 years of scientific investigation, often by extremely partisan investigators, not a single study has ever found any large group of people/households with any behaviours that could be ascribed to a culture or genetics of poverty. This failure does not result from lack of research or lack of resources. For example, the Transmitted Deprivation Programme of the 1970's lasted over 10 years, commissioned 23 empirical studies and cost over £5m at today's prices. ... There are also of course many families which have problems (sometimes multiple problems) who could benefit from additional help and services. However, any policy based on the idea that there are a group of 'Problem Families' who 'Transmit' their 'Poverty/Deprivation' to their children will inevitably fail, as this idea is a prejudice, unsupported by scientific evidence.

What is the outcome of the CJS approach to children and families?

As previously noted, England and Wales have one of the lowest minimum ages of criminal responsibility, meaning that children are caught up in the CJS earlier than in other countries, and this includes being imprisoned much earlier. Chapter 7 highlights how being in prison can lead to increased negative health outcomes, and Clinks (2021) details how poor conditions in prison lead to and exacerbate poor mental and physical health, with long-lasting and traumatising effects. Linked to this is the fact that the CJS has become more punitive, meaning that it jails more people, leading to a huge increase in the rate of imprisonment to a level higher than it has ever been. In combination, this suggests that what is most relevant to children and families' involvement with the CJS is this combination of the low age of criminal responsibility and the increase in punitiveness, which together have increased the likelihood that children and families will have contact with the CJS. It should be noted that these increases have occurred almost in parallel with the claim that the family is the site of crime, and research suggests that these two factors can be specifically linked.

This is because imprisonment has specific and enduring negative consequences not just for the individual but also for their family (Mowen and Visher, 2016). For example, research has shown that it can lead to the loss of family income, the severing of family bonds, stigma, mental health problems, drug use and further contact with the CJS (Miller and Barnes, 2013), as well as negative issues related to education, physical health and deprivation (Turney and Goodsell, 2018). Additionally, Mowen and Visher (2016) argue that children can be especially affected by the imprisonment of a parent, leading to issues such as lack of emotional support and family interactions, and research has shown that 'the children of incarcerated parents are significantly more likely to suffer from mental health problems, academic underperformance, anti-social or aggressive delinquency, drug use and contact with the criminal justice system' (Miller and Barnes, 2013:672). In specific relation to the CJS, research has shown that having a parent in prison is linked with serious and violent delinquency, drug use and getting into trouble with the police. The research indicates that youths with incarcerated parents are also more likely to get into trouble in school and in their neighbourhood. Most recently, Murray et al (2012) has found that parental involvement in the CJS is predictive of youth property offences (such as theft). One explanation of this, as detailed by Turney and Goodsell (2018), is that the children of a parent in prison are suffering from disadvantages before their parent goes to prison, and imprisonment simply makes these problems worse, which suggests that it is prior disadvantage, and not a parent being in prison, that causes the increased harms. Another explanation lies with the importance of the nuclear family at the heart of policy. If the male breadwinner is supposed to act as the figurehead of the family who undertakes the important roles of socialisation and structure, the growth in imprisonment means that this role can no longer be performed. In this context, it is perhaps not surprising that problem families have become a concern at a time of increased imprisonment, particularly male imprisonment.

Additionally, the growth in imprisonment has often been compounded by changes that make it hard for families to maintain contact, despite the fact that maintaining such contact can be beneficial for the family (Duwe and Clark, 2011). However, prisoners' families can have problems visiting for various reasons, including location, cost and procedures, and these barriers may increase family conflict (Mowen and Visher, 2016). It is also important to understand that barriers also work to negatively change relationships within families, and this can have important negative consequences post-release in the context of the beneficial role that the family can play, as detailed in relation to desistance and recidivism (EUCPN, 2020). In this sense, intergenerational transmission is not the cause of crime in children and families, but rather it is the increased punitive nature of the CJS that is the cause of the intergenerational transmission of problems in families that can lead to further contact with the CJS.

How can a social policy approach improve criminal justice practice for children and families?

In the aftermath of David Cameron's speech about the cause of the riots, the government put forward the Troubled Families Programme (TFP) in 2012, a social policy programme to deal with families experiencing multiple problems, including crime, antisocial behaviour, truancy, financial exclusion, unemployment, mental health problems and domestic abuse. The government identified that there were 120,000 troubled families in the UK. A key point about the TFP was its focus on a 'broken society', which was outlined as caused by a collapse in family and the growth of an underclass, thus being heavily related to the belief of intergenerational transmission within families (Parr and Hayden, 2019).

The government initially hailed the TFP as a success, but a more detailed and objective evaluation of the programme rejected this claim (Crossley, 2015), and more recent evaluations are also unclear about the TFP's beneficial outcomes (Loft, 2020). Wider analyses of the effectiveness or otherwise of the TFP provide a good opportunity to outline how social policy could enhance criminal justice practice for children and families.

A key observation from the TFP is the breadth of problems that families face. As Loft (2020) observes, the most common problems faced by families relate to children needing help (88 per cent), worklessness (58 per cent) and health (48 per cent). Indeed, the TFP shows that crime and antisocial behaviour are the problems that occur the least. What this suggests is that the notion of crime being prevalent in such families is not evidenced. This highlights two problems with trying to link crime and family. The first is that where 'troubled families' exist as defined in the TFP, this is because of a multitude of problems rather than one specific problem. Linked to this is that the evidence does not support the notion that crime is rampant in such 'troubled families'.

A key feature of the TFP is its emphasis on changing behaviour through intensive intervention, without any concern for wider social or economic considerations (Lambert and Crossley, 2017). For example, families in the TFP are intensively monitored in their parenting skills, being subjected to parenting classes and intensive teaching of 'life-skills', and where there is a lack of compliance these are backed up by punitive measures such as welfare cuts and restrictions to welfare access (Nunn and Tepe-Belfrage, 2017). Of particular note here is the emphasis on the **conditionality** (Key Learning Box 10.4) of the TFP (Hargreaves et al, 2019), which is where service providers make entitlement to services and benefits conditional upon good behaviour, meaning that the TFP is punitive in nature. This punitive shift is also evident in other social policy areas, particularly in the growth of the use of **benefit sanctions** (Key Learning Box 10.4) (Stewart and Wright, 2018). This emphasis in social policy has appeared in parallel with the punitive shift in the CJS since the 1990s as has been detailed throughout this book. There is evidence that this approach in the form of benefit sanctions can have beneficial impacts, but the evidence is that these are short-lived, and in the longer term there are worsening outcomes. This is because punitive measures lead to short-termist behaviour that has an immediate negative impact and is unsustainable in the long term, such as moving into a low-paid job (NAO, 2016), which negatively affects an individual's health and well-being.

> **KEY LEARNING BOX 10.4** CONDITIONALITY AND BENEFIT SANCTIONS
>
> Conditionality in this context refers to where a benefit or service is only provided if certain actions are undertaken, which can also include changing behaviour. For example, in order to be eligible for Universal Credit, individuals are required to search for a job for a certain amount of time each week, and also attend interviews with their personal advisor. The rationale for conditionality is that the change in the behaviour that it requires is beneficial for the individual. Where an individual does not comply, benefit sanctions can be applied. This usually results in the partial or full withdrawal of a benefit or tightening of conditions for receipt. The key point here is that both conditionality and benefit sanctions have been increasingly used in social policy over recent years (Stewart and Wright, 2018).

A key reason outlined for the failure of the TFP is its stigmatisation of the very families that it claimed to want to help. Because of how stigmatisation works, this approach makes it less likely that families will either want to receive help that they need or be able to move beyond being a problem family. In particular, Bunting et al (2017) argue that the TFP failed because it was based on a deficit approach, meaning it considered that troubled families were caused by the failings of individuals, rather than the structural disadvantages that these families faced. By avoiding the realities of structural poverty, behaviour that could be seen as troublesome was perceived as troublesome in isolation even though it was a symptom of the negative material reality of individuals (Hargreaves et al, 2019). An example of this is provided by Parr and Hayden (2019:35):

> Other issues included children who were regularly reported missing to the police and poor home conditions. In one case, this included no access to hot water, resulting in a teenage girl avoiding school:
>
> Some of the unauthorised absences are in relation to [her] being home alone and not wanting to attend school as she could not have a bath. ... The parents both work and leave the property at 5.30am and the younger siblings are left in the care of the eldest sibling ... The

family report that they have trouble with the heating and the landlord has been advised. ... The family wish to move but housing options have told them they cannot be moved until the arrears are cleared.

What is evident here is how such stigmatisation can not only lead to individual problems, but also to entrenching structural inequalities, because of its ability to wield power over the actions of individuals (Barnwell, 2019). Parr and Hayden (2019) make the point that such circumstances as detailed here mean that the notion that problems with families can be intergenerational cannot and should not be ruled out but should be acknowledged. However, evidence does not support the notion of intergenerational transmission as is evident in much of the criminological approach detailed above, wherein problem families lead to problem families. Rather, they argue, it should be acknowledged that the needs of families are complex, chronic and enduring in nature, and require help that deals with these issues. If we refer to the Adverse Childhood Experiences (ACEs) discussed in Chapter 7, what we see is that when these negative factors occur in childhood, they not only lead to negative physical and mental health outcomes in later life, but also to maladaptive personality traits that can lead to crime. While some of these negative adversity factors are criminal in nature, such as child abuse and neglect, others are not, such as divorce and parental death, meaning that even experiencing non-criminal events can be associated with criminal behaviour, owing to the deleterious effect that such events can have on individuals. This brings us back to the quote by David Cameron at the beginning of the chapter about how certain types of families are the cause of crime. However, the evidence is actually to the contrary, wherein as Bunting et al (2017:38) observe: 'When David Cameron ... states that we only need to "join the dots" to understand that issues such as anti-social behaviour are attributable solely to parenting, we are being offered a simplistic, "common sense" understanding of complex social problems which ignore structural inequality as a potentially contributing factor.'

Summary

When looking at how children and families are considered in the CJS, it is important to locate these terms in their contemporary legal and social contexts. What is evident is that the criminal age of responsibility in England and Wales is low compared with many other countries and that family complexity has increased significantly. Criminal justice practice has to take account of these factors, and not just conceptualise the family as it was in the past.

The dominant perspective is that the family is a site of negative influence for children, as expressed through the notion of intergenerational transmission of crime. This conception indicates that children are socialised into crime and then transmit this socialisation to their own children. There is some relevant evidence for this, but also some important limitations.

Where the notion of intergenerational transmission makes itself apparent is in relation to the nature of the CJS itself, which since the 1990s has become more punitive in nature. This has seen a huge increase in the rate of imprisonment, which when linked to the fact that England and Wales have one of the lowest minimum ages of criminal responsibility, means that not only are more people being imprisoned, but also that they are being imprisoned much earlier.

From a social policy perspective, the TFP was specifically introduced as a policy to deal with such intergenerational transmission, with criminality being an important factor that the programme aimed to reduce. The TFP also reflects a focus on punitive measures in social policy, as has been increasingly evident in the CJS. The beneficial outcomes of the TFP are hard to discern, and analysis of the reasons for this lack of evidence highlight some important lessons that indicate social policy could enhance criminal justice practice for children and families.

First, where the stigmatisation of children and families occurs, this not only makes it harder to work with children and families, but it can also exacerbate the disadvantages that they face, owing to stigmatisation's ability to wield power over individuals. Additionally, to cast the notion of intergenerational transmission in terms of behavioural understandings is problematic, as it misses the fact that the needs of families are complex, chronic and enduring in nature, and cannot be attributed solely to parenting. This focus on social policy highlights that a good starting point in improving criminal justice practice for children and families is considering how the CJS treats children – as this is currently having a detrimental intergenerational effect on families.

References

Anker, A.S.T. and Andersen, L.H. (2021) 'Does the intergenerational transmission of crime depend on family complexity?', *Journal of Marriage and Family*, 83(5): 1268–1286. https://doi.org/10.1111/jomf.12770.

Barnwell, A. (2019) 'Family secrets and the slow violence of social stigma', *Sociology*, 53(6): 1111–1126. https://doi.org/10.1177/0038038519846443.

Berg, M.T. and Huebner, B.M. (2011) 'Reentry and the ties that bind: An examination of social ties, employment, and recidivism', *Justice Quarterly*, 28(2): 382–410. https://doi.org/10.1080/07418825.2010.498383.

Beveridge, W. (1942) *Beveridge Report*. CMD 6404. London: HMSO. Available from: https://www.parliament.uk/about/living-heritage/transformingsociety/livinglearning/coll-9-health1/coll-9-health/ [Accessed 19 July 2022].

Bowlby, J. (1969) *Attachment and Loss: Attachment*. Ann Arbor, MI: Basic Books. https://books.google.co.uk/books?id=FYEuAAAAMAAJ.

Bunting, L., Webb, M.A. and Shannon, R. (2017) 'Looking again at troubled families: Parents' perspectives on multiple adversities', *Child & Family Social Work*, 22: 31–40. https://doi.org/10.1111/cfs.12232.

Cameron, D. (2011) *PM's Speech on the Fightback after the Riots*. Available from: https://www.gov.uk/government/speeches/pms-speech-on-the-fightback-after-the-riots [Accessed 2 August 2022].

Cherney, A. and Fitzgerald, R. (2016) 'Finding and keeping a job: The value and meaning of employment for parolees', *International Journal of Offender Therapy and Comparative Criminology*, 60(1): 21–37. https://doi.org/10.1177/03066 24X14548858.

Clinks (2021) *Written Evidence from Clinks*. Available from: https://committees. parliament.uk/writtenevidence/36351/html/ [Accessed 28 July 2022].

Collier, N.L. and Mears, D.P. (2022) 'Delinquent by the dozen: Youth from larger families engage in more delinquency – fact or myth?', *Crime & Delinquency*: 001112872210880. https://doi.org/10.1177/00111287221088036.

Copp, J.E., Johnson, E.I., Bolland, A.C. and Bolland, J. (2021) 'Household member arrest and adolescent externalizing behaviors: The roles of family and peer climates', *Children and Youth Services Review*, 129: 106207. https://doi.org/ 10.1016/j.childyouth.2021.106207.

Crossley, S. (2015) *The Troubled Families Programme: The Perfect Social Policy?* London: Centre for Crime and Justice Studies. Available from: https://www. crimeandjustice.org.uk/publications/troubled-families-programme-perfect-soc ial-policy [Accessed 4 August 2022].

DCLG (Department for Communities and Local Government) (2014) 'Understanding troubled families'. Available from: https://www.gov.uk/governm ent/publications/understanding-troubled-families [Accessed 2 August 2022].

Duwe, G. and Clark, V. (2011) 'Blessed be the social tie that binds: The effects of prison visitation on offender recidivism', *Criminal Justice Policy Review*, 24(3): 271–296. https://doi.org/10.1177/0887403411429724.

EUCPN (European Crime Prevention Network) (2020) 'Toolbox – family-based crime'. Available from: https://eucpn.org/toolbox-familybasedcrime [Accessed 1 August 2022].

Farrington, D.P., Jolliffe, D., Loeber, R., Stouthamer-Loeber, M. and Kalb, L.M. (2001) 'The concentration of offenders in families, and family criminality in the prediction of boys' delinquency', *Journal of Adolescence*, 24(5): 579–596. https:// doi.org/10.1006/jado.2001.0424.

Franco-Paredes, C., Ghandnoosh, N., Latif, H., Krsak, M., Henao-Martinez, A.F., Robins, M., Barahona, L.V. and Poeschla, E.M. (2021) 'Decarceration and community re-entry in the COVID-19 era', *The Lancet Infectious Diseases*, 21(1): e11–e16. https://doi.org/10.1016/S1473-3099(20)30730-1.

Gana, O., Saeed, K.N. and Halid, H. (2021) 'Reintegration after prison: Encouraging employers to hire ex-offenders to be a part of the society', *Albukhary Social Business Journal*, 2(2): 1–9. https://doi.org/10.55862/asbjV2I2a001.

Gordon, D. (2011) *Consultation Response; Social Mobility & Child Poverty Review.* Policy Response Series No. 2. Available from: https://www.poverty.ac.uk/ sites/default/files/attachments/WP%20Policy%20Response%20No.%202%20C onsultation%20Resp%20Social%20Mobility%20%26%20Child%20Poverty%20 %28Gordon%20Oct%202011%29.pdf [Accessed 3 August 2022].

Haines, K., Case, S., Smith, R., Joe Laidler, K., Hughes, N., Webster, C., Goddard, T., Deakin, J., Johns, D., Richards, K. and Gray, P. (2021) 'Children and crime: In the moment', *Youth Justice*, 21(3): 275–298. https://doi.org/10.1177/1473225420923762.

Hargreaves, C., Hodgson, P., Mohamed, J.N. and Nunn, A. (2019) 'Contingent coping? Renegotiating "fast" disciplinary social policy at street level: Implementing the UK Troubled Families Programme', *Critical Social Policy*, 39(2): 289–308.

Hobbs, D. (2002) 'Organized crime families', *Criminal Justice Matters*, 50(1): 26–27. https://doi.org/10.1080/09627250208553415.

Jaspers, E., van der Lippe, T. and Evertsson, M. (2022) 'Gender inequality, households, and work', in K. Gërxhani, N. de Graaf and W. Raub (eds) *Handbook of Sociological Science: Contributions to Rigorous Sociology*. Cheltenham: Edward Elgar Publishing, pp. 176–195. https://doi.org/10.4337/9781789909432.

Kelly, E. (2019) 'The age of criminal responsibility in England and Wales is the lowest in Europe at just 10 years old', in J. Treadwell and A. Lynes (eds) *50 Facts Everyone Should Know about Crime and Punishment in Britain*. Bristol; Chicago, IL: Policy Press, pp. 66–69.

Kiernan, K., Crossman, S. and Phimister, A. (2022) *Families and Inequalities*. Available from: https://ifs.org.uk/inequality/families-and-inequalities/ [Accessed 2 August 2022].

Kroese, J., Bernasco, W., Liefbroer, A.C. and Rouwendal, J. (2021) 'Growing up in single-parent families and the criminal involvement of adolescents: A systematic review', *Psychology, Crime & Law*, 27(1): 61–75. https://doi.org/10.1080/1068316X.2020.1774589.

Lambert, M. and Crossley, S. (2017) '"Getting with the (Troubled Families) Programme": A review', *Social Policy and Society*, 16(1): 87–97. https://doi.org/10.1017/S1474746416000385.

Loft, P. (2020) *The Troubled Families Programme (England)*. Briefing Paper Number 07585. London: House of Commons Library. Available from: https://commonslibrary.parliament.uk/research-briefings/cbp-7585/ [Accessed 2 August 2022].

Merton, R.K. (1948) 'The self-fulfilling prophecy', *The Antioch Review*, 8(2): 193. https://doi.org/10.2307/4609267.

Miller, H.V. and Barnes, J.C. (2013) 'Genetic transmission effects and intergenerational contact with the Criminal Justice System: A consideration of three dopamine polymorphisms', *Criminal Justice and Behavior*, 40(6): 671–689. https://doi.org/10.1177/0093854812468434.

Mowen, T.J. and Visher, C.A. (2016) 'Changing the ties that bind: How incarceration impacts family relationships', *Criminology & Public Policy*, 15(2): 503–528. https://doi.org/10.1111/1745-9133.12207.

Murray, C. (1990) 'The emerging British underclass', in C.A. Murray and R. Lister (eds) *Charles Murray and the Underclass: The Developing Debate*. London: IEA Health and Welfare Unit in association with the *Sunday Times*, pp. 24–53.

Murray, J., Loeber, R. and Pardini, D. (2012) 'Parental involvement in the Criminal Justice System and the development of youth theft, marijuana use, depression, and poor academic performance', *Criminology*, 50(1): 255–302.

NAO (National Audit Office) (2016) *Benefit Sanctions*. HC 628. Available from: https://www.nao.org.uk/report/benefit-sanctions/ [Accessed 4 August 2022].

Nunn, A. and Tepe-Belfrage, D. (2017) 'Disciplinary social policy and the failing promise of the new middle classes: The Troubled Families Programme', *Social Policy and Society*, 16(1): 119–129. https://doi.org/10.1017/S147474641 6000452.

ONS (Office for National Statistics) (2011) *Social Trends 41*. London: The Stationery Office.

Parr, S. and Hayden, C. (2019) 'Multiple needs, "troubled families" and social work', *People, Place and Policy*, 13(1): 29–41.

Rowe, D.C. and Farrington, D.P. (1997) 'The familial transmission of criminal convictions', *Criminology*, 35(1): 177–202. https://doi.org/10.1111/j.1745-9125.1997.tb00874.x.

Segeren, M., Fassaert, T., de Wit, M. and Popma, A. (2020) 'Constellations of youth criminogenic factors associated with young adult violent criminal behavior', *Crime Science*, 9(1): 2. https://doi.org/10.1186/s40163-020-0111-2.

Shulman, E.P., Steinberg, L.D. and Piquero, A.R. (2013) 'The age–crime curve in adolescence and early adulthood is not due to age differences in economic status', *Journal of Youth and Adolescence*, 42(6): 848–860. https://doi.org/10.1007/s10964-013-9950-4.

Stewart, A. and Wright, S. (2018) *Final Findings: Jobseekers*. Economic and Social Research Council. Available from: http://www.welfareconditionality.ac.uk/wp-content/uploads/2018/05/40426-Jobseekers-web.pdf [Accessed 27 January 2023].

Turney, K. and Goodsell, R. (2018) 'Parental incarceration and children's wellbeing', *The Future of Children*, 28(1): 147–164.

11

Ten ways in which a social policy focus can improve criminal justice practice

Introduction

The key objective of this book is the improvement of criminal justice practice. It has attempted to do this principally by clearly outlining that there are significant interconnections between social policy and criminal justice practice. The aim has been to show that understanding and working with these interconnections can and does lead to improvements in responses to crime and criminal behaviours for criminal justice practice, which has beneficial outcomes not just for criminal justice practice, but also for wider society. Understanding these interconnections is very important for anyone who has an interest in working in and improving criminal justice practice.

The focus of this concluding chapter is to draw together the key issues from the previous chapters to provide ten key ways in which understanding and applying key social policy concepts can improve criminal justice practice.

1. The importance of understanding that criminal justice practice service users have social policy needs

We can demonstrate the beneficial outcomes of understanding the interconnection between social policy and criminal justice practice for practitioners and the wider community by analysing those most likely to come in contact with the Criminal Justice System (CJS). What this shows is how closely those with social policy issues are also those who come into contact with the CJS and therefore criminal justice practice. It is very often the case that the types of service user that practitioners come across have significant welfare needs. For example, a report by Clinks (Drinkwater, 2017) identifies that issues such as housing, debt and financial management, problematic substance misuse and poor mental health are significant areas of need for service users of voluntary sector criminal justice organisations. What is apparent from this list is that they can all be specifically related to Beveridge's original 'five giant evils', such as squalor, want and disease. This suggests that the groups most likely to have a high level of welfare needs are also those who are most likely to need assistance from criminal justice practitioners (Baker and Barrow, 2006), indicating that there is a clear interconnection. This can include not just those who are poor, but also those with intellectual or physical disabilities, those from diverse cultural backgrounds, those with low levels of education, women who have special needs in relation to discrimination, pregnancy and responsibility for children, young people, children and older people (Baker and Barrow, 2006).

There is also evidence that contact with the CJS can be significantly reduced by meeting other social policy needs. For example, while 85 per cent of the general population have literacy skills equivalent to at least that of an 11 year old, only 46 per cent of newly assessed prisoners do (*Inside Time*, 2015). And in relation to numeracy, while 50 per cent of the general population have the skills equivalent to at least that of an 11 year old, only 39.8 per cent of prisoners do (*Inside Time*, 2015). This indicates that low educational attainment is a significant factor in criminal activity, and that another giant evil identified by Beveridge, namely ignorance, is also linked to contact with the CJS, as it relates to employment, housing and mental health. This suggests that meeting these needs could prevent contact with the CJS.

An additional relevant point to note is that criminal justice practitioners often find that each problem they are dealing with is one of a cluster (Baker and Barrow, 2006). By this is meant that individuals who have contact with the CJS are also very likely to have problems in other areas of their life, particularly in relation to their welfare needs, such as a lack of income, low qualifications, substance misuse and mental illness. This means that trying to solve their criminal justice problems often means trying to solve their welfare problems. In the absence of measures that specially deal with these, there is often a failure of criminal justice practice outcomes. The way in which these welfare issues often need to be met is through social policy interventions in health, education, housing, education and social care. Therefore, understanding and dealing with the welfare issues that a service user is having while in contact with the CJS can and often does lead to beneficial outcomes for individuals and practitioners alike.

2. The importance of focusing on social security, not just security

As detailed in Chapter 4, criminal justice practice and social policy are connected by their concern with the security of the individual, communities and society. However, the notion of security in criminal justice practice is very different from the notion of security in social policy. For criminal justice practice, it is concerned with protection from a threat to physical existence, essentially meaning stopping crime. In contrast, for social policy the focus is on social security, meaning protection from social threats such as poverty, unemployment and ill health.

Hopefully, what has become evident from this book is that a significant amount of the work of criminal justice practitioners is with those who have significant social needs, such as poverty, unemployment and ill health. For example, in Chapter 5, we see how homelessness can lead to involvement with the CJS, in Chapter 6 we see how employment is important to desistance, in Chapter 7 we see how those with health issues are significantly over-represented in the CJS, in Chapter 8 we see how drug misuse is underpinned by social needs, in Chapter 9 we see how poverty limits the ability to respond to crime, and in Chapter 10 we see how it is families with problems rather than problem families that are relevant to criminal justice practice.

All this should make it clear why there is a need for criminal justice practice to consider a wider definition of security that includes the social issues that individuals, communities and societies need protection from. An exclusive focus on security as an absence of physical threats means ignoring many factors that make physical threats a reality. The best example of this is in relation to substance abuse, where evidence shows overwhelmingly that the best way to protect from the physical threat that this poses, such as causing harm to self and others, is to deal with the social causes of substance abuse. As is evident from the analysis here, without dealing with these social issues, criminal justice practice is bound to fail.

This highlights the importance to criminal justice practitioners of understanding the wider social context of the issues faced by those they work with. Furthermore, making policies that may solve such problems is the essence of social policy. However, for these policies to be truly effective requires a focus in criminal justice practice on deep and meaningful engagement with the reality of social insecurity, including its causes, which means a transformation in criminal justice practice from a narrow focus on physical security to one that includes a wider concern with social security.

3. The importance of working towards less punitive practice

The book has outlined that since the mid-1990s there has been a decisive shift in the CJS towards a more punitive focus. This means a move away from the rehabilitation of offenders towards the punishing of offenders, as is evident from the significant increase in the prison population set out in Chapter 3. This punitive shift has been rationalised as a way to effectively deter and punish crime. There is a wealth of evidence, however, that this shift has done little to prevent or reduce crime, but has actually done much to significantly increase social harm – and at great expense (Bradley and De Nohora, 2022). In particular, when considering the current CJS approach to substance abuse as set out in Chapter 9, it is arguable that the punitive approach has made the situation worse. The evidence is that from both a social and an economic perspective, the punitive shift has been very expensive for the CJS.

Additionally, it became evident during COVID-19 that there was a focus in many countries towards 'decarceration', which refers to efforts to limit the number of people who are imprisoned, through releasing prisoners early or simply jailing fewer people in the first place (User Voice and Queen's University Belfast, 2022). This suggests two key points. First, that if there is a will towards jailing fewer people, then it is something that can happen. Secondly, and perhaps most importantly, the incarceration of those who are decarcerated could have been avoided in the first place, or at least it could have been less severe, meaning that incarceration is often more about the appearance of being tough on crime than focusing on what actually works.

Similarly, there has been a punitive shift in social policy, as exemplified in the application of the TFP and the use of conditionality and benefit sanctions as outlined in Chapter 10. The outcomes identified in relation to social policy are somewhat similar to those identified for the CJS, in terms of worsening outcomes and more expense in the long term. Evidence from the punitive approach in social policy reinforces the point made about the punitive approach in the CJS, and by extension criminal justice practice, that it contributes to the production and entrenchment of disadvantage.

Many criminal justice practitioners may justifiably say that this shift to the punitive approach is out of their hands, and their responsibility is simply to apply the policy as it stands. There are two responses to this.

First, it is true that the shift to a more punitive approach is largely the work of policy makers, specifically the Ministry of Justice and the Home Office, and many criminal justice practitioners simply apply this policy. However, this book has defined criminal justice practice in a broad way, not only including those individuals who work in statutory organisations, but also a range of non-statutory agencies such as lawyers, victims' organisations, charities such as Nacro and research organisations such as the Centre for Crime and Justice Studies. As detailed in Chapter 2, it is possible for such organisations to successfully work to make the CJS less punitive, as was made evident when the Howard League for Penal Reform overturned the ban on prisoners having access to books. From social policy, there are numerous organisations that have been successful in changing government policy so that it is less punitive, such as the Child Poverty Action Group in relation to children, Shelter in relation to housing and Gingerbread in relation to lone parents. The history of social policy has taught us that policy can be influenced by those working within statutory organisations and also those working outside them.

The second key point is in relation to how criminal justice practice is implemented. The work of Lipsky (1980) highlights how professional discretion can be used as a practical tool by practitioners to make policy work in a way that is more amenable to their core beliefs. What this means is that while professionals may have limited say about the overarching policy, they can use their powers of discretion to shape and effectively change how the policy is enacted at street level. Social policy provides an example of how this can work to shape and change policy. If we refer to the Troubled Families Programme (TFP) outlined in Chapter 10, Hargreaves et al (2019) outline how practitioners working on the TFP enacted the policy in ways that limited its punitive aspects in order to make it work, thereby highlighting how professionals can function as agencies of resistance. This makes evident to criminal justice practitioners how they can use their discretion to shape criminal justice practice in ways that are less punitive.

4. The importance of a focus on the structural rather than individual causes of disadvantage and crime

It has been a long-standing debate in criminal justice practice whether criminals are born as criminals or whether they are made criminals by the circumstances they find themselves in. The focus on one of these explanations over another has important implications for practitioners in terms of the what, why and how of practice. To simplify this debate, the former relates to individual explanations of crime that locate the cause of crime in factors within the control of individuals, such as personal characteristics, behaviours and vulnerabilities. This means that the cause of crime is determined as the consequences of an individual's actions. The latter relates to structural explanations that locate the cause of crime to factors outside the control of individuals, such as lack of housing, low wages and unemployment. This means that the cause of crime is determined as the consequence of wider issues over which an individual has little or no power.

This has also been a long-standing debate in social policy, and there are some important points to note that are of relevance to criminal justice practice. In Chapter 5, we identified that since the 1980s the primary concern when dealing with homelessness has been to concentrate on issues that affect the individual rather than the structural causes of homelessness itself. However, the more recent Housing First approach addresses homelessness on the basis that the priority is to provide stable housing, which then enables other issues to be dealt with. This is a structural approach, and there is evidence that suggests it provides a number of positive benefits, including those that are specifically related to criminal justice outcomes such as a reduction in offending behaviours and decreased workloads for criminal justice practitioners (Homeless Link, 2019).

Chapter 9 analyses dealing with crime through the crime reduction approach. The key observation is that this approach focuses on individuals taking responsibility for reducing crime, which means victims may be blamed – which is not relevant in the context of the constrained circumstances of those living in poverty. Additionally, the analysis details that there are specific circumstances that can lead to living in poverty, such as low pay and chronically insecure work, which it would be hard to argue are things that are caused by the individual. Rather, these are factors that most people have no control over. This also points to the need for a more relevant approach for criminal justice practitioners, one that deals with the underlying causes of both poverty and crime.

These analyses should highlight to criminal justice practice that the primary cause of crime is located within society's structure, not in the nature of individuals, and this should be the concern of practice. Specifically, it should draw attention to the fact that it is only by first working to enable those they work with to overcome such deliberate and organised powerlessness will positive outcomes for practice become possible. Criminal justice practice should therefore encompass the belief that crime is created not by the individual but by specific facets of society, such as insecure work and low pay, which cannot be controlled by most people in society but nevertheless underpin their lack of power. This makes it clear that the conditions of crime are caused by individuals' lack of power, rather than their individual inadequacy or deviancy.

5. The importance of the de-stigmatisation of service users and clients

A collective theme throughout this book has been the negative and prejudicial attitudinal responses in society to those within the CJS. These attitudes range from demeaning to outright hostile. The main significant negative outcome that such perceptions cause is stigmatisation. The key point about this is that it can and does have important negative implications on the social and economic outcomes for individuals, in terms of limiting the possibility of desistance and participation. More specifically, stigmatisation can also lead to the pathologisation of those in criminal justice, meaning they are viewed as medically or psychologically abnormal. The key point for criminal justice practice is that such stigmatisation and pathologisation work to limit its possible positive outcomes, for example by limiting rehabilitative employment possibilities. As detailed in Chapter 10, these can also directly lead to contact with the CJS, as children with parents in prison are more likely to become involved in the CJS than those with parents not in prison owing to stigma and labelling, with the families of those involved in crime more likely to be under the close watch of criminal justice authorities than the families of those who are not involved in the CJS.

The emphasis in criminal justice practice on the individual rather than the structural causes of crime undoubtedly influences such stigmatisation. Being judged by others as the cause of your situation when this might not be the case inevitably has negative consequences. Feeling that they are being judged is an isolating and debilitating experience for people who are facing adversity, and this often leaves individuals feeling alone and anxious.

Stigmatisation has been a prevalent issue in social policy, as evident in the emphasis on 'benefit scroungers' and 'workshy' individuals. It has a long history that goes back to the use of workhouses for those in poverty in the 19th century. As with the CJS, such stigmatisation has severe negative consequences, such as disengagement, denigration and division (Bolton et al, 2022). The relevance for criminal justice practice here is that evidence from social policy shows that being stigmatised by welfare practitioners inevitably has negative consequences (Sealey et al, 2022). In particular, stigmatisation by practitioners can lead to submissive expectations being placed upon individuals, meaning an expectation to behave and act in certain ways. What then occurs is false compliance, which works to limit outcomes for both the individual and the practitioner, although this may only become apparent later on when there is a failure of the intervention and the need for re-involvement of both parties.

Stigmatisation, then, is exacerbated by the failure of those working with individuals to recognise the skills and insights of those they are working with, thereby according them a lower status than others. De-stigmatisation can occur when skills and abilities are recognised. For example, the de-stigmatisation of physical disability has been driven by the changed perception of disabled people, as it is no longer assumed they lack skills and abilities but rather have the same skills as able-bodied people (Smith and Sealey, 2022). To negotiate with complex procedures, while dealing with life experiences that limit your daily activities or approach to life, requires determination, persistence and an ability to understand and relate to a large number of institutions and individuals. Service users and clients have an array of skills, live in pressured environments and often have high expectations and competing demands placed upon them. Stigmatisation, in contrast, may restrict people in the CJS from attaining wider inclusion in society.

6. The importance of a universal rather than selective approach to criminal justice practice

Moving to a risk-based approach in the CJS is a move away from a universal towards a more selective focus for criminal justice practice. This means that rather than being concerned with providing services for all, the focus is only on those who are at risk or defined as a risk. For example, Jones and De Zoete (2018) outline how many programmes for those at risk of crime, such as school exclusion and gang membership, focus only on high-risk individuals and not on the general population as a whole. Social policy provides many services and benefits that are both universal and selective, and this provides a good opportunity to consider the implications of this shift for criminal justice practice.

The main advantage of providing services that are universal from a criminal justice practice perspective is that they reach much of the population, meaning that services have the potential to effect change in a wide range of individuals and therefore provide opportunities for primary prevention opportunities. On the other hand, the main advantage of a selective focus is that it provides the opportunity for intensive targeted work with those who are at risk. We can compare these advantages by considering how education and council housing are provided, as these are, respectively, examples of universal and selective services.

Up to the age of 18, education is universal, and as a consequence of this the majority of people are able to read and write. Consider the impact if education was provided on a selective basis, meaning only some people were entitled to it. Providing education universally means that society as a whole benefits, and also that the majority of individuals have an interest in how the service is provided and maintained, and this is exemplified by how important an issue education is for the general public. In contrast, when services are selective, they rarely focus on those who are healthy and wealthy, but are more often focused on those who are poor and powerless. The example of council housing set out in Chapter 5 typifies this, as becoming more selective has led to its 'residualisation', meaning that only a narrow group of people are eligible for it. These are the very poor, rather than a broad mix of people, and as a consequence the service has become stigmatised (Sealey, 2015). Richard Titmuss has made the observation that 'services for the poor end up being poor services' (Titmuss, 1973), and this is something we can see in the shift from universalism to selectivism in council housing. The danger for criminal justice practice in focusing on risk in such a selective way is that services benefit fewer people and services become less of a concern for society in general. As a consequence, services become poor and ineffective.

This is significant because there has been a general trend away from universal CJS policies towards more selective CJS policies, and the austerity policies of the 2010 Coalition government intensified this trend in a number of ways. The analysis presented here suggests this trend will significantly limit CJS policies in the future.

7. The importance of approaching crime as a public health issue

As hinted earlier, there has been a growing recognition by criminal justice practitioners of the relevance to criminal justice practice of the public health approach to preventing diseases and injuries (Schuller, 2013).

Public health is focused on preventing, protecting and improving the health of individuals and the community they live in by tackling issues that cause significant harm. It does this by identifying threats to health and putting in measures to prevent them occurring, usually before they have the opportunity to take effect. An example of this is the use of vaccines in public health, as this protects against an identified threat by preventing it from taking effect. Public health also works to improve people's health when they have existing conditions that limit their health. An example of this is helping people to quit smoking, because smoking has been identified as limiting health. A crucial way in which public health works is by building up evidence to support activities that prevent, protect and improve people's health. Health measures are therefore only put in place if there is evidence that they work, as opposed to measures that are put in place because there is a feeling that something needs to be done to deal with a problem. Crucially, public health measures do not just focus on medical interventions, but can draw on a broad range of non-medical measures from a variety of fields.

Before outlining how a public health approach would work, it is perhaps relevant to outline key differences between this and the criminal justice approach. These are shown in Table 11.1. A clear distinction is that the public health approach focuses on the population in terms of the cause of the disease and its treatment, whereas the criminal justice approach focuses on the individual. To explore this further, it is useful to observe that the key difference between a health approach and a public health approach is that the former is viewed as an individual concern, whereas the latter refers to measures that focus on improving the health of the public as a whole, because the issue under consideration affects everyone rather than just an individual. To illustrate this contrast, consider different approaches to dealing with someone who trips up on a pavement. If just one person trips up in a single incident, then the simple solution is to deal with the injuries that transpire from that specific accident. However, if this becomes something that happens to lots of different people in lots of different places over a period of time, dealing with the injuries individually would not be enough, as the injuries would continue to occur. This is because tripping up on pavements

Table 11.1 Simplified comparison of differences between public health and CJS approaches to crime

	Public health approach to crime	CJS approach to crime
What is crime?	Crime is a disease	Crime is an action that breaks the laws of a society
Who commits crime?	People who are ill	Criminals
Why does crime occur?	Crime occurs as a response to socio-economic factors	Crime occurs primarily because of individual criminal behaviour
How should crime be dealt with?	Crime should be treated and cured	Crime should be punished
Who is responsible for dealing with crime?	The whole community	The CJS
How should crime be prevented?	'Upstream' prevention measures through treatment and/or education	'Downstream' prevention through deterrence

is no longer an issue that occasionally affects an individual, but has become an issue that affects the population. This means it has become a public health issue. If we understand public health issues in this way, it becomes evident that crime is a public health issue.

There are various examples of public health interventions that have been successful in a variety of both health- and non–health-related contexts. This includes smoking cessation programmes, human papillomavirus vaccination, congestion charging, cancer screening programmes, the soft drinks sugar levy (Royal Society of Public Health, 2022) and more recently COVID-19 vaccination. However, the public health approach has also been successfully applied to a specific aspect of crime through the Scottish Violence Reduction Unit (SVRU). This was founded in 2005 as a response to increasing murders and following a report by the World Health Organization (WHO), which named Glasgow as the 'murder capital' of Europe. Since adopting the public health approach that 'violence is preventable, not inevitable', murders have fallen to their lowest level since 1976, with a 39 per cent decrease since 2011 (SVRU, 2022). This suggests that public health interventions can be used to reduce crime.

8. The importance of dealing with crime in a multi-agency way

A key rationale for treating the link between health and crime as a public health issue is the societal costs of violence-related injuries, in relation to both short-term and long-term costs (Potter and Krider, 2000). The logic of the public health argument is that many of the same techniques associated with successful public interventions such as smoking cessation and teenage pregnancy can be successfully applied to crime.

The public health approach would gather evidence to detail why an issue is happening, and then put in place measures to prevent, improve and support people that draw on evidence and work in a multidisciplinary way. Public health relies on knowledge from a broad range of disciplines including medicine, epidemiology, sociology, psychology, criminology, education and economics. So, for example, the measure to deal with people tripping up on pavements would not only involve working with doctors, but could also involve urban planners to redesign the streets, sociologists to consider why people are falling over more and educationalists to consider ways to educate people about walking.

Using the public health approach, crime would be viewed as a threat to the health of the whole community and everyone who lives within it, not just as a threat to order within the community. This means that the focus is not only on the effect of crime on the perpetrators through punishment, but also on victims of crime, either directly or indirectly. A public health perspective views crime as occurring not simply because of individuals' intentions, motivations and characters, but because of the coming together of many factors within an individual's environment and life. This means that crime is treated as an infectious disease that can be cured by using scientific evidence to identify what causes it and finding interventions that work to prevent it spreading. However, unlike in health, the cure does not necessarily lie in medical interventions but rather in a variety of non-medical actions.

9. The importance of focusing on primary upstream rather than secondary downstream interventions

The focus in public health on primary upstream interventions contrasts with the CJS focus on secondary and tertiary downstream measures after the risk of crime has been identified or when crime has already occurred. The use of risk management assessment tools such as the Offender and Assessment System (OASys) tool that prison and probation services use is a good example of this, as it requires staff to complete a risk and needs assessment towards prioritising interventions that target criminogenic risk factors. The problem with such risk-based approaches is twofold. First, there is a move away from an individualised approach to service users, meaning that the personal approach to assessing risk is replaced by an approach that classifies risk in bands. Secondly, this approach to risk management downplays social and economic circumstances and other factors that we have seen can play an important role in occasioning crime (Bullock, 2011).

For public health, there are three levels of prevention: primary, secondary and tertiary. Whereas primary prevention is designed to prevent something happening in the first place within the population, secondary prevention focuses on intervention for those who are showing early signs of problematic behaviour but where this may not yet meet the threshold to be classified as such, whereas tertiary prevention focuses on reducing the problematic behaviour after it has occurred. It can be thought of in terms of the differences between primary healthcare (having access to your GP to prevent a health problem occurring), secondary healthcare (going to the hospital with a specific problem that is a one-off but may develop more seriously) and tertiary healthcare (being an outpatient for a chronic or enduring condition).

The distinction between upstream and downstream measures, as adopted from *The Marmot Review* (Marmot 2010), is important to understand. Upstream measures refer to those that take place before any harm occurs. An example of this is provided by Jones and De Zoete (2018), who relate how firefighters now offer 'Safe and Well' visits while installing smoke alarms in the homes of the more vulnerable. These 'Safe and Well' visits include fire safety advice and how to reduce hoarding and clutter as a way to prevent a fire rather than fighting it later – with inevitable and often tragic human costs. In contrast, a downstream measure simply focuses on planning a safe escape from the fire. Thus, the crucial difference between the two is measures that are put in place to prevent an event happening and measures that happen after an event has happened.

The benefits of such an approach can be wide ranging, as detailed by Marmot (2010:140):

> Investing in ill health prevention can, if implemented effectively, improve health and life expectancy as well as reduce spending over the long term, as NICE agrees: 'Promoting good health and preventing ill health saves money. ... Increased investment in public health is key to increasing efficiency in the health service. A small shift in resource towards public health prevention activity would offer significant short, medium and long-term savings to the service and to the taxpayer.'

10. The importance of optimism that practice can effect change

This book has been written during a long period of austerity, during which there have been deep cuts to the funding and scope of both CJS and social policy provisions by central government since 2010. This has been followed by a deep cost of living crisis. It is apparent that austerity has had a significant impact on the issues analysed in this book, either through cuts in finances, cuts in services or cuts in support. In this sense, austerity has failed on its own terms: it is a false economic model (Stirling, 2019) that has brought about even greater deficits than those it purported to solve. It is easy to be pessimistic in such a context.

However, the history of social policy reminds us that the welfare state emerged from real problems within society. In particular, it was the levels of poverty, disease and ill health that led to the creation of the welfare state in the first place. It is unquestionable that the situation in relation to poverty, disease and ill health is significantly better now than it was in the past as a consequence of the social policies that were put in place to deal with them; these policies continue to make a real difference to the lives of many people, and contribute significantly to the development of society.

The major social and economic changes that are occurring in society suggest that there will be a real need for different social policies that can ameliorate their worst effects. Making policies that can solve such problems is the essence of social policy. As a social policy lecturer, I remain optimistic that social policy will continue to do so, despite the impact of austerity and the cost of living crisis.

References

Baker, D. and Barrow, S. (2006) 'Proxy models of legal need: Can they contribute to equity of access to justice?', *Journal of Social Policy*, 35(2): 267–282. https://doi.org/10.1017/S0047279405009529.

Bolton, R., Whelan, J. and Dukelow, F. (2022) 'What can welfare stigma do?', *Social Policy and Society*, 21(4): 1–14. https://doi.org/10.1017/S1474746422000185.

Bradley, G.M. and Noronha, L. de (2022) *Against Borders: The Case for Abolition*. New York: Verso.

Bullock, K. (2011) 'The construction and interpretation of risk management technologies in contemporary probation practice', *British Journal of Criminology*, 51(1): 120–135. https://doi.org/10.1093/bjc/azq056.

Drinkwater, N. (2017) *The State of the Sector*. Available from: https://www.clinks.org/sites/default/files/2018-08/clinks_state-of-the-sector-2017_final-web1.pdf [Accessed 5 August 2022].

Hargreaves, C., Hodgson, P., Mohamed, J.N. and Nunn, A. (2019) 'Contingent coping? Renegotiating "fast" disciplinary social policy at street level: Implementing the UK Troubled Families Programme', *Critical Social Policy*, 39(2): 289–308.

Homeless Link (2019) *Housing First and Its Impact in the Community*. London: Homeless Link. Available from: https://homelesslink-1b54.kxcdn.com/media/documents/Housing_First_and_its_impact_in_the_community_2019.pdf [Accessed 25 July 2022].

Inside Time (2015) 'Vital statistics: English and Maths skills of prisoners', *insidetime*, 30 November. Available from: https://insidetime.org/vital-statistics-english-and-maths-skills-of-prisoners/ [Accessed 5 August 2022].

Jones, P. and De Zoete, E. (2018) *What Does a 'Public Health' Approach to Violence Really Mean?*, Catch22. Available from: https://www.catch-22.org.uk/news/public-health-approach-to-violence/ [Accessed 5 August 2022].

Lipsky, M. (1980) *Street Level Bureaucracy: Dilemmas of the Individual in Public Services*. New York: Russell Sage Foundation. Available from: https://www.jstor.org/stable/10.7758/9781610447713 [Accessed 4 August 2022].

Marmot, M. (2010) *Fair Society, Healthy Lives: The Marmot Review*. London: UCL.

Merrington, S. and Stanley, S. (2000) 'Doubts about the What Works initiative', *Probation Journal*, 47(4): 272–275. https://doi.org/10.1177/026455050004700408.

Potter, R.H. and Krider, J.E. (2000) 'Teaching about violence prevention: A bridge between public health and criminal justice educators', *Journal of Criminal Justice Education*, 11(2): 339–351. https://doi.org/10.1080/10511250000084961.

Royal Society of Public Health (2022) 'Top 20 public health achievements of the 21st century'. Available from: https://www.rsph.org.uk/our-work/policy/top-20-public-health-achievements-of-the-21st-century.html [Accessed 5 August 2022].

Schuller, N. (2013) 'Is crime a question of health?', *Safer Communities*, 12(2): 86–96. https://doi.org/10.1108/17578041311315067.

Sealey, C. (2015) *Social Policy Simplified: Connecting Theory with People's Lives*. London; New York: Palgrave Macmillan.

Sealey, C., Fillingham, J. and Unwin, P. (eds) (2022) *Social Policy, Service Users and Carers: Lived Experiences and Perspectives*. Zurich: Springer Nature Switzerland AG.

Smith, J. and Sealey, C. (2022) 'Living with long-term disability and care – a perspective on the adequacy of provision and areas for improvement', in C. Sealey, J. Fillingham and P. Unwin (eds) *Social Policy, Service Users and Carers: Lived Experiences and Perspectives*. Zurich: Springer Nature Switzerland AG, pp. 103–124.

Stirling, A. (2019) *Austerity is Subduing UK Economy by more than £3,600 per Household this Year*, New Economics Foundation. Available from: https://neweconomics.org/2019/02/austerity-is-subduing-uk-economy-by-more-than-3-600-per-household-this-year [Accessed 5 August 2022].

SVRU (Scottish Violence Reduction Unit) (2020) 'About us'. Available from: http://www.svru.co.uk/about-us/ [Accessed 5 August 2022].

Titmuss, R.M. (1973) *Commitment to Welfare*. London: Allen & Unwin.

User Voice and Queen's University Belfast (2022) 'Coping with COVID in prison: The impact of prisoner lockdown'. Available from: https://www.uservoice.org/consultations/coping-with-covid/ [Accessed 4 August 2022].

Index

www.ingramcontent.com/pod-product-compliance
Lightning Source LLC
Chambersburg PA
CBHW080541030426

42337CB00024B/4811